The Presidents' Wives

THE
PRESIDENTS'
WIVES

Reassessing the Office
of First Lady

Robert P. Watson

LYNNE
RIENNER
PUBLISHERS

BOULDER
LONDON

Published in the United States of America in 2000 by
Lynne Rienner Publishers, Inc.
1800 30th Street, Boulder, Colorado 80301
www.rienner.com

and in the United Kingdom by
Lynne Rienner Publishers, Inc.
3 Henrietta Street, Covent Garden, London WC2E 8LU

Library of Congress Cataloging-in-Publication Data
Watson, Robert P., 1962–
   The Presidents' wives : reassessing the office of First Lady / by
Robert P. Watson.
     p. cm.
   Includes bibliographical references (p.   ) and index.
   ISBN 1-55587-860-1 (hc : alk. paper)
   1. Presidents' spouses—United States—History. I. Title.
E176.2.W37   1999
973'.09'9—dc21   99-27842
                                               CIP

British Cataloguing in Publication Data
A Cataloguing in Publication record for this book
is available from the British Library.

Printed and bound in the United States of America

5 4 3 2

Contents

Illustrations

Tables

Photographs

Boxes

1

The President's Partner

*The failure of political scientists and historians to consider the
political role of first ladies neglects the role of a key player in the
president's inner circle.*

—Karen O'Connor, Bernadette Nye, and Laura Van Assendelft,
Presidential Studies Quarterly

Conventional wisdom has held that first ladies have not occupied a central
position in political affairs or U.S. history and have functioned as little
more than feminine window dressing to the office of the presidency. But in
the early 1920s, long before the country experienced Hillary Rodham
Clinton, the epitome of the modern, activist first lady, and a dozen years
before the reign of Eleanor Roosevelt, widely considered to be the first
powerful White House spouse, there was Florence Harding.

The Power Behind the Throne

Many bold assertions have been attributed to Mrs. Harding. For instance,
on the eve of Warren Harding's ascension to the nation's highest office, she
is said to have commented to her husband, "Well, Warren, I have got you
the presidency, what are you going to do with it?"[1] On another occasion,
she apparently quipped, "I know what's best for the President, I put him in
the White House."[2] During Harding's presidency political cartoonists even
depicted the couple as "the Chief Executive and *Mr.* Harding." If these
quotes are in fact accurate, are Mrs. Harding's words and, perhaps more
important, the actions underlying them aberrations in U.S. history?

Consider the administration of President Harding's predecessor,
Woodrow Wilson. In June 1919, at the close of World War I, President

Wilson, accompanied by his wife, Edith, traveled to Paris to sign the Treaty of Versailles. Wilson was seeking to establish the League of Nations, an organization that he hoped would ensure world peace. Although he was successful abroad, he encountered opposition back home from Republicans in the U.S. Senate. In an effort to build popular support for the League and thereby counter Republican opposition, Wilson, again accompanied by his wife, initiated a whistle-stop campaign across the country in September of that year. Exhausted by the hectic schedule, the president suffered a stroke after a speech in Pueblo, Colorado, on October 2 and nearly died. The debilitating stroke left Wilson partially paralyzed, largely bedridden, and unable to perform many of the tasks of governance for many months.

However, rather than resign the presidency or pass the powers of the office to Thomas Riley Marshall, his politically weak vice president, Wilson turned to his wife. Edith Wilson discouraged her husband from resigning and not only supported him morally and physically but carried out many of the tasks of the presidency. Wilson remained in almost complete seclusion until January 1920. In fact, it would not be until April 1920 that the president met formally with his cabinet. During this time, Edith screened her husband's visitors, served as an intermediary between the president and his cabinet, and consulted with Wilson's advisers and cabinet secretaries about policy matters. Ignoring public epithets of "Her Regency" and "President-in-Fact," Mrs. Wilson withheld the severity of her husband's illness from the public, denied access to the president to government officials and the press, and continued functioning as surrogate president.[3]

The severe denouncements of her actions and power serve as testimony to the central role First Lady Edith Wilson played during her husband's critical rehabilitation. Yet even before the stroke, Edith functioned as Woodrow Wilson's most trusted adviser and member of "The Inquiry," Wilson's inner circle of advisers and policymakers. There are some great ironies and important lessons behind Edith Wilson's story, one of them being the fact that Woodrow Wilson is widely viewed to have been a stubbornly independent individual and a strong leader. He was the president, after all, who would rather not join his brainchild—the League of Nations—than compromise with Senate Republicans on his vision for "his" organization. Considered one of the ten greatest presidents by most historians,[4] Wilson was not known for taking the advice of others or for being much of a team player. Yet he regularly took his wife's advice and briefed her on the most intimate details of public policy and war.

Despite his lifelong opposition to women's suffrage, Wilson appears to have softened on the issue because of Edith's support for women's rights. Ironically, even while he and Edith were dating, only months after the death of his first wife, Ellen, the president revealed secrets of the war to his new companion and enlisted her assistance in encoding and decoding sensitive White House wartime correspondence.[5] Perhaps the most compelling irony of Mrs. Wilson's role in her husband's presidency is that her stewardship of the office during Woodrow Wilson's long convalescence occurred in 1919, the year before the passage of the Nineteenth Amendment to the Constitution, which gave women the legal right to vote. The lesson of Mrs. Wilson's power is that first ladies have often functioned as a power behind the throne of the American presidency.

The historical record is filled with examples of a power operating behind the throne of the presidency, a power that the public, the White House press corps, and presidential scholars have either overlooked, minimized, or been completely unaware of. It stands to reason that such stories should be a part of every American child's civic education. The feats of the first ladies would fit in well with the nation's political lure and heritage, right alongside George Washington's crossing of the Delaware River, Abraham Lincoln's Gettysburg Address, and John F. Kennedy's inaugural speech. A strong case presents itself for revisiting what we thought we knew about the first ladies. It also compels us to reexamine the institution of the U.S. presidency and the state of the presidential marriage. To that end, this book is dedicated to reassessing the hidden history of the presidency and examining the unknown institution of the White House: the first lady. After all, the office is a viable part of the presidency, the U.S. political landscape, and even the nation. And it has been so since the founding of the nation.

A New View of the First Lady

Scholarly attention to the institution and those individuals occupying the office started in the late 1980s and has grown during the subsequent decade.[6] For instance, during First Lady Hillary Clinton's first term, a $1,000-a-plate fund raiser at the U.S. National Botanical Garden was held in honor of the new National Garden in Washington, D.C., a monument dedicated to the first ladies. Former First Ladies Johnson, Ford, Carter, Reagan, and Bush joined Hillary Rodham Clinton in the media ceremony that showcased the first ladies as much as it dedicated the new National Garden. The garden has now taken its place on the capital city's Mall near Independence Avenue in a city full of monuments to national achievements, public service, and political leaders. Even before this event, in April 1984, a conference titled "Modern First Ladies: Private Lives and Public Duties" was held at the Gerald R. Ford Presidential Library.

In 1985, NBC aired a one-hour prime-time special on Nancy Reagan's life as first lady. Today there are a growing number of video documentaries of the first ladies to complement the vast collection of presidential documentaries. For instance, as part of its "Biography" series, A&E network has produced video biographies on the lives of several first ladies, including Jackie Kennedy and Hillary Clinton. On June 8, 1998, the National First Ladies' Library was opened at the Saxton McKinley House in Canton, Ohio, the former residence of First Lady Ida Saxton McKinley. This national archive is dedicated to the lives and legacies of the United States' first ladies and houses a growing collection of archival data. Today the First Lady Portrait Gallery, located on the ground-floor corridor in the White House, is a popular attraction for visitors and guests at the White House and a tribute to the lives and service of the presidential spouses. But perhaps the most telling testimony to the changing public perspective on the first lady exists at the Smithsonian Institution's National Museum of American History. Here, the long-standing, popular first ladies exhibit has a new look. Once simply a collection of first ladies' gowns, a new, more comprehensive exhibit documents the many roles of the first lady and highlights her political activities and achievements.[7] The first lady has arrived on the political stage.

Educators are also slowly beginning to take an interest in the wife of the president. For example, Louisiana State University at Shreveport dedicated its 1997 American Studies Summer Institute to "First Couples in the White House: Presidents and Spouses." The theme for the institute in 1998 was "George *and* Martha Washington."[8] Professional academic conferences in the field of political science have begun to include an occasional presentation on the first ladies, and scholarly journals in the disciplines of political science and history are likewise publishing articles on the topic.[9]

An interest in the first lady has also been sparked in the political arena. During the 1988 presidential campaign a first ladies forum was proposed early in the campaign season, signaling the political relevance of candidates' spouses. Political pundits even joked that the two presidential candidates—George Bush and Michael Dukakis—were not nearly as interesting or as capable as their wives. In fact, the entire field of prospective first ladies in the 1988 presidential race was impressive. Democratic nominee Michael Dukakis's wife Kitty had lectured at Harvard University. Both Hattie Babbitt, the wife of Bruce Babbitt, former Arizona governor, and Jeanne Simon, wife of Illinois senator Paul Simon, were lawyers. Al Gore's wife, Tipper, was an author, and Jill Jacobs, the spouse of Joseph Biden, a senator from Delaware, was pursuing her second master's degree at the time of his candidacy and even retained her maiden name. Elise du Pont, the spouse of Pierre "Pete" du Pont, who entered the Republican presidential race in 1988, was also a lawyer. In recent years, many other spouses of presidential hopefuls have had successful careers of their own.

Another debate between the prospective first ladies was suggested during the 1996 presidential race because of the high profiles and official portfolios of the candidates' wives. Both spouses—Hillary Rodham Clinton and Elizabeth Dole—were well-known and powerful public figures who held law degrees from prestigious universities. Elizabeth Dole was a former cabinet secretary in both the Reagan and Bush administrations and Hillary Clinton had been recognized as one of the nation's most influential attorneys. The political enthusiasm for the presidential spouses continues to grow as we begin to realize the power first ladies have wielded throughout history and to the present day.

Studying the first ladies reveals the trials and tribulations of being wife to the president, sheds light on presidential decisionmaking, and offers some insightful tales of the shaping of the nation. There is also the personal history of those who occupied the nation's second most difficult job. In their lives we find tragedy as well as triumph, extraordinary feats as well as ordinary events. Many of the first ladies were notoriously ordinary. Yet most accomplished much both in and out of office.

The group of capable and heroic women who have been called first lady is impressive. For instance, as a college student at the University of Vermont, Grace Coolidge cofounded a chapter of Pi Beta Phi fraternity and, after graduation, went on to become a teacher of the deaf. Just out of college, Hillary Rodham Clinton worked as a lawyer on the staff of the House Judiciary Committee investigating the impeachment of President Richard Nixon. Abigail Fillmore, a former schoolteacher, was so disturbed by the lack of books in the executive mansion that she pressured Congress into appropriating funds for a White House library, establishing what has since become a national archive and treasure. Eleanor Roosevelt appears to have been a major force behind the progressivism of her husband's famous New Deal programs and was one of the nation's first civil rights advocates in the White House. Several first ladies, including Eleanor Roosevelt and Rosalynn Carter, traveled abroad alone on behalf of the president in the formal capacity as presidential envoys. In January 1943 Lady Bird Johnson purchased KTBC, a small radio station near her home in Austin, Texas. The future first lady ran the station, doing everything from cleaning the offices to managing the business. The station was successful and made the Johnsons a considerable amount of money, which Lady Bird used to purchase other stations that would eventually become part of the Johnsons' media empire.

However, such examples of the presidential spouses do not tell the whole story. In fact, much of the interest is driven more by social curiosity

and celebrity sensationalism than by serious, objective analysis and therefore omits the importance of this dynamic political office. It is doubtful that
the public fully appreciates the extent of influence, power, and sacrifice
experienced by the women of the White House and the degree to which
first ladies have shaped U.S. history. Unfortunately, accounts of the first
lady by the media focus almost exclusively on scandal and controversy, her
private life, or the traditional functions of the office such as social hostessing. She is typically portrayed as little more than an ornamental part of the
presidency. We know her as a handshaker and loyal wife. The public knows
more about her latest hairstyle and taste in fashion than about her political
influence in official Washington. Not surprisingly, most aspects of the first
ladyship remain misunderstood or unknown. Indeed, presidential scholars,
historians, and political scientists have largely ignored the first lady in their
studies, viewing her as trivial and not worthy of serious scholarly
attention.[10]

Yet, dating back to Abigail Adams, spouse of the second U.S. president, or perhaps even to Martha Washington, the influence of first ladies on
national events and presidential decisionmaking has been much more pro-
found than we have been led to believe. Many powerful and influential
women have resided in the White House. First Ladies Abigail Adams,
Sarah Polk, Helen Taft, Ellen Wilson, Edith Wilson, Florence Harding,
Eleanor Roosevelt, and Rosalynn Carter, to name a few, have functioned as
the president's most trusted political confidante. Many first ladies served
not only as White House hostesses but also as policy advisers. Even Hillary
Rodham Clinton, thought to be a brand-new type of first lady, is less the
trailblazing activist than she is simply the extension of a long line of White
House spouses who have served their husbands and nation as presidential
partners.

The first ladies represent an intriguing group of women responsible for
many political contributions to the presidency. These spouses have hosted
formal affairs of state, renovated the White House, raised families, supported their husbands through the many challenges of the presidency, and
served as leading public figures. They have done all this without pay and
often without any prior training, institutional supports, or proper recognition. As a group, the first ladies have generally been a capable lot, excelling
in both their White House duties and personal lives. It is not unreasonable
to suggest that as a group, given what they had to do, they were as highly
capable and competent as the presidents themselves. Many even discharged
their public responsibilities better than their husbands discharged their own
presidential duties and, subsequently, enjoyed an equal if not higher degree
of popularity during their day and age. It is time for their accomplishments
to be celebrated and for the first ladies to assume their rightful place in U.S.
history.

The Title of First Lady

The first lady remains such an unknown institution of the White House that basic questions such as who can technically be considered a first lady and the origins of the title remain unclear. Indeed, the genesis of the title *First Lady* remains a point of contention, with competing theories and arguments surrounding its development.[11]

There are numerous claims as to the exact date of the first use of the term. These tend to encompass four basic arguments, each of which corresponds to a different period in time: (1) the first is the "prewar thesis," which points to the year 1849 as the time the title was first used; (2) the second can be termed the "Civil War thesis," because this argument generally places the initial use of the title around the time of the Civil War (1861–1865); (3) the "postwar thesis" places both the origin of the title and its growing popularity in the decade of the 1870s; and (4) the "twentieth-century thesis" identifies the early 1900s as the period when widespread use of the title began.

According to advocates of the prewar thesis, the earliest reference to the first lady dates back to 1849 when, at the death of Dolley Madison, President Zachary Taylor referred to her as "our First Lady for a half-century" during her eulogy.[12] Although Taylor did use the term, if this was in fact the genesis of the title, it appears not to have gained widespread acceptance for some time. Nor was the title used during Dolley Madison's service in the White House. There are few historical accounts of the title being used during the period leading up to the Civil War. On May 8, 1858, the magazine *Harper's Weekly* published a likeness of Harriet Lane, niece and White House hostess for bachelor president James Buchanan, with a caption reading "Our Lady of the White House."[13] However, *Harper's* had not used the title *First Lady,* and the term *Lady of the White House* did not endure.

Not long after, on March 31, 1860, Frank Leslie's *Illustrated Newspaper* used the term *First Lady* in reference to Miss Lane. This may mark the first time the title was used to describe the hostess of the White House while she was living. Yet, because Harriet Lane was the niece of the president, the title had not yet been used for a living wife of the president. This usage would occur a year later, in 1861, when both the *New York Herald* and *Sacramento Union* newspapers spoke of Mary Todd Lincoln as "First Lady."[14] According to first lady scholar Betty Boyd Caroli, the title may have first been used during the Civil War by British journalists in describing Jefferson Davis's wife, Varina, as "First Lady of the Confederacy," a possible genesis of the title that is most ironic.[15] The Civil War thesis is also supported by historian Gil Troy, who places the date for the first use of the term at 1863.[16]

Box 1.1   First Ladies Around the World

Eva "Evita" Duarte Perón (1919–1952)

The infamous Evita was born of very modest means. Highly ambitious, young Eva moved to the capital city of Buenos Aires where she embarked on a career as a film and radio actor. Eva caught the attention of several rising political and military leaders, including Juan Perón, who became president of Argentina in 1945, in part because of Eva's determination and political acumen. As first lady, Eva championed the "shirtless" of Argentina and asserted herself as the power behind the Perón administration. Eva traveled around the nation building her husband's popularity and her own base of support, which exceeded that of her husband, among the middle and lower classes. Her obsession with power and hard work succeeded in forming the Peronista Feminist Party, enacting women's suffrage, giving voice to the downtrodden masses, and establishing her own welfare foundation as the largest in the country. At her untimely death in 1952 she was seen as a saint by Argentina's poor, who identified with Evita's rags to riches story.

Princess Grace of Monaco (1929–1982)

Grace Kelly was already famous when she married Prince Rainier in 1956. A wealthy, glamourous figure, Grace was a successful Hollywood actor who had an Academy award to her film credits. After becoming Princess Grace of Monaco, she immediately made her presence known, becoming a leader in the cultural life of the principality, a champion of many charities, including several children's organizations and the famous Princess Grace Foundation, and head of Monaco's Red Cross. Although not born of royal blood, Grace successfully performed her duties as a princess. Because of her work, Monaco achieved notoriety as an international cultural center. Unfortunately, Princess Grace's story met a tragic end when she died in a car accident.

Madame Chiang Kai-Shek (Soong Meiling) (b. 1897)

Perhaps the most powerful woman in modern China, Soong Meiling received an American education, graduating from Wellesley College in 1917. In 1927 Soong became the second wife of Nationalist Chinese leader Chiang Kai-Shek. Throughout their long marriage Soong served as his most influential adviser, softening his militaristic ambitions and introducing him to Western culture and politics. She even served in the formal capacity as head of the Chinese Commission on Aeronautical Affairs. Madame Chiang Kai-Shek's influence extended beyond the Great Wall, when, during a 1943 visit to the United States, she became only the second woman and the first person from China to address a joint session of the Congress. Soong was intelligent, the author of numerous works, and dedicated to the support of wounded soldiers, women, orphans, and war relief. But perhaps her most remarkable accomplishment came in 1936 after her husband was kidnapped in Sian when she risked her life personally and successfully negotiating with Chiang's kidnappers for his release.

Imelda Romualdez Marcos (b. 1930)

A former beauty queen, in 1954 Imelda married Ferdinand Marcos, who would go on to lead the Philippines from 1966 to 1986. As first lady of the Philippines, Mrs. Marcos was widely recognized as one of the most powerful politicians in her country and its leading diplomat during her extensive international travels. Imelda served her country in several formal positions, including governor of Metro Manila in 1975 and an elected member of the National Assembly in 1978. Imelda oversaw government spending on a variety of projects and, like her dictator husband, became embroiled in scandals of fraud, corruption, and worse, causing them to flee their country. After Ferdinand's death in 1989, Imelda returned from her exile in Hawaii, whereupon she ran unsuccessfully for the Philippine presidency but successfully for a seat in the legislature.

Raisa Maximovna Gorbachev (b. 1932)

Whereas the wives of previous Soviet leaders were rather unremarkable, drab women who served in obscurity, Raisa Gorbachev was a media-savvy, "Western-style" woman who earned an advanced degree at Moscow State Pedagogical Institute and even taught at Moscow State University. As was true of many American first ladies, Raisa came from a powerful family and her marriage to Mikhail in 1954 helped advance his career. Raisa accompanied her husband during his travels and appears to have been one of his most trusted confidantes. While Mikhail will be remembered for presiding over the collapse of the USSR, during which time his actions quite possibly averted a nuclear confrontation with the United States, Raisa will be remembered for her modern approach to the office and for providing counsel to her husband during the critical closing chapter of the Cold War.

In 1870 journalist Emily Briggs, writing under the pen name "Olivia," called Julia Grant the "First Lady" in a newspaper column.[17] This occurrence is mentioned by presidential historian Stephen Robertson as a possible point of origin for the title.[18] Many leading scholars of the presidency and first lady identify 1877 as the year the title was initiated.[19] Proponents of this thesis claim that reporter Mary Clemmer Ames, in an article about Rutherford B. Hayes in the newspaper *The Independent,* referred to Lucy Hayes as "First Lady of the land" in reference to a recent cross-country trip Mrs. Hayes had taken.[20] Historian Stanley Pillsbury, writing in *The Dictionary of American History,* also uses 1877 as the date of origin, but maintains that the term *First Lady* was first used to describe Lucy Webb Hayes at her husband's inauguration.[21] The advocates of the postwar thesis maintain that by the 1880s the title appears to have gained popularity.

Arguments for the fourth thesis often credit a 1911 play by Charles F. Nirdlinger, *The First Lady of the Land,* about First Lady Dolley Madison, for popularizing the title.[22] Another theater production in 1935 by Katherine Dayton and George S. Kaufman titled *First Lady* further solidified the term's acceptance by a wide audience.

Prior to the use of the title *First Lady,* presidential spouses were known by a variety of formalities. For example, Martha Washington was known as "Lady Washington," a term reflecting the period's popular equivocation to royalty. The second presidential spouse, Abigail Adams, was called "Mrs. President" or "Her Majesty," titles that, at times, were used disparagingly by the political enemies of John and Abigail Adams.[23] The popular Dolley Madison was occasionally called "Lady Presidentress." And Harriet Lane, though technically not a first lady, was even known as the "Democratic Queen."

With the exception of the last title, such royalistic terms disappeared in the 1830s with the rise of Jacksonian democracy and the era of the common man. This period favored more humble terms for the spouse of the president, such as simply "Mrs.," that were in keeping with the democratic spirit of the young nation.[24] Contemporary critics such as historian Gil Troy echo these sentiments, seeing the title and office as too regal and an "extra-Constitutional improvisation."[25] The list of critics also includes several first ladies who have been uncomfortable with the title. For example, Jackie Kennedy, despite the image of the American Camelot she and her husband projected, so disliked the term that she forbade the White House staff from using it altogether.[26] However, first ladies such as Barbara Bush preferred *First Lady* to other titles.[27]

Irrespective of the origins of the title *First Lady,* today the term is commonly used by the public, the press, and the White House. Beginning with Webster's *New International Dictionary* in 1934, dictionaries began adopting the title. By the 1960s the term was even used to refer to leading or powerful women in a variety of professions and the spouses of state governors. Today, the title is also used internationally to describe the spouses of male political heads of state. Remarkably, however, *The Congressional Directory,* a who's who listing of everyone working in official Washington politics that has been published every year since 1834, did not even list the first lady until the March 1965 edition. Even more remarkable is that the 1953 edition, though it omits First Lady Mamie Eisenhower, lists a secretary named Mary Jane McCaffree as the "Acting Secretary to Wife of the President."[28] Such examples point to the uphill struggle first ladies have faced in gaining respect for their public service and the general neglect of the office by the press and the political establishment.

Despite the widespread use of the term, the title needs further clarification. The term *First Lady* always used to be capitalized. Today the term is sometimes capitalized, and sometimes lowercased. This book uses the format of leading scholarly journals in the field of the presidency, such as *Presidential Studies Quarterly,* which use the lowercase except when referring directly to a particular first lady or using the term as a title. The title may be in need of another change. The term *lady* is almost never used in day-to-day conversation, in print, or even in formal settings, especially in the United States. It is a dated phrase that conjures up images of a privileged aristocracy and the Old World. In such cases, the term *lady* carried with it a set of expectations, including that of refraining from any sort of political activity. Moreover, it seems that the title *Presidential Spouse* or *First Spouse* or even terms such as *Presidential Mate* or *Presidential Partner* not only are more appropriate descriptions of the office but may soon by necessity replace the title *First Lady.* It appears inevitable that a married, heterosexual woman will one day be elected to the presidency and thus her husband's service will make the title obsolete. In this book, the title *First Lady* will be used for historical accuracy, but the title *Presidential Spouse* will be proposed for future adoption.

In the Service of Their Country

Among our nation's first ladies are women of affluence and high social standing, individuals well educated for their times, and those with a variety of talents, musical, linguistic, artistic, and otherwise. There have also been mothers, grandmothers, and women of modest birth. Some first ladies have been unlikely public figures; others seem to have lived a life designed to prepare them for the office. Of course, there have been successes and failures, both in and out of office. There are also many fascinating, unusual, and inspiring accounts of real women facing seemingly unreal challenges.

A total of five presidential spouses died prior to their husband's tenure in the White House: Martha Jefferson, Rachel Jackson, Hannah Van Buren,

Ellen Arthur, and Alice Roosevelt. All of these deceased spouses had spent many years married to their husbands prior to their deaths and were help-mates in their husbands' lives and careers. (See Box 1.2 for marriage data on all presidential spouses.) Three first ladies died in the White House: Letitia Tyler, Caroline Harrison, and Ellen Wilson. Interestingly, all three of the widower presidents would later remarry, two while still in the White House: John Tyler and Woodrow Wilson. Two first ladies who outlived their president husbands would also remarry in the years after the White House: Frances Cleveland and Jackie Kennedy, both of whom were consid-erably younger than their first husbands. There have been a total of five incidents of divorce associated with the presidential marriage, all occurring before the presidential years. Three eventual first ladies, Rachel Donelson (Jackson), Florence Kling (Harding), and Betty Bloomer (Ford), were divorcees when they married their second husbands. President Ronald Reagan's first wife, Jane Wyman, was previously divorced. Reagan and Wyman later divorced before Reagan married Nancy Davis and went on to become the president. Three first ladies, the early mothers of this nation, were widows when they met their future-president husbands: Martha Washington, Martha Jefferson, and Dolley Madison. Some first ladies, such as Martha Washington, Martha Jefferson, Dolley Madison, and the divorced Florence Harding, brought children from previous marriages into their presidential marriages. Most first ladies have outlived their husbands. Four first ladies were widowed as a direct result of their husbands' service as president (Lincoln, Garfield, McKinley, and Kennedy were assassinated in office). Four others were widowed perhaps as an indirect result of that serv-ice (W. H. Harrison, Taylor, Harding, and F. D. Roosevelt died in office of natural causes).

First ladies do not receive a salary for their service. (The idea has been proposed from time to time and was even championed by Rosalynn Carter and Betty Ford. These efforts, such as a 1946 proposal by Representative James G. Fulton of Pennsylvania, have been defeated.) However, there are many tangible benefits enjoyed during their service, not the least of which is living in the White House, a mansion filled with historical works of art and Americana and staffed with skilled chefs, butlers, and a number of per-sonal attendants. There is also the notoriety that comes from being the spouse of the president, even though this notoriety is often a mixed bless-ing. For instance, even after her husband's death, during her visits to the Capitol, Dolley Madison was invited by a unanimous vote in Congress to be seated on the floor of the legislature rather than in the visitor's gallery.

One form of official recognition for a first lady's service is a govern-ment pension. Interestingly, the first lady's pension predated the granting of pensions to presidents. The first presidential spouse to receive a pension after her husband's death was Anna Harrison, who, on June 30, 1841,

Box 1.2   The Presidential Marriage

> *"You can't have been together for almost thirty years without being an influence on each other."*
> —President Ronald Reagan speaking of his wife, Nancy

Number of Years Married Prior to Serving in the White House:

George & Martha Washington: 30.3

John & Abigail Adams: 32.3

Thomas & Martha Jefferson: (10.5 prior to her death)

James & Dolley Madison: 14.5

James & Elizabeth Monroe: 41

John Q. & Louisa Adams: 27.5

Andrew & Rachel Jackson: (37.5 prior to her death)

Martin & Hannah Van Buren: (12 prior to her death)

William & Anna Harrison: 45.25

John & Letitia Tyler: 28

John & Julia Tyler: 0 (married while he was president)

James & Sarah Polk: 21

Zachary & Margaret Taylor: 38.75

Millard & Abigail Fillmore: 24.5

Franklin & Jane Pierce: 18.3

Abraham & Mary Lincoln: 18.5

Andrew & Eliza Johnson: 37.75

Ulysses & Julia Grant: 20.5

Rutherford & Lucy Hayes: 24

James & Lucretia Garfield: 22.25

Chester & Ellen Arthur: (20 prior to her death)

Grover & Frances Cleveland: 0 (married while he was president)

Benjamin & Caroline Harrison: 35.25

William & Ida McKinley: 26

Teddy & Edith Roosevelt: 14.75

Howard & Helen Taft: 22.75

Woodrow & Ellen Wilson: 27.6

Woodrow & Edith Wilson: 0 (married while he was president)

Warren & Florence Harding: 29.6

Calvin & Grace Coolidge: 18

Herbert & Lou Hoover: 30

Franklin & Eleanor Roosevelt: 28

Harry & Bess Truman: 26

Ike & Mamie Eisenhower: 35.5

John & Jackie Kennedy: 7.3

Lyndon & Lady Bird Johnson: 29

Richard & Pat Nixon: 28.5

Gerald & Betty Ford: 23

Jimmy & Rosalynn Carter: 30.5

Ronald & Nancy Reagan: 29

George & Barbara Bush: 45

Bill & Hillary Clinton: 17.25

received $25,000, an amount equal to the president's salary at the time. Anna received this pension because her husband had died in office. Before this time, widowed first ladies had been forced to support themselves. Martha Washington, who outlived her husband by two years, was fortunate enough to inherit great wealth and land holdings. After the death of James Madison, Dolley Madison organized her husband's papers that she had earlier saved from a fire at Montpelier (the Madison home) and appealed to President Andrew Jackson and the Congress to purchase the Madison presidential papers for the National Archives. The papers were bought for $30,000, in part because of their historical importance and in part because of Mrs. Madison's popularity and powers of persuasion.

Mary Todd Lincoln also received a pension in the amount of $25,000 on December 21, 1865, also because her husband had died in office. After her subsequent bankruptcy, this amount was amended to $3,000 per year on July 14, 1870. The fight for Mrs. Lincoln's annual pension was led by the powerful senator Charles Sumner. The $3,000 pension was raised to $5,000 annually on February 2, 1882. After her husband died in 1862, former first lady Julia Tyler struggled financially while supporting the South during the Civil War. In 1879 Julia lobbied Congress for a pension and in 1880 received a monthly allocation. The issue of financial supports for first ladies arose again in 1881 with the assassination of President James Garfield. Congressional action on March 31, 1882, granted $5,000 annual pensions to living, widowed former first ladies, including Lucretia Garfield, Sarah Polk, and Julia Tyler, which were to be administered by the U.S. secretary of interior. This established the precedent of granting pensions to all widowed first ladies, regardless of the cause of the president's death or whether it occurs in or out of the White House. (Frances Cleveland, who remained quite wealthy and remarried after the death of Grover Cleveland, turned down her $5,000 annual pension.) This practice has continued through the twentieth century. In 1958 Congress passed legislation that reinforced the granting of pensions to presidential widows. On January 8, 1971, widowed first ladies' pensions were increased to $20,000 per year, an amount that becomes void if she remarries before the age of sixty.[29]

There are other examples of formal recognition of the office. An act on April 3, 1800, provided widows of the president with the use of free mail for life. This has since been amended, yet through special legislation several former first ladies have been granted what is known as the "franking privilege," or free use of public mailings. The first lady and first family also receive Secret Service protection both in and out of the White House, as well as after their presidential years. In 1965 widows of presidents and their children under the age of sixteen were also granted Secret Service protection. In 1968 the Secret Service started guarding presidential candidates, and since 1976 the candidates' wives and families have been included in this detail. Some first ladies, such as Eleanor Roosevelt and Rosalynn Carter, were displeased with the constant attention and therefore attempted to reduce their Secret Service contingency in the name of privacy. In recent years, Secret Service detachments have been increased, testimony to, ironically, both the importance of and dangers inherent in the office of first lady.

The list of first ladies includes many exceptional women who lived full, productive lives and made many contributions to the White House and the nation. These contributions date to the founding of the nation. Consider the following example: Martha Dandridge Custis was a very wealthy and well-known widow, who is estimated to have been worth approximately $100,000 (a considerable amount of money in the mid-eighteenth century) at the time of her marriage to George Washington. Her second husband-to-be was an ambitious soldier, but he lacked a formal education and his social graces were somewhat unrefined by the standards of the very same Virginia aristocracy to which he aspired to belong. In marrying the widow Martha Custis, George Washington gained considerable wealth, vast land holdings, and access to the upper echelons of Virginia society. Throughout their lives together, the Washingtons shared a partnership based on mutual respect and admiration. Whether it was at Valley Forge during the most critical moments of the Revolutionary War or while hosting the formal events of the inaugural presidency, one person was beside him serving as a constant source of financial, social, and moral support. Indeed, Martha's fingerprints are all over George's career and thus the founding of the nation. She was the central figure in his historic life, to the extent that, had they not married, George Washington might never have gone on to help found the new nation, lead the colonial militia in the Revolutionary War, or serve as the first president. And the rest, as they say, is history.

Notes

1. The quote by Florence Harding is discussed in C. S. Anthony, *Saga,* 1990. See also R. K. Murray, *Warren G. Harding,* 1969. This book includes some general discussion of First Lady Florence Harding's influence and role in her husband's career and administration.

2. See Anthony, 1990, and Murray, 1969.

3. Edith Wilson faced severe criticism during the period after her husband's stroke. Mrs. Wilson discusses her decision to hide the severity of her husband's illness from the public and to carry on in support of him in her book *My Memoir,* 1939. In the book she denies that she ever made a significant decision on her own. J. L. Weaver provides an interesting assessment of Mrs. Wilson's personality and her ability to carry on in spite of the crisis and criticism in her article "Edith Bolling Wilson," 1985.

4. There have been numerous presidential rankings and most of them place

Wilson near the top. For a discussion of these ratings, see J. P. Pfiffner, *Modern Presidency,* 1993, or D. A. Lonnstrom and T. O. Kelly II, "Rating the Presidents," 1997. The presidential rankings are discussed further in Chapter 7 of this book.

5. Edith Wilson's role in such sensitive matters is discussed in Wilson, 1939. See also the informative chapters on Edith Wilson in Anthony, 1990, and L. L. Gould, ed., *First Ladies,* 1996.

6. There have also been several important books written about the first ladies since 1987. Perhaps the first groundbreaking analysis of the first lady's power was by B. B. Caroli, *First Ladies,* 1987. Other important books appearing after 1987 include: Anthony, 1990 and 1991; Gould, 1996; M. G. Gutin, *The President's Partner,* 1989; and G. Troy, *Affairs of State,* 1997.

7. The new exhibit is titled "First Ladies: Political Role, Public Image" and provides an excellent look at the many roles and contributions of the first ladies. The exhibit is also home to the always-popular collection of first ladies' gowns. Edith Mayo served as curator for this exhibit.

8. Dr. William Pederson served as the institute's director at the conference. The event, held from June 24 to July 17, 1997, was sponsored by the Louisiana Endowment of the Humanities and provided training for educators.

9. Since 1990 a few scholarly journals have devoted articles to the first ladies, most notably *Presidential Studies Quarterly,* which dedicated one-half of the Fall 1990 (Vol. 20, No. 4) issue to modern first ladies. In 1997 two different issues of the journal contained theoretical pieces on the first lady and *PSQ* has published a few other articles on the topic. A few other journals have also published studies of the first ladies. *Social Science Journal* devoted an entire issue (Vol. 37, No. 4, 2000) to "The First Ladies at the Turn of the Century." Similarly, academic conferences such as the Western Political Science Association Conferences in 1996 and 1997, the MidWest Political Science Association Conference in 1997, and the 1999 Southwestern Political Science Association Conference had presentations on the first ladies.

10. Several first lady and presidential scholars have commented on the lack of scholarly research on the subject. This includes L. L. Gould, "Modern First Ladies," 1990; R. G. Hoxie, "About This Issue," 1990; E. Mayo, "The Influence and Power of First Ladies," 1993; Troy, 1997; and R. P. Watson, "The First Lady Reconsidered," 1997.

11. The Constitution does not mention the title and there is no law or job description that mandates the use of a specific title for the president's spouse.

12. This eulogy is presented and discussed as part of the Smithsonian Institution's first ladies exhibit at the Museum of American History.

13. See the Smithsonian Institution's first ladies exhibit.

14. Ibid.

15. Caroli, 1987.

16. Troy, 1997.

17. Emily Briggs was a journalist who covered First Lady Julia Grant and is thought to have been one of the first to use the title. A history of her writings appears in her book *The Olivia Letters,* 1906.

18. S. L. Robertson, "The First Ladies," 1996.

19. Among those who point to the year 1877 as the possible origin of the term (in describing First Lady Lucy Hayes) are Caroli, 1987; D. C. Diller and S. L. Robertson, *The Presidents,* 1997; Gould, 1996; J. S. Rosebush, *First Lady, Public Wife,* 1987.

20. Mary Clemmer Ames used the title in a newspaper column titled "A Woman's Letter from Washington," 1877.

21. See S. R. Pillsbury, "The First Lady of the Land," 1976.

22. Ibid.

23. See B. A. Weisberger, "Petticoat Government," 1993.

24. Caroli, 1987.

25. Troy, 1997.

26. Caroli, 1987; Rosebush, 1987. Several of the biographies written on Jackie Kennedy also discuss Mrs. Kennedy's distaste for title *First Lady*.

27. Personal interview/questionnaire with First Lady Barbara Bush and Quincy Hicks, aide to Mrs. Bush, February 18, 1997.

28. *The Congressional Directory* is published by the United States Government Printing Office (Washington, D.C.). See the directories published in 1965 and 1953.

29. Courtesy of the White House Information Office.

President and Ida McKinley take their place on the reviewing platform in Plattsburgh, New York, as distinguished guests at the town's 1899 parade. Assisting her husband or acting alone, the first lady is a highly visible public figure (collection of the Library of Congress).

2

The Unknown Institution
of the White House

I hope that someday someone will take the time to evaluate the true role of the wife of a president, and to assess the many burdens she has to bear and the contributions she makes.

—President Harry S Truman

The first lady is considered one of the most powerful people in Washington. Her name has routinely appeared atop the annual Gallup Poll's "Most Admired Women," and her public opinion approval ratings often surpass those of the president, yet her political influence has been ignored by skeptics as well as by scholars. It could even be argued that she is the second most powerful person in the White House, but research on the subject is inadequate and a formal field of study is only beginning to take shape.[1] She is the missing link in our study of the presidency and a strong case exists to formalize the study of this unknown institution within the office of the president: the first lady.[2]

A Case for the Study of the First Lady

The move to formalize the study of the first lady faces resistance by some who perceive the subject as less than a legitimate scholarly endeavor. It has been dismissed as a source of celebrity gossip and little more.[3] This view is shared by part of the U.S. public and a critical press that see the first ladyship as window dressing for the presidency and have dubbed the office an "expensive folly" that is "offensive to taxpayers."[4] Similarly, a feminist critique calls for the elimination of the first ladyship altogether.[5]

19

Although the study of the first lady is long overdue, the relative absence of accessible information on the first ladies presents a problem. Information and documents on the first ladies are not nearly as abundant as such material for the presidents.[6] Part of the problem can be attributed to the lack of scholarly interest in the wives of presidents and the larger problem of a general omission of women from the pages of history. Culturally, women have suffered from subordinate status in U.S. society for the vast majority of the nation's history. Until the twentieth century, women in general and first ladies in particular tended to keep very low profiles. It must be remembered that not only did a "lady" not demonstrate any interest in politics or the news, but she was also not to appear in the news or be the subject of the news. (As Edith Kermit Roosevelt was fond of saying, a lady's name should "appear in print only three times, at her birth, marriage, and death.")[7] Moreover, women did not legally obtain the right to vote in the United States until 1920. Subsequently, there is comparatively little information available in early newspapers, books, and White House documents on the first ladies.[8]

Unfortunately, early writers and even present-day historians appear to have concurred with Edith Roosevelt's opinion and have omitted any discussion of women's lives. An example of this custom can be found in presidential memoirs. Presidents Monroe and Van Buren did not even mention their wives in their autobiographies.[9] Likewise, most presidential biographers have devoted little serious attention to the influence, power, politics, or contributions of the first lady. This trend has continued to the present time when, amazingly, many textbooks on the presidency and U.S. politics fail to mention the term *First Lady* even a single time. At best, textbooks mention the first lady in a passing reference or merely devote a short paragraph to her social endeavors. Even feminist writers and university women's studies programs have failed to include the first lady in the framework of feminist scholarship or treat the institution as a viable part of women's history. Courses on the first ladies are absent from university curricula and degree programs even when they are in fields such as political science, U.S. history, or women's studies.

A problem facing those interested in studying the history of women in the United States is a general lack of written documentation. Whether the subject is politics, war, or the westward expansion of early settlers of European descent, there is little discussion of the roles, contributions, and lives of women. American history was written of, by, and for men. Yet, compared with the written accounts for women in general in the early nineteenth century, the study of the first ladies provides a subject rich in documentation on the lives of women. As the most influential and scrutinized woman in the United States, the first lady also functions as a sort of barometer for the status of women in society and its shifting views of "womanhood."[10] Her roles, political activities, and treatment by the press and public reflect the status of women and societal expectations of women throughout U.S. history. Accordingly, research on the first lady could also help inform women's studies and women's history.

The political spouse has historically been the sole path to real political power available to women in the United States. This is a telling phenomenon. A consideration of how political leaders shared power with their spouses and how the spouses obtained and used power would provide insights on women and politics not found in other studies of women's history and political science. Traditional notions of leadership and power must be expanded to include notions of shared power or team leadership approaches such as those exercised by many political couples. The demands of modern politics often necessitate that the political spouse, especially when that spouse is a woman, abandon her own career in support of the "team's"—or her husband's—political office. Even reluctant political spouses often find that they are forced into at least some dimension of the political office or campaign. For instance, when Elizabeth Dole, wife of Robert Dole, the 1996 Republican presidential candidate, announced during the campaign that if her husband were elected, she would consider keeping her current job as head of the Red Cross, her statement became a controversial and newsworthy story.

Primary research sources on first ladies, as opposed to those for the presidents or other public figures, are difficult to find. For example, there is little documentation of the actual deeds or words of several first ladies. It is even believed that there is no authenticated likeness or portrait surviving for Thomas Jefferson's wife, Martha, or First Lady Margaret Taylor. Some presidents and first ladies compounded the problem by destroying their correspondence and personal letters. After George Washington's death, the intensely private Martha Washington burned many of the letters they had exchanged. A grieving Thomas Jefferson did the same after the death of his wife. Not only is there an absence of documentation on early first ladies, but the same is true of more recent presidential wives. For example, five twentieth-century first ladies left little written record of their White House days: Edith Roosevelt, Helen Taft, Ellen Wilson, Florence Harding, and Grace Coolidge.

Yet the good news is that media and scholarly accounts of the lives of first ladies do exist, and scholarship on the first lady is growing.[11] A flurry of recent books on the first ladies has revealed that many White House wives had considerable influence on their husbands' careers, decisions, and policies, leading us to reassess the role of the office and the first lady's influence on public policy. Considering the social forces limiting a woman's involvement in politics and influence in society, the level of political activism and influence of several pre-twentieth-century first ladies is remarkable. In fact, a new view of an "activist political partner" is emerging as possibly the rule rather than the exception for the female occupants of the White House.[12] This is no small matter, as such a position entails a complete reversal in our thinking about the first ladies. Scholarship on the first ladies also parallels the expansion of the study of the presidency into theories of the pluralist presidency, whereby the presidency is not viewed as a single institution but is understood through the many institutions, advisers, and forces (such as the first lady) that interact with and together make up the U.S. presidency.

The State of First Lady Scholarship

Until recently, the U.S. public and scholars knew little about the first ladies. This was especially true—and still is to a large extent—for pre-twentieth-century first ladies. Nor has adequate attention been directed toward the significant contributions first ladies have made to individual presidents, the U.S. presidency, or the institution of the first lady itself. But this situation is slowly changing. In 1990, for example, one-half of an issue of the prestigious journal *Presidential Studies Quarterly* was devoted to modern first ladies.[13] Edited by notable presidential historian Lewis L. Gould, the essays covered Eleanor Roosevelt, Lady Bird Johnson, and First Ladies Hoover, Ford, Carter, and Reagan. In this issue Gould theorized that one could learn much about the president by the way he managed the first lady's image and the political assets he gained from the first lady's image and roles.[14]

In the late 1980s and increasingly in the 1990s, books began to appear that addressed the topic in a more serious manner than that adopted by the early social and anecdotal works. Together, these books provide the basis for establishing a body of scholarship on the first ladies. However, the subject cannot be classified as a mature field of study. One of the goals of this book is to make an argument for both the legitimacy of the topic and the need for systematic study of the office. Relatedly, I call for the formalization of a field of study of the first lady. Currently, no framework exists to guide serious scholarly research on the subject, there is no coherent research agenda for the future, and no rationale has been offered for the formalization of a field of study of the institution of the first lady.[15] The slim body of scholarly literature on the first lady suffers from a lack of systematic study. Even among the recent, more serious books on the subject, few attempt to place the first lady into the larger context of the history of women or the institution of the presidency. These books focus more on individual first ladies than on the institution itself. The subject also suffers from having no "tightly argued thesis" or scholarly theories and models by which to test and subsequently advance the knowledge base on the topic, all necessary qualifications for any mature academic field of study.[16] Likewise, educational institutions at all levels are failing to incorporate the subject into the mainstream curricula. Graduate degree programs that produce future Ph.D.s in history and political science also earn a failing grade, because although they claim to produce well-trained presidential scholars, most require no coursework, readings, or research on the first ladies.[17] All of these factors must be addressed in order to advance the subject to the state of a mature discipline of study.

There are several fine biographies of the first ladies.[18] This collection, supplemented with autobiographies by former first ladies themselves, offers another starting point for studying the office. For example, Eleanor Roosevelt penned three autobiographical works (*This Is My Story,* 1937; *This I Remember,* 1949; and *The Autobiography of Eleanor Roosevelt,* 1961). Recent autobiographies by Rosalynn Carter, Betty Ford, Nancy Reagan, and Barbara Bush are helpful in assessing the challenges and activities experienced by these first ladies. The books also provide illustrations of the existence of a presidential partnership. Some presidential memoirs, especially those of recent presidents, are valuable and provide accounts of the importance of the presidential spouses. The first ladies have also left behind documentation including diaries and social papers on their years in the White House. Separate papers and White House social files on the first ladies now exist in many presidential libraries. In recent years, presidential libraries have opened access to archives containing valuable information on the first ladies. The Harding, Hoover, Roosevelt, Eisenhower, and Carter presidential libraries, for instance, all have accessible information on the first ladies. However, as of this writing, there are no separate papers for the first lady in the Truman, Coolidge, or Johnson libraries. In June 1998, the National First Ladies Library opened in Canton, Ohio, at the former home of First Lady Ida Saxton McKinley. This archive is dedicated to the study of the first lady and promises to be a valuable source of information, documents, and educational development on the first ladyship. The White House also administers a Web site for the first lady's official home page. This useful and easily accessible site contains biographical information on the first lady and collections of her speeches and activities, as well as informative links to pages on all the first ladies.[19]

Although progress has been made in the study of the first lady as a separate field of scholarship, the same cannot be said of first lady scholarship within the field of the presidency. A look at the voluminous literature base on the presidency reveals that the first lady has been almost completely ignored in presidential scholarship.[20] Rarely is she even mentioned, let alone considered as a worthy or useful topic of study. This lack of interest by presidential scholars has been both passive and active. Some presidential scholars have failed to come to the defense of the first ladies when they and their office have been attacked and misrepresented by the media. Other presidential scholars have actively dismissed or misdiagnosed the role and importance of the first lady.

This neglect of the first ladies is evident in the leading textbooks on the president to the extent that it appears to the reader that there never was such an individual or institution. The vast majority of the textbooks describe important institutions, advisers, and staff within the White House or the executive office of the president yet omit even a single reference to the first lady, whose influence, official budget, and staff often greatly exceed those referenced. Even a cursory review of books on the presidency—textbooks for college courses on the president, both scholarly and popular market books, and collector's series and reference books on the topic—reveals that the first lady is rarely mentioned or even listed in the indexes.[21] Only rarely will a book on the presidency include even a single paragraph under a heading such as "The President's Spouse." Considering the omission of even a simple reference to the first ladies in major textbooks and other books, it appears that the topic has been ignored in mainstream presidential scholarship.

Scholarly study of the first lady is necessary because the reality of the matter is that she has become an institution of the presidency, the U.S. political system, and, in a larger sense, U.S. society. Indeed, to study the first ladies is to study U.S. history.[22] Yet the first lady has been relegated to a footnote in history. Historically, the press and scholars have seen her as a ceremonial White House hostess and the quiet "good wife."[23] Even today, most of the discussion of the first lady in the media and in books fails to conceptualize her beyond the realm of her marriage, children, and hostessing talents. Moreover, although there have been several "activist political partners" as first ladies (Rosalynn Carter and Hillary Clinton, for example), whenever such a partner shows these characteristics, the pundits, press, and public speak of her as "nontraditional" and a "new type" of first lady or as breaking new ground by taking an "unprecedented" interest in politics and the issues.[24] But such pronouncements are simply not true. Except for Eleanor Roosevelt, Hillary Clinton, and perhaps Nancy Reagan, the power and influence of first ladies have been grossly underrated by the public, press, and presidential scholars, and their many contributions to their husbands' presidencies have largely been ignored or minimized. It is also wrong to assume that scholarly study of the first ladies should be limited to the era of Eleanor Roosevelt to the present. Several first ladies prior to Eleanor were active and influential in their husbands' administrations, most prominently, Florence Harding, Helen Taft, Sarah Polk, Dolley Madison, and Abigail Adams. The formal study of the first lady should not ignore the historical development of the institution of first lady. The first ladyship has had a unique history and the present state of the institution can be better understood by considering the precedents and customs established by previous first ladies.[25]

The formalization of a systematic study of the first lady is necessary but not easy. The call for study faces some of the same problems as does presidential scholarship: The field has a small number of cases with wide variance among them. Furthermore, at first glance, it seems that perhaps the only thing the first ladies have in common is that they have all been married to the president. However, there appear to be some generic challenges, experiences, and activities common to all first ladies. (This will be further examined in Chapter 3.) Such research should also consider those women who served in the capacity of White House social hostess but were technically not first ladies, such as Harriet Lane, the niece of bachelor James Buchanan, and Andrew Jackson's daughter-in-law, Sarah York Jackson, who served in place of Jackson's deceased wife, Rachel. Such research should not be disassociated from presidential scholarship; the office of first lady reflects the pressures on the president and the two fields can inform each other.[26] An example of this interaction is the general decline in the public prominence of the first lady after Mary Todd Lincoln that appears to correspond to the deterioration of the post–Civil War presidency. However, the vitality of the office of first lady appears not to have suffered to the degree that the presidency did in the latter half of the nineteenth century. Further research on the first lady may clarify such issues.

Scholarly research is needed in several areas, including (1) assessing the first ladies' political and public activities, roles, and influence; (2) identifying and classifying the various types of first ladies; (3) identifying and clarifying their approaches to the office; (4) identifying and classifying the measurements and determinants of success for a first lady; (5) understanding the historical development of the office; and (6) assessing any possible linkages of the presidential marriage with presidential job performance. Finally, such scholarship should consider a partnership approach to studying the office and begin discussion on the proper term or title for the office in the future, such as *First Spouse* or *Presidential Spouse*.

The Smithsonian Institution's revised first ladies exhibit in the National Museum of American History captures the essence and complexity of the first ladyship. The old exhibit showcased the inaugural gowns of first ladies. Ironically, this original display was itself somewhat groundbreaking, being one of the first and only displays in the Smithsonian dedicated solely to women. The Smithsonian dress collection was begun in 1912 by Cassie Myers James and Rose Gouverneur Hoes (a descendent of James Monroe), who attempted to track down the gowns worn by first ladies. The Smithsonian Department of Conservation then undertook a major examination of how the gowns were used by each first lady, the type of fabric used in the dresses, and where they were made. The gowns were then treated to preserve them and restore them to their original look. In addition to displaying the inaugural gowns, the new exhibit looks at the first lady's political roles and contributions, thus moving beyond a traditional focus of the office. Yet the popularity of the original Smithsonian display endures and is a tribute to the duality of the institution as both a political and social office. Not surprisingly, the new first lady exhibit was unveiled in 1987, the same year that saw the rise of the scholarly study of the first ladyship.

First Ladies and the American Presidency

The first lady is deserving of study simply because the institution has been a part of the presidency since the founding of the nation. Most presidents, after all, have been married and most of them have had their spouses with them while serving in the White House (see Table 2.1). This is true for first president George Washington, who with each action was establishing precedents and protocol while forming the new office. But he did not accomplish this alone. His wife, Martha, assisted him in carrying out the inaugural affairs of state and was the principal force in his life during their forty-year marriage. It is also true of the second president, who was the first to occupy the White House. Abigail Adams was beside her husband, John, during his presidency and remained his most trusted political confidante during their fifty-four years together.

Only two bachelors have been elected to the presidency: James Buchanan and Grover Cleveland, the latter of whom married while in the White House. Only a handful of presidents have occupied the White House without their spouses. For example, Ellen Arthur died just prior to Chester A. Arthur's vice presidency and Rachel Jackson died in the brief interim between her husband's election and inauguration. Martin Van Buren and Thomas Jefferson are exceptions; they lost their wives well before their White House days. The wives of Benjamin Harrison, John Tyler, and Woodrow Wilson died during their presidencies. However, Wilson and Tyler remarried before leaving the White House. In total, thirty-seven of the first forty-two presidencies had a first lady present in the White House. This fact alone demands that scholarly attention be given to the president's spouse.

The presidency can be studied as a team or partnership. The various presidential advisers and institutions of the White House form this team or plural presidency. So, too, does the first lady, whose relationship with the president transcends that of paid advisers and cabinet officers and even the team or pluralist approaches to the presidency or its study. Historian Gil Troy, for example, considers the perspective of the "presidential couple" as

Table 2.1   First Ladies of the United States

President	Term in Office	Presidential Spouses
George Washington	1789–1797	Martha Dandridge Custis Washington (1731–1802)
John Adams	1797–1801	Abigail Smith Adams (1744–1818)
Thomas Jefferson	1801–1809	Martha Wayles Skelton Jefferson (1748–1782)[a]
James Madison	1809–1817	Dolley Payne Todd Madison (1768–1849)
James Monroe	1817–1825	Elizabeth Kortright Monroe (1768–1830)
John Quincy Adams	1825–1829	Louisa Catherine Johnson Adams (1775–1852)
Andrew Jackson	1829–1837	Rachel Donelson Jackson (1767–1828)[a]
Martin Van Buren	1837–1841	Hannah Hoes Van Buren (1783–1819)[a]
William Henry Harrison	1841	Anna Tuthill Symmes Harrison (1775–1864)
John Tyler	1841–1845	Letitia Christian Tyler (1790–1842)[b] Julia Gardiner Tyler (1820–1889) (marriage: 1844)
James K. Polk	1845–1849	Sarah Childress Polk (1803–1891)
Zachary Taylor	1849–1850	Margaret Mackall Smith Taylor (1788–1852)
Millard Fillmore	1850–1853	Abigail Powers Fillmore (1798–1853)
Franklin Pierce	1853–1857	Jane Means Appleton Pierce (1806–1863)
James Buchanan	1857–1861	Harriet Lane(1830–1903)[c]
Abraham Lincoln	1861–1865	Mary Todd Lincoln (1818–1882)
Andrew Johnson	1865–1869	liza McCardle Johnson (1810–1876)
Ulysses S. Grant	1869–1877	Julia Dent Grant (1826–1902)
Rutherford B. Hayes	1877–1881	Lucy Ware Webb Hayes (1831–1889)
James A. Garfield	1881	Lucretia Rudolph Garfield (1832–1918)
Chester A. Arthur	1881–1885	Ellen Lewis Herndon Arthur (1837–1880)[a]
Grover Cleveland	1885–1889	Frances Folsom Cleveland (1864–1947) (marriage: 1886)
	1893–1897	
Benjamin Harrison	1889–1893	Caroline Lavinia Scott Harrison (1832–1892)[b]
William McKinley	1897–1901	Ida Saxton McKinley (1847–1907)
Theodore Roosevelt	1901–1909	Edith Kermit Carow Roosevelt (1861–1948)
William H. Taft	1909–1913	Helen Herron Taft (1861–1943)
Woodrow Wilson	1913–1921	Ellen Louise Axson Wilson (1860–1914)[b] Edith Bolling Galt Wilson (1872–1961) (marriage: 1915)
Warren G. Harding	1921–1923	Florence Kling Harding (1860–1924)
Calvin Coolidge	1923–1929	Grace Anna Goodhue Coolidge (1879–1957)

(Table 2.1 continues)

Table 2.1   Continued

President	Term in Office	Presidential Spouses
Herbert Hoover	1929–1933	Lou Henry Hoover (1874–1944)
Franklin D. Roosevelt	1933–1945	Anna Eleanor Roosevelt Roosevelt (1884–1962)
Harry S Truman	1945–1953	Elizabeth Virginia Wallace Truman (1885–1982)
Dwight D. Eisenhower	1953–1961	Mamie Geneva Doud Eisenhower (1896–1979)
John F. Kennedy	1961–1963	Jacqueline Lee Bouvier Kennedy Onassis (1929–1994)
Lyndon B. Johnson	1963–1969	Claudia Taylor Johnson (1912–)
Richard M. Nixon	1969–1974	Patricia Ryan Nixon (1912–1993)
Gerald R. Ford	1974–1977	Elizabeth Bloomer Ford (1918–)
Jimmy Carter	1977–1981	Rosalynn Smith Carter (1927–)
Ronald Reagan	1981–1989	Nancy Davis Reagan (1923–)
George Bush	1989–1993	Barbara Pierce Bush (1925–)
William Clinton	1993–	Hillary Rodham Clinton (1947–)

Notes: a. Spouse died prior to White House term.
b. Spouse died during White House term.
c. President's niece.

a basis for his well-known, albeit critical, examination of the first ladies and presidents.[27] Even though Troy is concerned with the existence of a partnership or presidential couple, he does not deny its existence or power. As such, a co-presidency or associate presidency model or, as I advocate, the perspective of a presidential partnership would provide another approach for analyzing the presidency.

Not only is the first lady's office budget and staff larger than many of the so-called key advisers and institutions that presidential scholars study, but as presidential spouse she assumes a role vastly more vital to the president's career and the success of the White House than any formal adviser. Consider how many public opinion polls have been taken of the president's chief of staff or secretary of the treasury. Not many; even conservative, traditional first ladies generate more polls. How many senior aides have been with the president since the start of his political career? Again, not many. Likewise, how often has the president's popularity been tied to the popularity of a staffer? Rarely. And how many key advisers have campaigned alongside the president throughout the duration of the election cycle? The answer is obvious. Thus the character of the presidential marriage should be examined and used to inform presidential scholarship. It is natural for the first lady, as the person closest to the president, to emerge as a major influence in the president's political life. Many presidents had been married to their wives for decades when they were elected to the presidency. It makes sense, then, that the president's personal character, beliefs on and agenda for the family, and commitment to women's issues might be examined through his relationship with his wife. Additionally, the presidential marriage and the symbolic role society forces on the first lady offer a basis for examining society's shifting views on womanhood, gender, and marriage.

Presidential Partners

Early books on the first ladies failed to recognize the existence of a partnership in the presidential marriage and were limited in scope to social histories of individual first ladies. But such perspectives are changing, and support for the existence of a partnership in the presidency is building. The emergence of the perspective of a White House partnership will assist our understanding of both the first ladyship and the presidency, especially presidential decisionmaking, leadership, and character. This new approach can be termed the *presidential partnership* model. As presidential scholars move from the notion of a singular to a plural presidency and as more information on the contributions made by first ladies becomes available, such a model will gain widespread acceptance.

Evidence of the existence of a partnership are found in the words of presidents themselves. Many presidents have praised their wives for their roles and actions. Jimmy Carter, for instance, publicly admitted that his wife, Rosalynn, was his most trusted adviser.[28] Rosalynn, for her part, readily admitted to influencing her husband's decisions as well as those of high-ranking government officials.[29] According to Mrs. Carter, a first lady can influence officials, the public, or issues simply by discussing them or devoting her attention to them, such is the power and visibility of the office. Or a first lady's influence might take the form of a working partnership. Rosalynn Carter assisted her husband in this capacity from the time he started his political career in 1962 in the Georgia state senate, through his governorship of that state, to his presidency by helping him with his official correspondence, making phone calls for him, and campaigning alone for him.

Consider even those first ladies, such as Bess Truman or Pat Nixon, thought to have been apolitical and uninterested in the presidency. Harry Truman gave his wife, Bess, the nickname "The Boss" and admitted that he never made an important decision without consulting her. Even Richard Nixon, a president who generally did not involve his wife in the political or policy affairs of his office, conceded the existence of a partnership during his 1960 campaign for the presidency. The Republican National Committee's press releases during that campaign featured such slogans as "When you elect a President you are also electing a First Lady" and "The First Lady has a working assignment." In practice, this partnership approach has been occurring in one form or another since the Washington presidency. Historically, the partnership was often defined more by social functions and moral support. More recently, it has become a political partnership, as can be seen in Bill and Hillary Clinton's merger of the East and West Wings of the White House. (Hillary Clinton broke with precedent when she relocated her office in the vicinity of the president's office. In the modern era, first ladies have had offices in the East Wing; the West Wing contained the presidential office.) Hillary Clinton's well-known campaign promise of "We are a partnership" and her husband's pledge during his 1992 bid for the White House that by electing him, voters would get "two for the price of one" further reflect the existence of a presidential partnership. Author and daughter of former President and First Lady Truman, Margaret Truman, speaking of the power and partnership role of first ladies, goes so far as to say that "without Dolley, Madison would almost certainly have been a one-term failure."[30]

Presidential scholar James David Barber's important book *The Presidential Character: Predicting Performance in the White House* and related works such as Alexander and Juliette George's *Presidential Personality and Performance* are premised on predicting and explaining presidential behavior through analysis of presidential character.[31] This approach considers a compilation of factors, such as the president's worldview, personality, style, and leadership. Clearly, one of the factors either influencing or reflecting the president's personality and character is his wife. It would thus benefit scholars like Barber to consider the presidential marriage. As R. Gordon Hoxie, longtime head of the Center for the Study of the Presidency, asserts, "Analyzing the work of first ladies provides a valuable and insightful path to knowledge about the American Presidency."[32]

The Paradoxes of Being the President's Spouse

The absence of a clearly defined role and constitutional guidance concerning the duties and functions of the president's spouse is both an asset and a liability for the occupant of the office.[33] Similarly, this ambiguity is both an asset and a liability insofar as first ladies might exploit the powers of the office. Although this ambiguity may allow a particular first lady to frame the office in a manner that suits her personality, abilities, and political objectives, it also means that any approach is open to criticism and controversy. Yet the reality of the matter is that a few legal parameters and many social customs concerning the nature of the office do in fact exist. The institution has a long and viable history that cannot be ignored, and numerous media, social, and political forces are functioning to define the parameters of the first ladyship, especially with respect to her public roles and political activities. The challenge is for the president's spouse to juggle these many complex and often conflicting factors while somehow not crossing the hypersensitive, dynamic, and nearly invisible line between what is and what is not an acceptable approach to what has emerged as one of the most demanding, difficult, and politicized jobs in the United States.

It is not surprising, then, that the first lady has been deemed "the wild card of American politics."[34] Besides being married to the president, perhaps the one thing that all presidential spouses have had in common is that they faced a great challenge in coming to the White House. A second commonality is that they all faced criticism. Each one has been attacked by the press, public, and the president's political enemies. The first lady has been open to a variety of attacks, many of which have been unfair and unfounded as well as highly personal in nature and, in many ways, without precedent in other institutions of U.S. society. Perhaps the defining factor in examining the office is that every one of its occupants has had to attempt to function within a paradoxical, unrealistically attainable set of expectations from a public still uncertain about what it really expects from the office. The first ladyship is an institution filled with paradoxes.

One such paradox is that technically none of the first ladies have asked for the job. Presidents and elected officials are in office because they sought the office. They campaigned for the privilege; indeed, many spent most of their adult lives and professional careers pursuing the opportunity. A first lady, however, serves only because of marriage. Whereas the president is elected by the entire nation and can be sure that at least a significant percentage of the public—or electoral college—supports him, the first lady has no such sense of security, mandate, or public confidence. The first lady is "elected" by only one person: the president.

Another paradox is that many first ladies have served at great personal expense and only out of a sense of duty to their spouse or to the nation. Some have been downright reluctant to enter the White House. For example, Anna Harrison was highly distraught over the election of her husband, William, to the presidency. She literally and unsuccessfully begged his friends and supporters to leave him alone in peaceful retirement. Jane Pierce so dreaded the office that she fainted upon learning of Franklin Pierce's nomination. Margaret Taylor worried so much about her husband Zachary's declining health that she prayed that he would lose the election. In a cruel twist of fate, he won, only to die sixteen months into his term. Even Martha Washington, the beloved "mother of her country" who impressed almost everyone with her competent service, hid the fact that she disliked the office and longed to be rid of the presidency and return to her beloved home in Virginia.

First ladies have had justifiable reason to be concerned about the office, as they have faced the daunting task of becoming national celebrities. But they have had another, more pressing reason for not embracing the presidency. The presidency brings with it threats to the health and safety of the president and his immediate family. Four presidents, after all, have been assassinated in office: Abraham Lincoln, James Garfield, William McKinley, and John Kennedy; four others have died of natural causes while in office: Zachary Taylor, William Henry Harrison, Warren Harding, and Franklin D. Roosevelt. Several presidents have narrowly escaped death from attempted assassinations: Lynette "Squeaky" Fromme tried to assassinate President Gerald R. Ford on September 5, 1975, and John Hinkley Jr. shot Ronald Reagan on March 31, 1981. As dismaying as it may be, all presidents, and thus their spouses, have faced the specter of assassination and the extreme mental and physical stress that comes with the office. Despite such concerns, several first ladies enjoyed their tenure in the White House, accepting and even appearing to thrive on the challenges and demands of what Margaret Truman calls "the second hardest job in America."[35]

There are other paradoxes surrounding the roles and responsibilities of the first ladyship. Because there is no formal job description, few legal precedents, and no constitutional guidance available to the first lady, essentially all of her activities are open to criticism and questioning.[36] Other than the "Bobby Kennedy rule," which imposes limitations on the first lady's ability to hold formal political office in her husband's administration, there is little official guidance that can assist first ladies in defining their office. By contrast, the president's roles and functions are at least marginally mandated by law and the Constitution. Tradition helps frame some responsibilities of the Office of First Lady, along with such factors as public opinion and societal values. But as society changes, so do public expectations, and subsequently, so does the office. The office also evolves with each personality occupying it and the preferences and agenda of the particular president. Most recent first ladies, for example, have created new responsibilities for and dimensions to the job. But because the sole avenue to the office is through the wedding ring, questions arise about the constitutionality of some of these responsibilities and dimensions as well as the basis of any political power wielded by first ladies.[37] Power in a democracy is not to be vested in unelected individuals or family members of elected officials; thus a first lady's political power might be illegitimate. She is, after all, unaccountable to the citizenry.[38] However, this argument has been questioned and related examples exist in the many staff positions that have evolved in the executive office of the president.[39] There are few corollaries for such spousal power internationally, in U.S. corporations, or other public or non-profit institutions. Congressional spouses do not draft legislation, corporate spouses do not lead board meetings, and military spouses do not command troops.

Legal uncertainty accompanies any formal actions taken by the first lady because her office is, in the words of historian Gil Troy, an "extra-constitutional position."[40] The first lady is beyond the structural checks and balances of the U.S. political system. Some critics of the office have gone as far as to suggest the office should not exist because it is an affront to democracy; others are no less hostile in deeming it "philosophically twisted in concept and . . . politically outrageous in practice."[41] Although some legal criticism is certainly valid, much of it seems to come from the traditional chauvinistic displeasure with women in positions of power and leadership. However, such prominent feminists as Germaine Greer have also attacked the first ladyship.[42] Paradoxically, Greer's call for abolishing the office is in direct contradiction to the chauvinistic position; Greer sees the first ladyship as demeaning to women and the first lady's means of empowerment as antithetical to the ideals of the feminist movement. Herein the first lady is considered to be an archaic and negative model by which all U.S. women are judged: that is, the perfect wife wearing lipstick, makeup, and high heels, standing loyally by her man. She has no identity except through her marriage, and her base of power is solely the result of marriage. This particular critique seeks to liberate women and the presidential spouse in particular from the "decorative servitude" that perpetuates a culture whereby women are conceptualized foremost as wives. Even those first ladies who were quite powerful and functioned as activists were forced to exercise their influence behind the scenes, hidden from the glare of public opinion or media introspection.

Despite the criticism and controversy, the public still demands a wide variety of roles for the first lady, and the specific duties seem to change with the whims of political necessity and shifting public attitudes. So with no legal, constitutional, or formal mandate for the first lady to follow, it appears that the specific roles and responsibilities of the first lady have been driven largely by public opinion and other factors such as the particular inclinations and talents of individual first ladies, the events of the times, and the president's view of his spouse's job. The public and press demand active, public roles for the first lady, and when first ladies act accordingly, the public and press are often critical of these very roles. The office is defined by paradoxes. In this respect, it parallels the presidency, an office also defined (and plagued) by paradox, according to Thomas Cronin and Michael Genovese's *The Paradoxes of the American Presidency* (New York: Oxford, 1997).

An Office Under Siege

It is not surprising that the office of first lady has been and remains under attack. Such hostility comes from a variety of sources and institutions. The critiques pertain to almost anything the first lady does (or does not do), but many of the attacks appear to be related to the first lady having power and influence, or at least the perception of such. The paradox is that the public seems to admire strong and visible first ladies, yet when the first lady exercises or even gives the appearance of exercising real power, she is attacked for it. This is the case even when such power arises from actions and roles demanded by the public or when she is acting in support or defense of the president, something spouses are otherwise supposed to do.

Every first lady seems to have been subjected to criticism. It comes with the "job." Even the strong and intelligent Abigail Adams was criticized for (what else but) being strong and intelligent. She was derogatorily called "Madame President" and "Her Majesty" by powerful enemies of her husband, such as Albert Gallatin.[43] Abigail was thought to be too political, and politics was not something in which a lady of the times was supposed to participate. Abigail was an exception for her times; she often fought back against her critics and her husband's political enemies. She was even critical of venerable figures like Gallatin and Thomas Jefferson. So upset was the first lady with the attacks from the press that they drove her to support censoring the press and argue in favor of the Alien and Sedition Acts (which were passed in 1798), one of the rare lapses in political judgment for the otherwise intelligent and astute Mrs. Adams.[44]

More recently, Nancy Reagan was vilified as the "Dragon Lady" and "Queen Nancy." In part such criticism was due to the first lady's extravagant, high-society lifestyle, something that seemed odd juxtaposed with the austere cuts in social programs advocated by her husband. But the attacks were also a result of the perception that she wielded real political power in the Reagan administration. Interestingly, the attacks came not just from Democrats and Ronald Reagan's opponents but were echoed by Republicans and Reagan insiders concerned about the first lady's influence over the president. Of course, the same ugly and personal epithets were not hurled at the president's most influential advisers, Donald Regan, Michael Deaver, Cap Weinberger, and George Shultz. Similarly, Sarah Polk, who served back in the 1840s, was accused of "ruling" her husband and influencing his political decisions. Even James Polk's vice president, George Dallas, complained that "she is certainly mistress of herself and I suspect of somebody else also."[45] Sarah Polk's obvious interest in politics and role as adviser to her husband even landed her in hot water with women. Female guests at the Polk White House were often put off when the first lady failed to remain with the ladies after dinner, preferring instead to adjourn with the men to discuss politics.

Even today the first lady is forced to juggle the roles of traditional wife and modern woman, seeking an elusive balance between the two. The first lady is caught between the unease many Americans have with women in power and the reality of contemporary society whereby women work, head households, and lead corporations. As first lady scholar Myra Gutin states, "The first lady treads a narrow line," and even the social causes she is expected to champion had better be safe, conservative, and "feminine" in nature.[46] Not only do active, strong first ladies run the risk of breaching some narrow parameter of what constitutes the proper role for spouses and women in general in U.S. society, but such activism could also harm the president. It is more likely that an unpopular first lady will be a political liability to the president than that an immensely popular first lady will benefit the president. Some historians feel that the perception of a strong and successful first lady could negatively affect public opinion toward the president; such a spouse leads the public to assume that the president is "henpecked," does not "wear the pants," or is weak.[47] Ronald Reagan, for example, was perceived as being too dependent on his wife. Much of this attitude stemmed from Nancy Reagan's perceived overprotective and domineering manner. Regardless of how they approach the first ladyship, presidential spouses must also be careful not to "threaten, eclipse, or overwhelm" the president.[48] First ladies must be concerned with their appearance, style of dress, social events, and so on, all the while balancing the catch-22 of not being too overwhelming or too underwhelming.

The problem is that the variety and scope of criticism seem limitless. Moreover, the range of faultfinding covers the entire realm of options and actions, leaving first ladies to face blame no matter what they do or don't do. For instance, first ladies have been attacked for being too uppity, yet at the same time too bland. They have been criticized as too active and too passive. In recent years, Barbara Bush was seen as too old-fashioned and frumpy; Nancy Reagan, too powerful; Rosalynn Carter, too tough; Betty Ford, too outspoken; Pat Nixon, too passive; and Hillary Clinton, too active. Whereas Nancy Reagan, Mary Lincoln, and Elizabeth Monroe were criticized for their excessive tastes in clothing, Edith Roosevelt and Rosalynn Carter were judged harshly for just the opposite. Even the popular Dolley Madison, who was widely admired for her impressive social hosting, was at the same time criticized for her impressive entertaining style. Julia Tyler was thought to be too young (she was in her early twenties), and Martha Washington, too old (she was in her late fifties). Martha was even criticized for the number of horses pulling her carriage and the type of food she served at official and unofficial events. Many accounts exist, however, that compliment her for her taste in carriages and menus. Harriet Lane was criticized for being too happy, whereas Jane Pierce was criticized for being too unhappy. Dolley Madison was judged to be too flirtatious, whereas Elizabeth Monroe was too aloof. There is no shortage of criticisms, and all first ladies can expect to be attacked for something. The adage "You can't please all of the people all of the time" might be paraphrased, in the case of the first ladies, to read, "You can count on your actions—and your inactions—upsetting some of the people all of the time."

Many of the attacks have been highly personal in nature and, by most measures, unfair. For example, the press made fun of Eleanor Roosevelt for her physical appearance and unfashionable attire. Cartoonists depicted the first lady with huge, ugly, protruding teeth. Pat Nixon was called "Plastic Pat" for appearing to be the perfect housewife. Shockingly, Julia Grant, by all accounts a very warm, admirable, and competent social hostess and supportive partner to her politically marginal husband, Ulysses, was teased in the press about being cross-eyed. Margaret Taylor was also the brunt of political satirists who portrayed her as an illiterate hick. In the press she was often caricatured smoking a corncob pipe, even though it appears that Mrs. Taylor never did smoke a pipe.[49] Rachel Jackson's divorce was the subject of ugly rumormongering and personal attacks from both the press and Jackson's political rivals. Yet Rachel's first husband was highly abusive, and her relationship with Andrew Jackson appears to have been warm and genuine. First Lady Ida McKinley, who suffered from epilepsy, was not spared. Her condition and health, along with a host of inaccurate charges— she was accused of being an English spy, a lunatic, and a Catholic—were topics for press sensationalism and negativism. Mary Todd Lincoln endured the lowest of such personal attacks. She was brutalized by her husband's critics, the press, and Washington society on both personal and political levels unprecedented in U.S. politics. Her attire, hosting, family life, and friendships were all open to condemnation. The South criticized her for being pro-Union, and the North never truly trusted this former belle from a prominent southern family. She was simultaneously accused of being pro-North and pro-South, uncouth and too fancy. She was even accused of treason by the North and received a considerable amount of hate mail and death threats from the South.

Although the hostility Mary Todd Lincoln experienced is an extreme example of what first ladies face, a recent parallel to Mrs. Lincoln might be the personal and political attacks on Hillary Clinton. For instance, the Republican Party conventions of 1992 and 1996 were filled with Hillary Clinton bashing to the point that she was demonized as a threat to the very future of the American family and the Republican-preferred traditional notion of womanhood. The public was treated to a debate over whether or not the first lady, who happened to be a Yale-educated lawyer, should have forgone her legal career in order to have stayed home and baked cookies. Other parallels to the poor treatment of Mrs. Lincoln are found in First Ladies Lou Hoover and Eleanor Roosevelt, both early champions of civil rights, who were the target of many southern segregationists and the southern press for, among other things, inviting blacks to the White House for tea. Because of such acts of "defiling" or "crusading," the first ladies were vilified in newspapers from Alabama to Tennessee, and state legislatures from Texas to Georgia passed resolutions condemning such efforts at integration.[50]

Criticism has resulted from the first lady's public actions. After citizens repeatedly invaded the White House grounds and even the living quarters of the first family by entering the White House uninvited and at all hours, First Lady Frances Cleveland had a gate erected and restricted public access to the grounds. Even though the hours in which the executive mansion remained open to visitors were generous and much of the building was still accessible, Mrs. Cleveland was criticized for her actions. First ladies have also been victims of political agendas. Lucy Hayes, a well-educated, intelligent woman who had earlier shown signs of embracing the women's movement, was criticized by early suffragettes for not further supporting women's suffrage during her years in the White House. She was also derogatorily branded "Lemonade Lucy" for her refusal to serve alcohol in the White House and her support of the temperance movement.

Some first ladies effectively countered the attacks and others did not. Some retreated under the barrage, whereas others laced up the gloves. Dolley Madison charmed her husband's enemies and won many supporters. Hillary Clinton, bowing to the relentless pressure of her critics, retreated from some of her more political and feminist activism and resorted to the image-enhancing task of baking cookies for reporters during the Christmas holidays and thereby appeased her critics. Eleanor Roosevelt fought back, adopting the practice of permitting only female reporters access to her press conferences. This strategy both helped the careers of female journalists, who tended to be excluded from most political and news stories, and had the effect of creating allies for the first lady among grateful female reporters. Betty Ford, clearly an exception to the rule, continued to hold her own views and speak her mind on such sensitive issues as abortion rights and the Equal Rights Amendment, even if her opinions differed from those of her husband. After being criticized for her open support of the controversial ERA, Betty rebutted, "Being ladylike does not require silence."[51] Abigail Adams also had strong words and little patience for her critics. Nancy Reagan wrote a book titled *My Turn* after leaving office, which, as the title suggests, answered her many critics.

It seems probable that many first ladies felt overwhelmed by the challenges of the office. After all, first ladies served at great personal sacrifice.

There were also economic considerations. Public hosting and formal socials were not funded by the government during the nineteenth century; such occasions were a personal expense to be borne by the first family. Many early first families found the high costs of official entertainment a drain on their personal savings.

As might be expected, some first ladies did not necessarily enjoy their years of service. Martha Washington did not like public life. She found the formalities dull and restrictive and complained of the loss of her cherished privacy. Mrs. Washington wrote about her life in the capital, "I live a very dull life here." She also observed, "I think I am more like a state prisoner," and she referred to her time as presidential spouse as her "lost years."[52] Abigail Adams shared Mrs. Washington's feelings, noting during her service that she was "sick, sick of public life."[53] Abigail's daughter-in-law and wife of the sixth president, Louisa Adams, even likened her life in the White House to "a bird in a cage."[54]

Other first ladies enjoyed the White House, feeling that their years spent there were among the happiest of their lives. Among those who most enjoyed the experience were Dolley Madison, Julia Tyler, Julia Grant, Frances Cleveland, Grace Coolidge, and Mamie Eisenhower. Regardless of whether they liked or disliked their years as first lady, most presidential spouses served dutifully, accepting the challenges, loss of privacy, and personal sacrifices on behalf of their husbands and country.

Studies of journalists and media coverage of politicians suggest that perhaps sexism among male reporters may factor into press attacks on strong, successful first ladies such as Hillary Clinton. Yet the findings are far from conclusive, because some of the criticism has come from female reporters.[55] Two things are apparent: (1) Criticism has always been a part of the job, and (2) in general, the extent of criticism has grown, corresponding to the expanded media coverage of the presidency in the modern, televised age. Television has brought the presidents and their families into the living rooms of average Americans, thus personalizing the office. The effect has been to enhance the president's power. Presidents have used the mass media to their advantage, offering the country warm, personal glimpses into the private lives of the first family. However, such accessibility has also had the effect of making the presidential family part of the political process and, thereby, open to excessive media introspection. By the 1970s and 1980s, the new style of adversary journalism was being felt by both presidents and first ladies, who had become targets of an increasingly scandal-driven, competitive press. This effect was furthered in the 1990s with the advent of a no-holds-barred, sensationalized, tabloid journalism that reawakened the old specter of William Randolph Hearst, the penny press, and yellow journalism. No story is off limits, no private aspect of a politician's personal life is kept sacred, and the first ladyship has experienced brutal political and personal attacks. Not only has this exacted a terrible price on the presidency—whereby many prospective candidates have turned away, unwilling to subject themselves and their families to the ugly attacks of an intrusive and unprincipled press—but the effects have also been felt by first ladies.

Conservatives have brought criticism to a new level of unabashed sensationalism by declaring a personal war on First Lady Hillary Clinton. Radio talk show host Rush Limbaugh has called Mrs. Clinton a "man-hater" and a "femi-nazi." Limbaugh's unscrupulous attacks even resorted to mean-spirited criticism of the Clintons' teenaged daughter, Chelsea. Even well-known columnists like William Safire assaulted Nancy Reagan's role in her husband's administration in a manner that amounted to little more than thinly veiled sexism and misplaced aggression. Safire and others continued in this manner during the early months of the Clinton administration, with accusations of a "Hillary Problem" or a "Hillary Factor."[56] Safire even suggested that Hillary would not let her husband have any say in his own presidency and wondered if Mrs. Clinton might not even take over the president's office. Even Ted Koppel, the staid, notoriously objective host of ABC's popular news show *Nightline,* allowed conservative guests on his show to participate in a bashing of Hillary Clinton that was highly personal in nature, without foundation, and far from professional. A news show about the first lady was reduced to a circus of derogatory name calling and ugly comments about Mrs. Clinton's looks and her hairstyle.[57]

The media has attacked the institution of the first lady as being too powerful, even if it has helped create that institution and forced first ladies into such activism. First ladies no longer have the option of refusing to participate in campaigns and other political activities. One day we read about the office being too political and too powerful, and the next day we read that the first lady is little more than an ornamental part of the presidency. Neither the media nor presidential scholars have accurately portrayed the institution and its true nature. But such depictions influence public opinion and expectations of the office and, in turn, shape the office of first lady.

What has evolved is an institution of the White House, with a large, powerful staff, offices, and budget that rival those of many senior presidential advisers, yet that same institution is not even supposed to be a formal job. It is an office that is expected to perform numerous challenging tasks with serious political consequences, yet it is subject to criticism whenever some nondelineable, gendered, political line is crossed. The first lady is the most scrutinized woman in the United States and must watch her every step. The public allows only a very narrow margin for error. These paradoxes point to a need to better understand the public perceptions, roles, and responsibilities of the first ladyship.

Studies of the office must consider public opinion and the public image of the first ladies. They must also somehow include the private relationship between the president and the first lady because the first lady's official capacity and unofficial influence are inseparable. In short, it is an office defined by controversy, criticism, and paradox. In the words of First Lady Rosalynn Carter: "I had learned when Jimmy was in the state Senate that you're going to be criticized no matter what you do. If you stay in the White House and pour tea, you'll be criticized because you don't get out. If you get out a lot, you are trying to do too much. I had learned even before I got to the White House to do what I thought was important, because the criticism is going to come."[58]

Notes

1. Several scholars of the first ladyship and presidency have noted the lack of systematic research on the first ladies. See, for instance, L. L. Gould, "Modern First Ladies," 1990; L. L. Gould, "First Ladies," 1986; R. G. Hoxie, "About This Issue," 1990; E. Mayo, "The Influence and Power of First Ladies," 1993; G. Troy, *Affairs of State*, 1997.

2. Several other scholars have called for further study of the first lady, including B. B. Caroli, *First Ladies*, 1987; Gould, 1990, 1986; Hoxie, 1990; and Mayo, 1993.

3. For a discussion of the lack of scholarly interest in the first lady and some of the criticisms of the first ladies and the first ladyship as a field of study, see Gould, 1990, 1986; C. S. Anthony, "First Ladies, Third Degree," 1994; Mayo, 1993; B. A. Weisberger, "Petticoat Government," 1993.

4. See the aforementioned sources, but in particular, see Gould, 1990, and A. M. Rosenthal, "The First Ladyship," 1994.

5. Prominent feminist Germaine Greer has even called for abolishing the office altogether. See her article "Abolish Her," 1995.

6. Literature and studies on the first lady are increasing. Within the past few years a number of presidential libraries have opened collections of the first ladies' papers. For a discussion of the comparative lack of information on the first ladies, see P. F. Boller Jr., *Presidential Wives*, 1988; M. C. Ryan and N. K. Smith, *Modern First Ladies*, 1989. The status of documents on the first lady is improving with organizations like the new National First Ladies Library, located in the Saxton McKinley House in Canton, Ohio, that are compiling literature on the first ladies.

7. See M. Truman, *First Ladies*, 1996.

8. Historically, women (the first ladies) were rarely discussed in newspapers. Consequently, there are few newspaper or written accounts of many of the early first ladies. But there are enough to assist my study of the subject. Presidential libraries have started organizing the first ladies' papers and making them available to the public. The White House and First Ladies Library both have helpful home pages with links to a variety of sources on the first ladies.

9. Custom held that it was not respectful or proper to discuss one's wife in books and a lady was not to be discussed in the newspapers. Therefore, a few of the early presidents, apparently in observance of custom, hardly even mentioned their

wives in their autobiographies and memoirs. However, there are exceptions: Some newspaper accounts exist of early first ladies and these presidential wives do appear in presidential memoirs.

10. See Caroli, 1987; Greer, 1995; J. S. Rosebush, *First Lady, Public Wife,* 1987.

11. A. E. Anderson and H. V. Baxendale, *Behind Every Successful President,* 1992; C. S. Anthony, *Saga,* 1990 and 1991; Caroli, 1987; L. L. Gould, *First Ladies,* 1996; M. Gutin, *The President's Partner,* 1989.

12. Caroli, 1987; Gutin, 1989; B. H. Winfield, "Madame President," 1994.

13. See Fall 1990 issue, Vol. 20, No. 4.

14. *Presidential Studies Quarterly* has published articles on the first ladies in issues other than the 1990 issue. For example, it published articles in 1986 and in two issues in 1987 (Fall, Vol. 27, No. 4, and Summer, Vol. 27, No. 3). *PSQ* is published by the Center for the Study of the Presidency, based in New York City.

15. Caroli, 1987; Gould, 1996, 1990; Mayo, 1993.

16. Ibid.

17. I examined the curriculum at approximately two dozen Ph.D.-granting programs in political science and found that they did not offer courses on the first lady. For further discussion, see R. P. Watson, "Incorporating the First Ladies," 1998.

18. Scholarly sources include Caroli, 1987; Gutin, 1989; Anthony, 1990 and 1991; Gould, 1996; and Troy, 1997. Popular sources include Rosebush, 1987; Boller, 1988; M. Truman, 1996; and M. B. Klapthor, *The First Ladies,* 1994.

19. The Web site can be accessed at *http://www.whitehouse.gov.*

20. In my review of approximately three dozen popular books on the presidency, I found that many books fail to even mention the first ladies in the index or table of contents. Most textbooks either completely fail to discuss the first lady or devote only a paragraph or two to the president's spouse.

21. For instance, the following important books on the presidency fail to discuss the first lady: Barber's *The Presidential Character;* Watson and Thomas's *The Politics of the Presidency;* Edwards and Wayne's *Presidential Leadership;* and Pfiffner, *The Modern Presidency.* The same is true of some older classics, such as Koenig's *The Chief Executive* and Corwin's *The President.*

22. See Gould, 1996, 1990.

23. Boller, 1988; Caroli, 1987; Gould, 1986; Winfield, 1994.

24. C. S. Anthony, "First Ladylike," 1993; Mayo, 1993; Winfield, 1994.

25. R. P. Watson, "The First Lady Reconsidered," 1997.

26. Gould, 1996, 1990; Hoxie, 1990.

27. Troy, 1997.

28. The Carters regularly discussed their partnership marriage. See President Jimmy Carter's memoir *Keeping Faith,* 1982, and First Lady Rosalynn Carter's autobiography *First Lady from Plains,* 1984; B. D. Ayers Jr., "The Importance of Being Rosalynn," 1979; H. Sidey, "Second Most Powerful Person," 1979.

29. Ibid.

30. M. Truman, 1996.

31. J. D. Barber, *The Presidential Character,* 1985; A. L. George and J. L. George, *Presidential Personality,* 1998.

32. Hoxie, 1990.

33. Troy, 1997.

34. Anthony, 1993.

35. M. Truman, 1996.

36. Anthony, 1990 and 1991; Rosebush, 1987; Rosenthal, 1994; Winfield, 1994.

37. Rosenthal, 1994; Troy, 1997.

38. Ibid.

39. A. Borrelli and J. M. Martin, *The Other Elites,* 1997.

40. See Troy, 1997.

41. See Rosenthal, 1994.

42. See Greer, 1995.

43. Weisberger, 1993.

44. Abigail Adams regularly provided political advice to her husband. In fact, he solicited it, recognizing and valuing her opinion. She appears to have had good political instincts with the exception of her support of the Alien and Sedition Acts and her bickering with critics.

45. Quote appears in M. Truman, 1996.

46. See Gutin, 1989.

47. See Troy, 1997.

48. See Greer, 1995, and Troy, 1997.

49. The record is mixed, but it appears that Margaret Taylor did not smoke a pipe. Some scholars feel that she was too ill to have smoked. For a further discussion of the matter, see H. Holman, *Zachary Taylor,* 1966; Gould, 1996; M. O. Whitton, *First First Ladies,* 1948.

50. For instance, the *Mobile Press,* in an article titled "The White House Tea," complained that these acts "offered to the south and to the nation an arrogant insult." The *Commercial Appeal* (a Memphis-based newspaper) suggested on June 17, 1929, that the nation should "drop the 'White' from the White House." The *Birmingham Age-Herald* criticized First Lady Hoover on June 14, 1929, in an article titled "What Do They Say?" Relatedly, the Georgia House of Representatives passed a resolution expressing "regret over recent occurrences in the official and social life of the national capitol, which have a tendency to revive and intensify racial discord." See Gutin, 1989, for a further discussion of these racially based attacks. A. M. Black provides a nice discussion of Eleanor Roosevelt's response to the question of racism in the South in her article "Championing and Champion," 1990.

51. "The Last Word on First Ladies," 1992.

52. J. E. Fields, *"Worthy Partner,"* 1994.

53. Abigail's complaints about life in the White House are discussed in C. W. Akers, *Abigail Adams,* 1980; P. L. Leven, *Abigail Adams,* 1987; L. E. Richards, *Abigail Adams,* 1928; and L. Withey, *Dearest Friend,* 1981.

54. S. Mitchell, ed., *New Letters of Abigail Adams,* 1947.

55. H. L. Gates, "Hating Hillary," 1996; A. Mundy, "The Two Mrs. Clintons," 1996.

56. William Safire repeatedly attacked Hillary Clinton during the 1992 campaign and in 1993.

57. Ted Koppel devoted two shows of ABC's *Nightline* to Hillary Clinton in March 1993.

58. I conducted a questionnaire/interview with Rosalynn Carter. The information was provided by Deanna Congileo, associate director of public information at the Carter Center on February 25, 1997.

3

History of the First Lady

The president's spouse has the potential to become an important component of the contemporary presidency.

—George Edwards and Stephen J. Wayne,
Presidential Leadership: Politics and Policy Making

The history of the first ladyship provides a good starting point by which to begin formulating theories and models to guide the scholarly study of the office. Unfortunately, little is known about the historical development of the office of first lady and the roles and responsibilities of early first ladies. Scholarly study of the subject typically commences with Eleanor Roosevelt (first lady from 1933 to 1945) or dates back only to around the start of the twentieth century. However, in order to understand the contemporary office fully, it is necessary to study all first ladies serving since the founding of the nation. Indeed, nineteenth- and even eighteenth-century first ladies set precedents that shaped the early office, many of which are followed to the present day. Moreover, the development of the office of first lady as an institution of power and influence as well as an office responsible for social hosting and the advent of a presidential partnership in the White House pre-date women's suffrage, the rise of modern feminism, and the tenure of First Lady Eleanor Roosevelt.

Challenges to the Office

One of the first themes that becomes apparent in a study of the history of the institution is the great challenges that the office poses for its occupants. As I discussed in Chapter 2, many spouses felt overwhelmed by the numerous demands of the first ladyship, the sudden and intense public attention for which few people could ever be prepared, and the stress and changes brought on by living in the White House. Early first families also faced financial loss in accepting the presidency. The first couple was expected to entertain lavishly, yet in the early days of the republic, payment for such entertainment came out of the pocket of the president. The costs of living in the White House and fulfilling the social affairs of state were often in excess of the means of first families. Though it is true that many presidents and their spouses were quite wealthy, not all of them were. Jefferson, for example, although extremely wealthy upon entering the White House, was so generous with his own fortune in entertaining, donating his vast library, and later founding the University of Virginia that he died a man of common means. Interestingly, in his retirement, Jefferson was refused a pension or financial reimbursement for his many public services by an unappreciative Congress.

The early White House was not the building of splendor it is today. (See Box 3.1 for a history of the executive mansion.) With limited staff, few amenities, and little consideration of family living accommodations and necessities (like the logistics of washing clothing), early first families often experienced a decrease in their standard of living by moving to the executive mansion. Abigail Adams, the first presidential spouse to actually live in the newly constructed White House, found the building damp, drafty, and designed more for appearances than for livability. Out of necessity, she used the East Room to hang laundry to dry.[1] Only six rooms were completed at the time. Moreover, at its founding, the capital city of Washington, D.C., was little more than a struggling, small community literally carved out of swampland.

The office has also posed a great challenge to its occupants' health. A few of those first ladies who did not enjoy their White House years felt this way in part because of illness. The White House is very demanding on those in good health but has been nearly unbearable for those in poor health. This is true for both presidents and first ladies. Many pre-twentieth-century first ladies were unfortunate enough to enter the White House already in poor health. In an era of low life expectancies and poor health care, it is not surprising that many first ladies suffered from sickness, weakness, and symptoms associated with old age. After all, many entered the White House late in life, often past the average life expectancy for the times, and had endured several childbirths. Margaret Taylor and Anna Harrison, for example, had been married to career military men and spent most of their adult lives traveling from one rough frontier military outpost to another, living without comfortable amenities and raising large families in dangerous and primitive conditions. The prospects of the presidency caused both wives to worry about their own health as well as that of their husbands. After the lives they had lived, and given the demands of the presidency, it is not surprising that Mrs. Taylor and Mrs. Harrison pre-

Box 3.1   The White House: The First Lady's House

The White House stands as a symbol of the nation, but it is also the home of the first family. It was first occupied in 1800 by John and Abigail Adams. The design for the executive mansion, perhaps the most well known residence in the world, was selected from a competition won by Irish architect James Hoban. George Washington himself helped oversee the planning and construction of the building he referred to as simply "the President's House." The popular name "the White House" was not officially inscribed on presidential letterhead until the time of President Teddy Roosevelt.

The White House has endured the challenges of the republic. On August 24, 1814, invading British troops during the War of 1812 set the building ablaze. First Lady Dolley Madison courageously helped save priceless objects from the flames and later encouraged the nation to rebuild the president's residence. During the Civil War the building again faced the threat of destruction. Union troops from Company K of the 150th Pennsylvania Volunteers, known as the "Bucktail Brigade," had to be stationed in and around the White House to guard President Lincoln, his family, and the executive mansion. The White House has seen many renovations during its 200-plus-year history, most of which have been headed by the first lady. Under the guidance of first ladies, the splendor of the building has grown, yet the history and legacy of the White House have been maintained.

The building is famous not only for its occupants but for its rooms and events. Guests are often entertained in the elegant East Room or the Yellow Oval Room on the second floor. An invitation to dine at the State Dining Room remains much sought after, and first ladies have held popular social receptions at the White House for as long as the building has existed. The White House has also played host to weddings, including those of Teddy Roosevelt's daughter Alice and Richard and Pat Nixon's daughter Tricia.

First families have faced the challenge of calling the White House home. The second floor houses the living quarters for the president's family. First ladies such as Lucretia Garfield, Mary Lincoln, Jackie Kennedy, Rosalynn Carter, and Hillary Clinton have raised young children in the White House. Today the eighteen-acre estate sitting at 1600 Pennsylvania Avenue in Washington, D.C., continues to offer public tours and to be the center of power of the United States. But it is also home to the first family and is, to a large measure, the "First Lady's House."

ferred quiet, convalescing retirements to the strain of living in the White House.

Evolution of the Office

There is a blending of internal and external forces at work that shape the office of first lady. It is important to consider the difference between these two forces as well as the difference between factors that influence individual first ladies and those that influence the office of the first lady. The dominant internal forces shaping the evolution of the Office of the First Lady are the president's and the first lady's view of the office. But the first ladyship is also a product of external forces, such as history and custom.[2] There are many societal or external forces that have been at work forging the nature of the office. Six particular external factors have significantly influenced the evolution of the office.

1. *Design of the Presidency.* The nature of the first ladyship has grown out of the unique design of the office of the president. Perhaps because the presidency is a fusion of two typically distinct offices—head of state and head of government—early presidents, with little staff and financial support, had to rely on their wives to perform many of the official ceremonial and social affairs of state. This remains true to the present time, though the vice president also assists the president in these matters. Relatedly, the absence of royalty and ceremonial national offices or figures has not diminished the United States' interest in having political celebrities. The first lady has thus functioned to an extent as the country's political co-figurehead and occasional head of state. In this capacity she has assisted the president by shouldering much of the burden of the official and ceremonial affairs of state and of the presidency.

2. *Long, Nationwide, Public Campaigns.* The very nature of U.S. politics, as opposed to, for example, the British system, whereby the party nominates the head of government, has created a system that necessitates an aggressive commitment to campaigning by the candidate for president. This need for extensive campaigning—largely a twentieth-century phenomenon—has created a new dimension to the first ladyship. The campaign must be national in scope, covering the huge geographic area of the United States, and reach the entire U.S. populace. In recent years the length of presidential campaigns has extended to over one year. Thus, the candidate's spouse has become a full-time co-campaigner. Starting with Eleanor Roosevelt and followed later by Lady Bird Johnson, the first lady has also emerged as a valuable solo campaigner, thus allowing presidential hopefuls to be two places at once. President Jimmy Carter hardly campaigned during

his bid for reelection in 1980, preoccupied by such matters of governance as the ongoing Iranian hostage crisis and the state of the economy. Instead, Carter relied on his wife to carry much of his campaign to the voters. Such campaigning does not end with the election of the president. With a relatively weak political party structure and an emphasis on public opinion in governance, the president is forced to constantly campaign for public and political support for his programs and agenda. In some ways, presidential popularity and public approval have allowed the president to govern without going directly to or through the party or Congress. Such strategies, however, wed the president to continuous campaigning, a degree of which has been performed by the first lady.

3. *Ideal of the American Family.* There is in U.S. politics a preference for a family-oriented leader. Male candidates for office must reinforce the socially preferred notions of masculinity, fatherhood, and family patriarch. This is especially true of the institution of the presidency because it is such a highly gendered (masculine) office. This ideal has required the first lady to fulfill the symbolic but necessary and highly visible role of the model wife, standing loyally beside her man. This has even been true of strong, independent, activist first ladies such as Eleanor Roosevelt, Rosalynn Carter, and Hillary Rodham Clinton, all of whom have still had to fulfill the more traditional aspects of the office. Because the first ladyship is a distinctly feminine office, certain functions such as hosting are seen as the purview of the wife and remain driven by society's social norms.

4. *An Office in the White House.* The proximity of the president's official residence and office has allowed first ladies physical access to power. Because the president's office and home are located in the same building, the president's spouse is accessible and close to the base of power of government. It could be said that because the president "works at home," it is only obvious that his spouse becomes familiar with, if not involved in, his work.

5. *Vague Legal Parameters of the Office.* The lack of constitutional guidance has left the role of the first lady relatively wide open. Particular first ladies have used their ambition and talent to forge various roles for themselves, including duties and activities that are highly political in nature.

6. *History and Custom.* The first ladyship has a long history and the precedents established by the early presidential spouses must be considered by each subsequent first lady. Of course there have been new dimensions to the office. One of the main trailblazers was Eleanor Roosevelt, who reshaped the office through her extensive travel, numerous press conferences, and outspoken political activism and advocacy.[3] Never before had the power and influence of first ladies been revealed in such a public manner. Previously, most of the power and influence wielded by first ladies had

been performed in private and was a well-kept secret. Regardless of such changes, the precedent for activism and for the very legitimacy of the office dates back to Martha Washington. Even Eleanor Roosevelt had limitations placed on her activities owing to the history of the office. For example, despite her extensive political travels and policy activities, Eleanor was still expected to host social events.

Whether or not the aforementioned factors allow for or encourage the role of the activist political partner is uncertain. An equally valid argument could be that these factors require the first lady to appear as the model wife. Either way, what is certain is that these factors have created an institution that is a central facet of the White House and the U.S. political system. They have also shaped a dual office, simultaneously social in nature, whereby first ladies are responsible for affairs of state and White House hostessing, and political in nature, whereby first ladies function as policy advisers and political confidantes to the president. They have also worked to create both a highly public and highly politicized office, one that is continuing to evolve.

Historical Periods of the First Ladyship

The growth of the office has been neither gradual nor predictable. Often, for years at a time, there has been little or no change in the office; consecutive first ladies have approached the office in rather the same manner. At other times, significant changes in the office occurred from one first lady to the next. Some changes occurred because of the actions of individual first ladies. Other changes occurred because of events that were often beyond the control of the first lady or president.

Perhaps the first ladies have had little in common beyond simply being married to the president (or being related to him, as was the case of most proxy or surrogate White House hostesses who served when the first lady was either deceased or ill). Then again, perhaps it is possible to identify some commonalities shared by all first ladies or at least those of a particular era. One such commonality that emerges is a shared approach to the office that can be grouped by historical period. Some scholars have recognized this commonality and have used a historical classification to study or assess the first ladies of different time periods in U.S. history. One such model of historical periods has been offered by Betty Boyd Caroli.[4] Caroli's classification is a twofold conceptualization of the history of the office: pre–twentieth century and twentieth century. She sees the twentieth century as the time in which the office of the first lady was developed. Historian Carl Sferrazza Anthony offers a two-volume study of the first ladies that delineates between the pre- and post-1961 time frame, marking the advent of the modern office around the time of Jackie Kennedy.[5] Anthony conceptualizes the history of the first ladyship along eleven identifiable eras in the nation's history prior to the year 1961. In doing so, he ties the institution to its period in time, suggesting a linkage to the events, politics, and social environment of the age.

In an effort to consider the first ladies' contributions to and the development of the office in historical context, I have identified six distinct periods in the development of the institution. This model is not without exception; some first ladies better fit the historical periods than others, and the development of the institution has been neither linear nor completely consistent in its pace of change and evolution. However, this model offers a historical overview and source for beginning our examination of the growth of the institution.

First Spouses: Shaping the Image and Role (1789–1817)

1789–1797	Martha Dandridge Custis Washington
1797–1801	Abigail Smith Adams
1801–1809	Martha Wayles Skelton Jefferson (deceased)*
	Martha "Patsy" Jefferson Randolph (daughter)
	Dolley Payne Todd Madison (wife of Secretary of State)
1809–1817	Dolley Payne Todd Madison

Martha Washington had no blueprint to follow in determining her role as first lady. She worried about the uncertainties surrounding both the presidency and her official and unofficial capacity as the president's wife.[6] George Washington had few precedents to follow during his inaugural presidency, but at least the office had been discussed by the founding fathers in Philadelphia and the Constitution provided some fundamental parameters for the office. This framework was more than Martha had to go by; the role of the president's spouse had not been considered. The new nation and the world were watching as the Washingtons established the nature and scope of both new offices.

The actions of "Lady Washington" and other early spouses shaped the institution as a public ceremonial office that was responsible for social functions and hosting formal affairs of state. The institution became highly visible, and the president's wife emerged as a public figure. Martha

Note: *First lady was unable to serve. (This note applies to following listings in this chapter as well.)

Washington was the most widely known and beloved woman living in the United States when her husband took the oath of office.[7] Although the institution evolved in an apolitical and unofficial capacity with respect to political and public affairs, these early spouses also forged a role as confidante and informal adviser to the president on political matters. This was especially true of Abigail Adams, an articulate, intelligent, and assertive lifelong counsel to her husband. Dolley Madison was also quite politically astute and gained nationwide fame as the capital city's leading hostess for over two decades. Martha Washington was far less active politically than Abigail Adams and Dolley Madison. However, she was the central figure in her husband's life and played a significant role in his career and presidency. An exception to this first era is Martha Jefferson, who died years prior to her husband's presidency. It appears that Mrs. Jefferson was not particularly interested in politics, but it is hard to tell because so little is known about her or her relationship with her husband.[8]

As a group, the early spouses were affluent and were seen in a queen-like capacity.[9] First Ladies Washington, Adams, and Madison were greatly admired, widely known, and competent, respected hosts. Dolley Madison, in particular, remains as one of the most popular and successful first ladies of all time. Martha and Abigail have also enjoyed continued admiration throughout the ages, making these first spouses some of the most celebrated women in the history of the country.

Absent Spouses: Idled by Illness and Death (1817–1869)

1817–1825	Elizabeth Kortright Monroe
1825–1829	Louisa Catherine Johnson Adams
1829–1837	Rachel Donelson Jackson (deceased)*
	Emily Donelson (Rachel Jackson's niece)
	Sarah Yorke Jackson (wife of adopted son Andrew)
1837–1841	Hannah Hoes Van Buren (deceased)*
	Angelica Singleton Van Buren (daughter-in-law)
1841	Anna Tuthill Symmes Harrison (too ill to move to capital)*
	Jane Irwin Harrison (widow of Harrison's son)
1841–1845	Letitia Christian Tyler (invalid, died 1842)*
	Priscilla Cooper Tyler (daughter-in-law)
	Julia Gardiner Tyler (married John Tyler in 1844)
1845–1849	Sarah Childress Polk
1849–1850	Margaret "Peggy" Mackall Smith Taylor (semi-invalid)*
	Betty Taylor Bliss (daughter)
1850–1853	Abigail Powers Fillmore (poor health)*
	Mary "Abby" Abigail Fillmore (daughter)

1853–1857	Jane Means Appleton Pierce (in mourning)*
	Abigail Kent Means (aunt and friend of Jane Pierce)
1857–1861	Harriet Lane (Buchanan's niece)
1861–1865	Mary Todd Lincoln
1865–1869	Eliza McCardle Johnson (poor health)*
	Martha Johnson Patterson (daughter)

The first ladies of this period were, as a group, less influential and less active both politically and socially than the first ladies of other periods. The roles and responsibilities during this time were not expanded, and the institution was much less visible than it was during the earlier period. This decline in the office appears to parallel the status of the presidency. This was the era of common man presidents, and the office reflected the prevailing humble spirit of the nation. This ethos proved true in one unintended respect: Many of the presidents were common in their performance. Likewise, the first ladies were not active participants in the formal or informal, political, and public business of the White House. The first ladies themselves were part of the reason for this inactivity; they tended to be of a different temperament and have different approaches to their offices than later, more active first ladies.

Another reason for this inactivity can be found in the name given to this period. Many of these women were in poor health during their years in the White House, which greatly limited their activity. Others died prior to their husbands' presidencies, and substitutes, typically young female relatives, served in their absence as "Lady of the White House," "Mistress of the White House," or surrogate White House hostess. For example, Rachel Jackson and Hannah Van Buren died prior to their husbands' presidencies. Letitia Tyler had a stroke prior to her husband's presidency and she was too ill to fulfill her expected duties. She died only a year into her husband's term. Several first ladies of the period, including Margaret Taylor, Abigail Fillmore, and Eliza Johnson, were strong, capable women and active and influential partners in their marriages but spent part of their White House tenures limited by serious illness. If they had not been incapacitated during their first ladyships, it is probable that these women would have distinguished themselves in the White House. Anna Harrison never even made it to the capital city, as she was too sick to accompany her husband to his inauguration and had little interest in the city or its politics. As fate would have it, President Harrison died after only a month in office and before she was fully recovered. Both during and just prior to their White House years, Mary Todd Lincoln and Jane Pierce experienced the loss of several close loved ones. Part of their first ladyships were spent in mourning. This was more troubling for Jane Pierce, who was so distraught that she rarely even made public appearances during her husband's administration.[10]

The exceptions of the period include Sarah Polk, Julia Tyler, and Harriet Lane. Each of these first ladies enjoyed good health and were active while in the White House. Lane became one of the most popular hostesses in the history of the White House and would most likely be better known today if her bachelor uncle's single-term presidency was not such a failure. Polk was also atypical in that she was an active, political presence throughout her husband's career and public life. In many ways, Sarah Polk functioned as a predecessor of the activist partners of the modern period like Eleanor Roosevelt, Rosalynn Carter, and Hillary Rodham Clinton. Julia Tyler, a very young, attractive woman when she married the widower president, became, not surprisingly, an overnight sensation. The nation and the press fawned over this new, charming first lady in a manner unlike that experienced by any of the other first ladies of this period.[11] But her marriage came toward the end of Tyler's single-term presidency, thus minimizing her ability to effect lasting changes in the office. Mary Lincoln was a controversial figure throughout her husband's presidency, something which limited her effectiveness during that turbulent period in history. Still, First Ladies Polk, Julia Tyler, and Lincoln, and White House hostess Lane were active and well known during their White House years and each made contributions to the presidency.

Transitional Spouses: Unfulfilled Possibilities (1869–1901)

1869–1877	Julia Dent Grant
1877–1881	Lucy Ware Webb Hayes
1881	Lucretia Rudolph Garfield
1881–1885	Ellen Lewis Herndon Arthur (deceased)*
	Mary Arthur McElroy (Arthur's younger sister)
1885–1886	Rose Elizabeth Cleveland (bachelor Cleveland's sister)
1886–1889	Frances Folsom Cleveland (married Grover in 1886)
1889–1893	Caroline Lavinia Scott Harrison (dies in 1892)*
	Mary Harrison McKee (daughter)
1894–1897	Frances Folsom Cleveland
1897–1901	Ida Saxton McKinley

The "Transitional Spouses" were generally well educated for their time and many were intellectually and socially gifted women. They held out the promise of a new age and of a new woman in the White House. This was the gilded age, a time of growth and development across the country. Urbanization, industrialization, and the rise of the suffragettes defined this period. Although these first ladies were generally more active and influential than their predecessors in the second historical period, their promise was not fulfilled through asserting their own identities, forging new facets of the institution of first lady, or contributing to the presidency. The first ladies of this period fell short of their potential; they did not make lasting impressions on the first ladyship or on the status of women in U.S. society.

Lucy Hayes was an intelligent, college-educated women who was supportive of women's liberation. However, as first lady she attempted and contributed little to this endeavor and was discouraged from further activism by her husband.[12] Lucretia Garfield was also well read and was an intellectual influence on her husband prior to his presidency, but as first lady, she was limited by poor health. Her husband's untimely assassination shortly into his term of office also prevented her from establishing her presence. As a young woman, Ida Saxton McKinley had been sent to prestigious schools in the United States as well as in Europe. She even had the practical experience of having worked in her father's bank to match her intellect and refinement. However, Ida appears to have had epilepsy, suffering from headaches and blackouts, which impeded her presence in White House affairs and political activities during the McKinley administration.[13] Her condition was complicated by a difficult second pregnancy and the death of her four-month-old child. Her deteriorating state and seizures prevented her from realizing her vast potential in the White House. Moreover, her husband's presidency is widely considered to have been a failure, marked by corruption and his death by assassination, factors that further limited the first lady from exerting lasting influence over the office.

The first ladies of this period were a well-liked, capable, and intelligent group. That they did not further influence the office or the country should not detract from the fact that they served well and appear to have benefited their husbands' presidencies. Considering the less than spectacular presidents of this era, it would seem that, as a group, the women of the White House from 1869 to 1901 were more competent in their respective tasks than the men of the White House. There were some contributions made to the office, the presidency, and the nation during this period. Julie Grant became something of a celebrity and is known as one of the best social hosts of the White House. Lucy Hayes emerged as a well-known public figure, traveling across the country and initiating the custom of the White House Easter egg roll. Caroline Harrison compensated for her dull, dour husband and charmed guests at the White House. She was intelligent, personable, and an active donor to charities. Mrs. Harrison left a legacy of accomplishments, including the redecoration of the White House, the initiation of the White House china collection, and the founding of the Daughters of the American Revolution. She even encouraged the prestigious medical school at Johns Hopkins University to admit women.[14]

Aspiring Spouses: Developing New Roles (1901–1945)

1901–1909	Edith Kermit Carow Roosevelt
1909–1913	Helen Herron Taft
1913–1921	Ellen Louise Axson Wilson (died in 1914)*
	Margaret Wilson (daughter)
	Edith Bolling Galt Wilson (married Woodrow Wilson in 1915)
1921–1923	Florence Kling Harding
1923–1929	Grace Anna Goodhue Coolidge
1929–1933	Lou Henry Hoover
1933–1945	Anna Eleanor Roosevelt

The first ladies of the early twentieth century forged new roles for the institution. Indeed, the foundation for the modern first lady as an active presidential partner was firmly established during this period. For example, Helen Taft and Florence Harding were highly ambitious, determined, and liberated women who were the primary forces behind their husbands' careers.[15] Both were active as campaigners, speechwriters, and advisers. It is not unreasonable to suggest that had they lived during the present time, they would have pursued elected office themselves. Florence Harding publicly admitted to being a suffragist, another milestone for first ladies. Edith Wilson functioned with an unprecedented amount of power on behalf of the president during the many months following his debilitating stroke when she conducted White House meetings and managed the president's business and communications. Such a role would have been unthinkable only a few years previously. Indeed, such a role remains unthinkable even today. A Stanford graduate with a degree in geology, Lou Hoover traveled extensively throughout the world with her husband, translating for him, contributing to a textbook he wrote, and serving in all capacities as his closest adviser and partner.[16] The Hoover marriage was the archetype of the political partnership, and Lou Hoover lived a full life as an adventurous, active public figure.

This is also the period of Eleanor Roosevelt, still the standard by which all other first ladies are measured.[17] Eleanor's political and social activism, independence, public speaking, and writing career are without equal in the office and perhaps among twentieth-century women in the United States. She did more to change the institution of first lady than perhaps any other single person, event, or historical period. Eleanor spoke on behalf of the president at the 1940 Democratic convention, as the first presidential spouse to give a speech at a convention of the political parties. The modern first ladyship owes much of its existence to Eleanor Roosevelt.

The sole exception to this period is Grace Coolidge, who, despite her impressive social skills, appears to have been severely limited in her public life by her stodgy, controlling, and overly prudent husband. Grace was prevented from participating in any part of her husband's presidency. With the benefit of hindsight, it seems Calvin Coolidge did this at great cost to his presidency and personal image.

Supportive Spouses: Model Wives in the Mass Media Era (1945–1974)

1945–1953	Elizabeth "Bess" Virginia Wallace Truman
1953–1961	Mamie Geneva Doud Eisenhower
1961–1963	Jacqueline Lee Bouvier Kennedy
1963–1969	Claudia Taylor "Lady Bird" Johnson
1969–1974	Patricia Ryan Nixon

In the post–Eleanor Roosevelt era, despite the precedents established and opportunities present for ambitious first ladies, the spouses of this period are defined largely by tradition and convention. The first ladies from 1945 to 1974 approached the White House with mind-sets that were different from those of their predecessors. For example, Bess Truman and Jackie Kennedy were extremely private individuals who were unenthusiastic about the public nature of the job. Though highly capable, Pat Nixon and, to a lesser extent, Lady Bird Johnson were often limited by very controlling husbands. Mamie Eisenhower appears not to have had the skills or disposition necessary for any policy or advisory dimension of the institution but was a success at campaigning and projecting the ideal of American womanhood and motherhood during the 1950s.

With the advent of television and the mass media culture, the institution of first lady became much more public during this period. Thus the first ladies became an intimate part of the public domain and a crucial element of the modern, televised presidency. They were the first to experience this new public dimension of the presidency: They appeared on television, graced the covers of popular women's magazines, and emerged as recognizable household names and faces. However, the public persona of the first lady reflected during this period tended to be that of a supportive wife. Most of these first ladies were not as active or as influential as the groups that served immediately before and after them, and they did not define themselves as individuals to the extent that some other first ladies did. Yet they were popular hosts and symbols of the state of womanhood during that time.

An exception is Lady Bird Johnson, who achieved notoriety and success with her beautification and conservation initiatives. She was also the first presidential spouse to hit the campaign trail on her own, campaigning across the South to offset the hostility to the president's support of the 1964 Civil Rights Act. As an activist and a political partner, Johnson has emerged as a woman with her own identity and a powerful public figure in her own right.

Modern Spouses:
Public Presidential Partners (1974–present)

1974–1976	Elizabeth Bloomer Ford
1976–1981	Rosalynn Smith Carter
1981–1989	Nancy Davis Reagan
1989–1993	Barbara Pierce Bush
1993–	Hillary Rodham Clinton

The modern first lady has emerged as an active, political partner of the president. Her influence is felt not only in the president's personal and social life but in his public life and political career as well. The modern first lady has become a highly visible and influential force in the White House and in U.S. society. Although the first lady has certainly not achieved status as an equal partner—at least in the public's eye—she often functions like an associate president. This is the period of Rosalynn Carter and Hillary Rodham Clinton, first ladies who have attended cabinet meetings, headed policy task forces, and scheduled policy meetings with the president and his senior advisers. But despite the political element of the modern first ladyship, these women are still expected to fulfill, simultaneously, the roles of loyal wife, mother, and White House social hostess. In fact, the modern office might be defined as a dual first ladyship; spouses are full-time policy advisers and political partners but also full-time wives, mothers, and bakers of cookies and servers of tea.

Modern first ladies are expected to have an interest in politics and the presidency. They are expected to campaign endlessly and enthusiastically for the president, putting in hours in excess of those worked by the professional, paid campaign managers. They are asked difficult policy questions during press conferences and interviews. They meet with voters, shake hands, give speeches, and are themselves the topics of the political headlines. The modern first ladies no longer have the luxury of avoiding such aspects of the office. Even Barbara Bush, who professed publicly to have no interest in policy matters, was repeatedly questioned in the media about her positions on current issues and her husband's policy agenda. Although her image was that of a traditional grandmother, Mrs. Bush traveled widely with her husband, gave commencement addresses, spoke publicly, and campaigned for Republican candidates and policies. In spite of this obvious political activism, she was still widely considered to have been an apolitical first lady. This fact is testimony to the political element of the first ladyship and the arrival of a dual aspect of the modern office. It is becoming the rule and not the exception that the first lady has surpassed the vice president and even the most senior advisers and cabinet secretaries in terms of visibility and perhaps even power and influence both in and out of the White House.

Surrogate First Ladies

For various reasons several first ladies have not been able to fulfill the many duties associated with being the wife of the president and hostess of the White House. A few first ladies experienced poor health during their White House years, and some presidents have been elected whose wives died before their bid for the office. This is especially apparent in the years from 1817 to 1869, when most presidential wives were unable to meet all of the expected hosting requirements of the White House. During this period both Presidents Jackson and Van Buren were widowers; John Tyler's first wife, Letitia, was, as her situation was described during her lifetime, a "semi-invalid" at the time of his election and died only one year into his term; and the wives of Presidents Monroe, William Henry Harrison, Taylor, Fillmore, and Andrew Johnson were all in poor health. Jane Pierce had no interest in politics or social hosting and she relegated herself to a self-imposed isolation while in the White House, grieving the recent loss of her young son Benny.

Consequently, several surrogate or proxy hostesses served as "lady" or "mistress" of the White House. Some White House surrogate first ladies served throughout the entire term of the president, covering every hosting duty associated with the first ladyship, whereas others merely assisted the first lady from time to time with planning and conducting White House events. As Box 3.2 depicts, typically a close female relative has fulfilled the duties of surrogate White House hostess. Of the sixteen women who served in a viable capacity as surrogate first ladies, all were relatives of either the president or the first lady. This list contains seven daughters, four daughters-in-law, two nieces, two sisters of the president, and one aunt of the first lady. In spite of the often unfortunate and somber situation that occasioned their need to serve as White House hostesses, these surrogates served with distinction, earning praise from the social commentators of their day, political visitors to the White House, and the U.S. public. This praise is all the more impressive given that many of these surrogate first

Box 3.2   White House Hostesses Who Were Not First Ladies

White House Hostesses
for Widower and Bachelor Presidents
Martha Jefferson Randolph (1772–1836)
   President (Term): Thomas Jefferson (1801–1809)
   Period of Service: 1801–1809 (Dolley Madison also assisted with
      formal hosting)
   Relationship to President: Daughter
   Reason for Service: Wife, Martha, died years prior to Jefferson's
      presidency
Emily Donelson (1808–1836)
   President (Term): Andrew Jackson (1829–1837)
   Period of Service: 1829–1836
   Relationship to President: Wife's niece
   Reason for Service: Wife, Rachel, died prior to Jackson's presi-
      dency
Sarah Yorke Jackson (1805–1887)
   President (Term): Andrew Jackson (1829–1837)
   Period of Service: 1836–1837
   Relationship to President: Daughter-in-law
   Reason for Service: Wife, Rachel, died prior to Jackson's presi-
      dency; hostess Emily Donelson died in 1836
Angelica Singleton Van Buren (1816–1878)
   President (Term): Martin Van Buren (1837–1841)
   Period of Service: 1837–1841
   Relationship to President: Daughter-in-law (and relative of Dolley
      Madison)
   Reason for Service: Wife, Hannah, died prior to Van Buren's presi-
      dency
Harriet Lane (1831–1903)
   President (Term): James Buchanan (1857–1861)
   Period of Service: 1857–1861
   Relationship to President: Niece
   Reason for Service: Buchanan was a bachelor
Mary Arthur McElroy (1842–1917)
   President (Term): Chester A. Arthur (1881–1885)
   Period of Service: 1881–1885
   Relationship to President: Sister
   Reason for Service: Wife, Ellen, died prior to Arthur's presidency

(continues)

Rose Elizabeth Cleveland (1846–1918)
President (Term): Grover Cleveland (1885–1889; 1893–1897)
Period of Service: 1885–1886
Relationship to President: Sister
Reason for Service: Cleveland was a bachelor at the time (he married Frances Folsom in 1886)

Other White House Hostesses
Jane Irwin Harrison (?)
President (Term): William Henry Harrison (1841)
Period of Service: 1841
Relationship to President: Daughter-in-law
Reason for Service: Wife, Anna, was too ill to travel from Ohio to the White House
Priscilla Cooper Tyler (1816–1889)
President (Term): John Tyler (1841–1845)
Period of Service: 1841–1844
Relationship to President: Daughter-in-law
Reason for Service: Wife Letitia was in very poor health, died in 1842
Letitia Tyler Semple (1821–1907)
President (Term): John Tyler (1841–1845)
Period of Service: 1841–1844
Relationship to President: Daughter
Reason for Service: Wife Letitia was in very poor health, died in 1842
Mary Elizabeth "Betty" Taylor Bliss (1824–1909)
President (Term): Zachary Taylor (1849–1850)
Period of Service: 1849–1850
Relationship to President: Daughter
Reason for Service: Wife, Margaret, was in very poor health
Mary "Abby" Abigail Fillmore (1832–1854)
President (Term): Millard B. Fillmore (1850–1853)
Period of Service: 1850–1853
Relationship to President: Daughter
Reason for Service: Wife, Abigail, was in poor health
Abby Kent Means (?)
President (Term): Franklin Pierce (1853–1857)
Period of Service: 1853–1857
Relationship to President: Wife's aunt and good friend
Reason for Service: Wife, Jane, was in mourning and not interested in hostessing

(continues)

Box 3.2 Continued

Varina Davis
  President (Term): Franklin Pierce (1853–1857)
  Period of Service: 1853
  Relationship to President: Wife of Secretary of War Jefferson Davis
  Reason for Service: Wife, Jane, was in mourning and not interested in hostessing

Martha Johnson Patterson (1828–1901)
  President (Term): Andrew Johnson (1865–1869)
  Period of Service: 1865–1869
  Relationship to President: Daughter
  Reason for Service: Wife, Eliza, was in poor health

Mary "Marnie" Harrison McKee (1858–1942)
  President (Term): Benjamin Harrison (1889–1893)
  Period of Service: 1892–1893
  Relationship to President: Daughter
  Reason for Service: Wife, Caroline, died in 1892

Margaret Wilson (1886–1944)
  President (Term): Woodrow Wilson (1913–1921)
  Period of Service: 1914–1915
  Relationship to President: Daughter
  Reason for Service: Wife Ellen died in 1914 (President Wilson remarried in 1915)

---

ladies were very young and had families of their own to tend to. The White House is an intimidating place and the social responsibilities are daunting for even professionally trained hosts. Some of these surrogate first ladies had little training in the social protocol of political hosting and some were barely past their adolescent years. Several surrogate hostesses, however, came to the White House well prepared in the art of social entertaining and well educated in the social graces. Thus the variety of individuals and approaches represented by the surrogate first ladies parallels the diversity found in the first ladies themselves.

Among the group who served as surrogate hostess include some interesting and unlikely women. Varina Davis, the wife of the secretary of war in the Pierce administration and Pierce's occasional hostess, was the spouse of none other than Jefferson Davis, the man who would go on to lead the Confederacy against the Union in the Civil War. Therefore, Davis's wife actually served in the capacity of first lady for two countries: the United States and the Confederate States of America. Varina Davis and her counterpart, Mary Todd Lincoln, were the United States' first ladies during the Civil War, representing, respectively, the Confederacy and the Union, the only time the nation had two first ladies. Another unlikely hostess was Priscilla Cooper Tyler, a struggling actor from a family of actors who had known difficult times. When starring as Desdemona in Shakespeare's *Othello,* she caught the attention of John Tyler's son Robert. Priscilla and Robert were married in 1839, and a mere two years later she was serving as surrogate first lady for President John Tyler's ill wife, Letitia. Priscilla wrote that she often felt amazed at how her life had worked out and that she was overwhelmed by being hostess of the White House.[18] Yet she was a charming, intelligent woman who played hostess to such celebrities as Charles Dickens.

The First Surrogate White House Hostess

The first surrogate to serve was Martha Jefferson Randolph, who hosted for her widowed father, Thomas Jefferson, the third president. Jefferson's wife, also named Martha, had died in 1782, eighteen years prior to his presidency, and Jefferson had never remarried. Daughter Martha was the oldest of Jefferson's six children and the only one to survive into adulthood. In a day and age when it was expected that a lady would preside over important social affairs, it was natural that Jefferson's White House social responsibilities would fall to his daughter, and she obliged. However, Martha, who married her cousin Thomas Mann Randolph in 1790, had a family of her own while serving in the White House. Her first child was born in 1791 and four more followed. Family obligations thus limited her time and service. Martha served officially and on a regular basis only during the winter social seasons of 1802–1803 and 1804–1805. Dolley Madison, the popular wife of Jefferson's secretary of state, James Madison, functioned as White House hostess most of the remainder of the time. This experience proved useful to Dolley, as her husband, James, would become the next president and she the next first lady. Even though the Jefferson years were not known for their social events—the president appears not to have placed much emphasis on formalities, customs, or social affairs of state—both Martha and Dolley did an admirable job fulfilling the formal social schedule of the White House. In fact, many years after Thomas Jefferson's presidency, the widower Martin Van Buren, while serving as President Andrew Jackson's secretary of state, asked Martha Jefferson to again serve as hostess for a state dinner in the capitol. (Martin Van Buren, as was the case of most early secretaries of state, went on to become the next president after Jackson.)

Martha was somewhat prepared for the challenges of hosting in the White House; she had attended a prestigious boarding school in Philadelphia and traveled with her father to France in 1784 when he assumed his ministerial post there. She also attended a well-known Paris convent for five years, until her father disenrolled her because of his alarm at her thoughts of becoming a nun. From there on she studied under the direction of secular tutors. Martha Jefferson had always taken her studies seriously and was remarkably well educated for a young woman of the period. Given Martha Jefferson Randolph's and Dolley Madison's able performances in the Jefferson White House, there seemed to be no serious opposition to the precedent for surrogacy they helped establish. Indeed, many future presidencies would benefit from the practice. It is not just an antiquated social convention that a woman should preside over social affairs. Rather, the need for and acceptance of surrogacy imply the importance of the first lady in the social affairs of the presidency, her importance as a public figure, and the central role she fulfills in the management of the White House.

Serving a Bachelor President

Perhaps the most famous surrogate first lady is Harriet Lane, niece of President James Buchanan, who served for her bachelor uncle during his entire presidential term, from 1857 to 1861. Lane was raised in Franklin County, Pennsylvania, and came from a family of successful merchants. After she was orphaned at either age nine or eleven (historical records are unclear), her favorite uncle, James Buchanan, assumed guardianship of her. Buchanan, or "Nunc," as she called him, found homes with relatives for her siblings but decided to raise Harriet as his own. The bookish, scholarly Buchanan saw to it that Harriet was well educated, enrolling her in the Visitation Convent in Georgetown. It is possible that Buchanan sought this avenue of education for his niece because there was no mother figure in her life and because, as a young girl, she was mischievousness, outgoing, and spontaneous.[19] Harriet's personality was such that, if she were growing up today, she would probably be called a tomboy as well as a flirt. As a young woman, she was very popular among the eligible bachelors of Pennsylvania and, later, in the nation's capital city. While Buchanan was serving as secretary of state and during his ministership to the Court of St. James, Lane often attended social functions with him and was thus given an intimate introduction to the world of diplomatic hosting and the social side of politics. It was during this period that she honed her impressive social skills. In fact, Harriet appears to have made quite an impression on those she met during her forays into social diplomacy. While still in her early twenties, she was even recognized in London with the rank of "Ambassador's wife" by Queen Victoria in 1854. This exposure helped give Harriet the confidence, poise, and knowledge of social affairs of state necessary for White House hostessing.

Harriet—or "Hal," as she was nicknamed—was only twenty-six when her uncle became president and she became White House hostess, but she appears to have been up to the challenge. She was known for her beauty, her fun-loving ways, and for being an outstanding hostess. The timing of the Buchanan administration, however, was a mixed blessing for Harriet. After the gloomy years of the Pierce administration, whose social activities were defined by a first lady who almost never even appeared in public and remained in mourning because of the death of her son, the capital city eagerly awaited the attractive, young, and charming new White House hostess. But these years were also highly sensitive times, with the specter of the Civil War looming over the Buchanan White House. Unlike her uncle, who faltered as president, Harriet remained upbeat and continued to fulfill her social responsibilities in spite of the loss of seven southern states that seceded from the Union by the end of Buchanan's term. She responded to the challenge, even earning the nickname "the Democratic Queen." With sectional tensions at a breaking point, she carefully organized seating arrangements at White House events so as to keep political enemies apart from one another. She also encouraged her guests not to discuss sensitive political issues at White House socials.

Surprisingly and perhaps because of her cautious bachelor uncle's influence, Harriet did not marry until 1866, when she was nearly thirty-six. She wed Henry Elliott Johnston, a banker from Baltimore. After leaving the White House, Harriet moved to Lancaster, Pennsylvania, where she and Johnston had five sons. These years were marked by tragedy. Her uncle died in 1869, her husband in 1884, and two of her sons died young and unexpectedly. Buchanan had left his prosperous estate in Pennsylvania to his niece, and she made good use of it, successfully managing the estate. After her husband's death, Harriet moved back to Washington, D.C., where she committed the remainder of her life to public service. This service continued even after her death in 1903; in her will she donated her impressive personal art collection to the Smithsonian Institution. Harriet's collection would later form the basis for the National Gallery of Art, which opened in 1941, earning her the posthumous nickname "First Lady of the National Collection of Fine Arts." She also donated a sizable sum of money to the Johns Hopkins Hospital in Baltimore for the construction of a home for invalid children. The home has become a world-renowned pediatric facility, and to this day, the hospital's Harriet Lane Outpatient Clinic serves needy children.

Surrogates Above and Beyond the Call of Duty

The other young women who served as surrogate hostesses in the White House made many contributions to the social arena of the presidency. Most had their own style, but few were as original as Martha Johnson Patterson, who allowed cows to graze on the White House lawn. Martha was serving in the difficult post–Civil War years for her ailing mother, Eliza Johnson, who had tuberculosis and was often too weak to perform the duties required of the first lady. Martha was a humble woman with a simple upbringing. The grazing cattle, which provided the White House with a source of fresh milk and butter, reflect both her pragmatic preferences and the tough economic times the nation faced.

The periods of service varied for surrogate first ladies. At times it was temporary. Rose Cleveland, whose older brother Grover was a bachelor when he was elected, served for less than two years during the first of his two, nonconsecutive White House terms. She returned to academic life when Grover Cleveland wed Frances Folsom during his first term in office. Jane Irwin, the widowed daughter-in-law of William Henry Harrison, never had much of an opportunity to practice her social skills in her father-in-law's administration. Harrison's presidency lasted only one month: He died following an illness from a cold he had contracted during his long inaugural address. Margaret Wilson served in the interim period after the death of President Woodrow Wilson's first wife, Ellen, and before the president remarried. Martin Van Buren, whose wife had died nineteen years before his presidency, started his term with no first lady and no surrogate. Consequently, the Van Buren presidency offered almost no entertaining. However, one year into his term he asked Angelica Singleton, who had just married his oldest son, Abraham, in 1838, to serve as a surrogate. A strikingly beautiful and graceful woman, she was an instant success and a very popular hostess.

Other surrogates served regularly throughout the entire presidential term and some even lived in the White House. Harriet Lane and Mary Arthur McElroy served for the full presidential terms of James Buchanan and Chester Arthur, respectively. Miss Lane remained unmarried while serving for her bachelor uncle and was the designated hostess for all four years of the Buchanan administration. Mrs. McElroy lived in Albany, New York, while functioning as hostess of the White House. Naturally very shy, Mary would travel to the capital only during the annual social season because she had her own family and husband's career to consider (she married John McElroy in 1861). Martha Johnson, daughter of President Andrew Johnson, also had a family: In 1855 she married David Patterson, a U.S. senator, making her simultaneously surrogate first lady and wife of a U.S. senator.

Most surrogates were successful, but not all. First Lady Jane Pierce did almost nothing during the first two years of her husband's term because she was still grieving the recent loss of her young son Benny. Consequently, she asked for assistance in carrying out the duties of the first ladyship. The person she asked was Abby Kent Means, her longtime friend and the second wife of her uncle. Mrs. Means did serve as White House hostess but appears to have fared little better than Jane Pierce. Abby Kent Means held regular receptions and a few socials, but with little success. It remains unclear as to whether the blame rests with Mrs. Means, the absent, reclusive First Lady Pierce, or the somber tone of a White House still in mourning for the death of the first family's son. It appears to be a combination of the three factors. The last two years of the Pierce administration were much the same, even with Mrs. Pierce's return to making public appearances. This first ladyship was marked by sparse entertaining, few social assets, and a sense of gravity even with the added help of Varina Davis.

Several of the surrogate first ladies were well educated. Rose "Libbie" Cleveland, sister of bachelor president Grover Cleveland, was a lecturer at the Houghton Seminary, an exclusive girls' school, and author of scholarly publications on such famous writers as George Eliot and other topics in the field of literature. When Mary "Abby" Fillmore entered the White House at the tender age of eighteen, she already spoke five languages and had attended schools in Massachusetts and New York. Mary Arthur McElroy was formally educated at such private academies as Mrs. Willard's Female Seminary in Troy, New York. Several of the surrogate hostesses came from powerful and wealthy families and were thus familiar with the art of political affairs and society life. Angelica Singleton Van Buren, for instance, came from a long line of powerful plantation families in South Carolina and was even a distant relative of Dolley Madison. An exception to this trend is Emily Donelson, who was only marginally educated, having briefly attended a school called The Old Academy in Nashville, Tennessee. Raised in a rural part of the country, she had little experience with formal social hostessing or society life. Emily had married her cousin at the age of sixteen and eventually had four children.

Surrogates found hostessing to be a difficult task. As if the responsibility of surrogacy were not difficult enough in and of itself, many faced additional obstacles. Mary Arthur McElroy, Chester A. Arthur's younger sister, took over a White House still suffering from the assassination of President Garfield. Moreover, the seceding president, her brother Chester, had lost his wife only eighteen months prior to his own presidency. These circumstances made for a very solemn environment within which to entertain. Fortunately, Mary proved to be a capable hostess and became a popular figure in the capital city. Emily Donelson served for President Andrew Jackson, who had just lost his beloved wife, Rachel, in the short months between his election and inauguration. The tone of the Jackson White House was made even more somber because Jackson's wife had been troubled by the scandal that surrounded her first marriage and divorce and her subsequent "unlawful" marriage to Andrew. Mrs. Jackson had been dreading the glare of attention she would receive as first lady and was thus anticipating only a minimal role in White House affairs, planning instead for Emily to assist with social events. To an extent, then, Emily was prepared to hostess, but she still had to overcome the untimely and tragic death of her aunt and the ugly attacks on the president and his deceased spouse perpetuated by the press and President Jackson's enemies. Tragedy often begets tragedy, and Emily would die with one year remaining in Andrew Jackson's second term. Consequently, Jackson's daughter-in-law, Sarah Yorke Jackson, was thrust into a similar difficult and somber situation to complete the remainder of Jackson's term as his social hostess.

Angelica Singleton Van Buren, while serving as surrogate hostess for her father-in-law, gave birth to an infant girl in the White House. Sadly, Angelica's newborn daughter died only a few hours later. She continued to serve despite the tragedy, and her surrogacy was known for successful, lively entertaining. Priscilla Cooper Tyler had the challenge of serving throughout the grave illness of President John Tyler's first wife, Letitia, and her convalescence from a major stroke. First Lady Letitia Tyler's only public appearance was at a wedding. She died in 1842 during Tyler's presidency.

Just as fate would pose further difficulties for surrogate first ladies, fate also aided them. Take, for instance, Mary Taylor. President Zachary Taylor's wife, Margaret, was too ill to travel to the White House and she had no interest in politics or her husband's presidency. In fact, she even strongly opposed his election to the office. So daughter Mary served as hostess. Mary was moderately well educated, having attended a boarding school in Philadelphia, but does not appear to have been especially capable. However, she benefited because her predecessor, Sarah Polk, had a bland personality and was a sober hostess. So Mary employed a degree of charm, showed interest in her social events, and was subsequently welcomed by an appreciative Washington populace, starving for a full social calendar.

That such surrogate first ladies were even called upon to serve points to the institutionalization of the office within the White House. Even though the added pressures of substituting for the spouse must have been considerable, most of the surrogates responded to the challenges and served the president and nation well. The women that served as White House hostesses in place of first ladies did not simply fill in for a deceased or ill presidential spouse; rather, they themselves made many contributions to the office.

Notes

1. L. Aikman. *The Living White House,* 1991.
2. Some scholars note that the office is shaped by outside forces, often beyond the control of the White House. See, for instance, S. L. Robertson, "The First Ladies," 1996.

3. A. M. Black, *Casting Her Own Shadow,* 1996.

4. B. B. Caroli, *First Ladies,* 1987.

5. C. S. Anthony, *Saga,* 1990 and 1991.

6. Martha's letters reveal her concern about the role she would fulfill as presidential wife and her uncertainty about the new office. Martha's letters to friends are collected and reprinted in J. E. Fields, *Worthy Partner,* 1994.

7. Martha's status was such that several newspapers covered her trip to New York City to join her husband for his inauguration. She encountered crowds of adoring fans, cheers of "Long live Lady Washington," and even cannon salutes. The trip took place from May 13–20, 1789, and is covered by such papers as the *Maryland Journal & Baltimore Advertiser* (May 22), the *Pennsylvania Packet* (May 26), and the *Gazette of the United States* (May 30). Martha is presented as arguably the most well known and admired woman of her time in the book by her grandson, G. W. P. Custis, *Recollections,* 1859.

8. On Martha Jefferson's death eighteen years before her husband's presidency, Thomas destroyed their correspondence. Historians say that Jefferson was so distraught, he never spoke of Martha after her death. A source for Jefferson's family life is E. M. Betts and J. A. Bear, *Family Letters,* 1966.

9. Many of the books and newspaper accounts of the first ladies written prior to the Civil War discuss the presidential wives as though they were queens or royalty. Early titles such as *Lady* or *Presidentress* and even the title *First Lady* are royalistic or at least date to the courts of Europe. Harriet Lane was even referred to as "the Democratic Queen."

10. Jane Pierce's mourning and lack of public appearances are discussed in Anthony, 1990; L. L. Gould, *First Ladies,* 1996. See also R. F. Nichols, *Franklin Pierce,* 1958; L. C. Taylor Jr., "A Wife for Mr. Pierce," 1955.

11. See R. Weager II, *And Tyler Too,* 1963.

12. E. A. Geer, *First Lady,* 1984; and A. Hoogenboom, *Rutherford B. Hayes,* 1995. See also the chapters on Lucy Hayes in Anthony, 1990; Gould, 1996; M. Truman, *First Ladies,* 1996. President Rutherford Hayes's diary is also useful in examining the Hayeses' relationship. T. H. Williams, *Hayes,* 1964.

13. See the chapters on Mrs. McKinley in Anthony, 1990; Gould, 1996. For a general description of her service as first lady, see M. Leech, *In the Days of McKinley,* 1959. Information on Ida McKinley and her health problems is available at the First Ladies Library, located at the former Saxton McKinley home in Canton, Ohio.

14. Caroline Harrison's many accomplishments are discussed in chapters devoted to her in Anthony, 1990; Gould, 1996. See also Caroli, 1987.

15. The lives and influence of these first ladies with their husbands are discussed in several books: J. I. Anderson, *William Howard Taft,* 1981; R. K. Murray, *Warren G. Harding,* 1969, F. Russell, *Shadow,* 1968. See also Mrs. Taft's autobiography, *Recollections,* 1914.

16. See "Hoover's Silent Partner," 1917; Herbert Hoover's *Memoirs,* 1951–1952.

17. There have been more books written about Eleanor Roosevelt than any other first lady. The rankings in Chapter 7 reveal that she was the overwhelming choice by presidential scholars as the top first lady of all time.

18. Priscilla Cooper Tyler's hostessing is discussed briefly in Weager, 1963.

19. Descriptions of Harriet Lane commonly refer to her in such terms. See, for instance, Anthony, 1990; Caroli, 1987; Gould, 1996; M. Truman, 1996; and M. B. Klapthor's *The First Ladies,* 1994.

From the time of Martha Washington, first ladies have been supporters of U.S. troops, especially the wounded in hospitals. Here, Florence Harding talks with a soldier at Walter Reed Hospital, March 30, 1921 (collection of the Library of Congress).

4

Official Duties

The role of first ladies in political decision-making has gone large-ly unreported.

—Karen O'Connor, Bernadette Nye, and Laura Van Assendelft,
Presidential Studies Quarterly

Members of the president's immediate and extended family often contribute to his bid for the office, helping campaign, appearing in public with the candidate, and offering much-needed moral support. This support carries over after the election into the White House and has at times involved actual service in the president's administration. For instance, several early presidents asked sons and sons-in-law to serve in the capacity of personal secretary or aide. First Lady Eleanor Roosevelt was even named by her husband, Franklin, to head the federal Office of Civil Defense. More recently, Bobby Kennedy, the younger brother of President John F. Kennedy, served as the president's attorney general. Today, however, such service is regarded as nepotism and an ethical conflict of interest. In fact, by law—through a measure sometimes known as the "Bobby Kennedy rule"—immediate members of the president's family can no longer be appointed to a position in the federal government. That such a clause exists, however, has not restricted recent presidential spouses from having influence in a nonofficial capacity.[1]

Neither has this clause limited the informal powers of a first lady. Modern first ladies often function much like cabinet secretaries, except that their scope of influence and informal powers typically exceed those of most cabinet members, whose influence is often limited to the jurisdiction of their respective federal agencies. The problem arises because the first lady lacks accountability to the electorate and the legislature and because she has no defined jurisdiction. For example, in 1993, shortly after Bill

Clinton's election to the presidency, he announced that his wife, Hillary, would be leading the effort to reform health care. The president justified the appointment by saying that he had full confidence in his wife and that she was the most intelligent, capable individual he knew for the task.[2] By most measures, Hillary's performance in leading the president's task force was exemplary, even drawing positive reviews from Republican critics of the president and health care experts.[3]

As task force leader, the first lady managed a large staff and budget. She had numerous heads of federal departments reporting to her, convened meetings across the country with experts, and was even called to testify before congressional committees examining the health care issue. However, opposition by congressional Republicans and the medical community to universal health care brought a legal challenge to the first lady's official role as task force chair. In 1993 the Association of American Physicians and Surgeons sued Hillary Clinton, claiming that the appointment of the first lady to head the reform effort violated the precedent of the Bobby Kennedy case.[4] Attorneys for the plaintiff maintained that Mrs. Clinton was acting as an "officer or employee" of the federal government, and because the first lady was an immediate family member of the president, she could not be appointed to head the task force.[5] However, the U.S. Court of Appeals for the District of Columbia disagreed, siding with the first lady and rejecting the physicians' claim. The court found that the offices of the president and first lady are complex and that the boundary between the first lady's official political roles and her unofficial ceremonial roles was blurred. The ruling recognized the centrality of the first lady as a major political figure and adviser to the president and, in effect, legitimized the political roles and responsibilities of the office.

To Act or Not to Act?

Aside from the Bobby Kennedy rule and the court case involving Hillary Clinton, there are few formal guidelines governing the functions of the first ladyship. The Constitution is silent on the official parameters of the first lady's activities and duties. This silence might be taken as an argument that the first lady can have no formal responsibilities. But constitutional silence has not precluded activism or the creation of offices in new areas of government or in the White House. Moreover, there is a significant dimension of the office that functions behind the scenes and in an informal or unofficial capacity. Clearly, the first lady has been an active participant in presidential affairs, both officially and unofficially. The presidential spouse has become the de facto social host of the White House and the chief White House designer, refurbisher, archivist, and preservationist. Even though they do not appear in writing, these aforementioned roles are so widely recognized that they are not questioned. In fact, the first lady has received public funding to carry out such duties, an acknowledgment of her purview over these matters. Although her policy and political influence is hard to assess, it is clear that the office contains a distinct political element and, despite its lack of formal powers, can influence the political processes in and beyond the White House.

First Lady's Duties

In determining what duties she should pursue—or how she should act—in the White House, the first lady must consider an array of factors. According to Barbara Bush, "Each First Lady defines her own roles and responsibilities—some take a very active role in their husband's career, others focus on an outside campaign or project."[6] Mrs. Bush believed her job was "to offer comfort and security to my husband . . . and . . . try to make a difference by promoting family literacy."[7] The office is not a blank slate and first ladies do have to consider a variety of factors in determining their roles. Among them are external factors beyond the immediate control of the first lady, including the forces of history and society. There are also internal concerns over which the first lady has more control, such as her own vision and objectives for her first ladyship or those of her husband.[8]

With no legal or constitutional guidance, it is hard to identify the formal or official roles of the president's spouse. The roles often change from one first lady to another, and between each presidential administration. Yet today all spouses are expected to perform at least a minimum level of campaigning, hosting, social activism, advocacy of pet projects, and public appearances. Such roles and public expectations are likely to change dramatically, however, if a women is elected president and a man serves as presidential spouse. Nevertheless, it is possible to identify a core set of duties assumed by first ladies. These duties are functions of the office, not necessarily the preferences or roles of individual first ladies per se.

Several scholars have attempted to classify these roles. The Smithsonian Institution curator who oversaw the development of the new first ladies exhibit at the National Museum of American History, Edith Mayo, organized the exhibit along five key roles central to the modern office: promoter of culture and historic preservation; social partner and the nation's hostess; campaigner; social advocate/advocate of social causes; assorted political roles.[9] Scholars of the first ladyship such as Myra Gutin[10] and the former chief of staff to First Lady Nancy Reagan, James Rosebush,[11] also identify a core group of responsibilities of the office. Gutin sees five roles: White House hostess; stand-in for the president; campaigner; social advocate; and a broad array of functions associated with being a symbol of her husband's presidency. Rosebush identifies the following roles: White House manager; diplomat; social hostess/national hostess; champion of causes/advocate of "pet" projects; political partner; wife. Karen O'Connor, Bernadette Nye, and Laura van Assendelft attempt to analyze activism in the office by studying three basic roles of the first lady: ceremonial role; president's political representative; and policy role.[12] All of these interpretations are helpful in attempting to identify the core roles and duties of first ladies.

Borrowing from these lists offered by other scholars, I have conceptualized eleven fundamental duties of the modern office.

1. Wife and mother
2. Public figure and celebrity
3. Nation's social hostess
4. Symbol of the American woman
5. White House manager and preservationist
6. Campaigner
7. Social advocate and champion of social causes
8. Presidential spokesperson
9. Presidential and political party booster
10. Diplomat
11. Political and presidential partner

This list includes roles that the public expects first ladies to perform and responsibilities commonly undertaken by twentieth-century first ladies, especially those serving since Eleanor Roosevelt (1933–1945). This is not to say that there were not duties affiliated with the early office; even during the first ladyship of Martha Washington, such roles as presidential confidante, social hostess, and public figure were already an integral part of the office. But given the continual evolution of the office and changing standards of the times, this list may not be applicable in its entirety to early first ladies. Moreover, this list may not be completely accurate in another fifty years, although if history proves to be as powerful as it has thus far in shaping the office, one can assume that the existing customs will continue to influence the office well into the next century. The exception to the continuation of existing roles, and indeed the next major change in the office, will occur when a married, heterosexual woman is elected to the presidency. It is doubtful that her spouse will have to adhere to the duties expected of female spouses. Finally, the list may not encompass the duties of all first ladies because there are variations in the approach to the office. Nevertheless, the list highlights the array of roles and core responsibilities of the office in general. A first lady who perhaps best exemplifies the list is Rosalynn Carter, a spouse who fulfilled a wide variety of roles. Of her first ladyship Mrs. Carter admits, "I played many roles as first lady of the United States; that of wife and confidante of my husband, mother, hostess, and almost full-time volunteer."[13]

Wife and Mother

Amidst all the controversy and glare of the White House, the first lady must also stay married, live her own life, and, at times, even raise children. This function of the office is often overlooked by those studying first ladies. It was included in this list, however, because such otherwise common tasks take on a uniqueness when they are performed in the White House and because these tasks reflect the dual nature of the office. That is, in addition to participating in presidential politics, first ladies must project a traditional image. The challenges of raising a family and keeping a family or marriage happy and healthy under the glare of the international spotlight and the pressures of the presidency are unimaginable to most people.

Moreover, as the embodiment of a traditional wife, the first lady must be careful not to overshadow the president or disagree with him in public. The first lady is expected to "stand by her man"; witness the behavior of liberated, modern first lady Hillary Clinton during the repeated allegations of Bill Clinton's marital infidelities.[14] Barbara Bush actually disagreed with her husband's opposition to gun control and abortion but remained silent in public about her views.[15] Nancy Reagan went so far as to state that her life did not begin until she married Ronald Reagan.[16] Mamie Eisenhower loyally endured her husband's long absences during World War II, the allegations of his affair with Kay Summersby during the war, their dozens of moves from town to town, state to state, and to the Philippines and Panama because of Ike's military career, and his practice of staying away from home in the evenings while he was playing cards with his friends.[17] Before they married, Ike even said to Mamie, "Mamie, there's one thing you must understand. My country comes first and always will. You come second."[18] First ladies have stood by their husbands through thick and thin and through the trials and tribulations of the presidency.

A total of fourteen first families have had school-aged children while serving in the White House; others have had grandchildren either visiting regularly or, as the case with the Washingtons, living in the White House. Recent first families have had the added problem of raising children in the age of television, when the White House has become open to public introspection on all levels. Caroline and John Kennedy Jr., Amy Carter, and Chelsea Clinton grew up in a White House surrounded by an intrusive press corps. Amazingly, First Ladies Kennedy, Carter, and Clinton managed to shield their children from much of the political limelight. (See Table 4.1 for those children from first families who pursued a career in public service.)

Table 4.1   Children from First Families Who Pursued Successful Careers in Public Service

Parents	Child	Occupation
John and Abigail Adams	John Adams	U.S. minister to Netherlands, Germany, St. Petersburg, and Great Britain U.S. senator (F-Mass.) Secretary of state President U.S. representative (F-Mass.)
John Quincy and Louisa Adams	Charles Adams	U.S. representative (R-Mass.) U.S. minister to Great Britain
Martin and Hannah Van Buren	John Van Buren	U.S. representative (D-N.Y.)
William Henry and Anna Harrison	John Harrison	U.S. representative (W-Ohio)
John and Julia Tyler	David Tyler	U.S. representative (D-Va.)
Abraham and Mary Lincoln	Robert Lincoln	Secretary of war
Ulysses and Julia Grant	Frederick Grant	U.S. minister to Austria-Hungary
James and Lucretia Garfield	James Garfield	Secretary of the interior
Benjamin and Caroline Harrison	Russell Harrison	State representative (R-Ind.)
Theodore and Edith Roosevelt	Teddy Roosevelt	Assistant secretary of the navy Governor, Puerto Rico Governor-general, Philippines
Howard and Helen Taft	Robert Taft Charles Taft	U.S. senator (R-Ohio) Mayor, Cincinnati
Herbert and Lou Hoover	Herbert Hoover	Undersecretary of state
Franklin and Eleanor Roosevelt	Franklin Roosevelt	U.S. representative (D-N.Y.) Undersecretary of commerce Chair, Equal Employment Opportunity Commission
	James Roosevelt Elliot Roosevelt	U.S. representative (D-Calif.) Mayor, Miami Beach
George and Barbara Bush	George Bush Jeb Bush	Governor, Texas Governor, Florida

Note: F = Federalist; R = Republican; D = Democrat; W = Whig.

Ronald Reagan's analogy of residing in the White House to "living above the store" highlights the great personal and family sacrifices made by first families. First ladies must manage to provide support and counsel to their husbands and families and somehow deal with the reality of living in the center of political power and governance. The value of the first lady's role of supportive wife and her efforts to create a home life in the White House are perhaps beyond estimation. When Lyndon Johnson had a heart attack, his wife changed his diet, made him stop smoking, and altered his schedule to protect his health. Nancy Reagan was famous for protecting her husband throughout his tenure as president, particularly after he was shot during an attempted assassination. Mamie Eisenhower made her husband relax more after his two heart attacks in office and arranged a quiet room in the White House for him to paint. Even if it is impossible to measure the influence the first lady has as a wife, it is nevertheless important to consider this role. Barbara Bush, for example, saw her duty as wife as her most important function as first lady.[19] Thanks to the first ladies, life has continued with some degree of normalcy for the first families in the White House, as it did when First Lady Eleanor Roosevelt installed a swing set on the White House lawn for her grandchildren.

Public Figure and Celebrity

For much of its fifty years of existence, the annual Gallup Poll of "Most Admired Women" has contained a first lady in the number-one spot, and former first ladies routinely occupy several of the top-ten positions in the poll.[20] First ladies grace the covers of some of the most popular magazines in the country, appear on the evening news broadcasts, and influence fashion trends, all of which speak to their enormous popularity. "First lady watching" is a pastime for many Americans, the U.S. press, and social publications. The first lady is a social and cultural trendsetter, and what she wears, how she styles her hair, and what she chooses to do often ignite a popular following. Nancy Reagan's power-conscious red dresses were synonymous with the 1980s. Barbara Bush's pearls and simple blue dresses became the style among women of the 1990s. And in the 1960s Jackie Kennedy ushered in an entire look with her pillbox hats and simple, elegant dresses. When Mrs. Kennedy appeared in public, fashion designers and clothing stores took notice; sales followed. Even Dolley Madison set off a fashion revolution with her bold tastes, bright colors, signature peacock plumes, and "the Dolley Madison turban."[21]

For a variety of reasons, first ladies have become leading celebrities. In the modern era they have emerged as public figures in their own right, recognized beyond their role as the wife of the president. Several early first ladies, such as Martha Washington, Dolley Madison, and Mary Lincoln, were, during their lifetimes, arguably the best known women in the country. The daily activities, socials, and travels of First Ladies Dolley Madison, Julia Tyler, and Frances Cleveland were followed closely by the press and public and were the source of gossip.

First ladies appear at public events, kick off holiday celebrations, and are asked to comment on all important events of the day. Edith Wilson was even asked by the U.S. Shipping Board to come up with names for eighty-eight ships, including new ships and those confiscated from Germany during World War I. As have most of the first ladies, Mrs. Wilson responded to her celebrity with poise. She named the largest ship the *Leviathan* and the smallest the *Minnow*. She went on to develop names from past presidents, U.S. cities, lakes, rivers, and mountains and even consulted an American Indian dictionary in order to generate names.

Nation's Social Hostess

Social events are an important part of the political process, as essential to diplomacy as are the formal diplomatic talks themselves. This is especially true in official Washington, where large, formal social galas, receptions, and dinners cater to the equivalent of a political who's who. The first lady presides over numerous social events, managing the menu, guest list, entertainment, seating arrangements, and so on. She must contend with a bewildering array of formalities in social etiquette and protocol, entertain a wide variety of guests, and host everything from casual teas for Senate wives to state dinners for hundreds of diplomats. All of these functions affect the president's political agenda and public image.

The magnitude of some White House socials is staggering. By custom, the early first ladies were expected to call on every guest who left her a calling card at the executive mansion. The practice was tiring, time consuming, and impractical. When Elizabeth Monroe decided to end social calling, she was criticized by the women of Washington, who felt snubbed by the breach of formal protocol. Protocol also dictated that women could attend White House socials only when the attending woman (the first lady) was present at the White House, thereby limiting a first lady's ability to travel. Mrs. Monroe also ended this custom and proceeded with her planned travels. Again, she was criticized for her actions; President Monroe was even forced to hold a cabinet meeting to resolve the matter. Despite introducing these changes, Mrs. Monroe was known for her formal, elegant socials, held in the style and manner of the European courts to which she was exposed while serving a diplomatic assignment in London and Paris with her husband. Julia Tyler was also known for her fancy social functions and formal protocol. Each guest's name was announced, and all visitors were introduced to the first lady, who sat on a raised platform. More than

2,000 guests were present at her New Year's Day party in 1845 and more than 3,000 people attended her final White House social. Julia Grant was also known for her lavish and formal affairs. She required female guests to wear hats and White House servants to wear white gloves, and men were not allowed to smoke or carry swords or guns, a practice common to gentlemen and military officers of the day. Mary Lincoln hosted approximately 4,000 guests at a White House function and in 1861 entertained Napoléon Bonaparte's nephew. Several first ladies invited prominent public figures to their socials. Ellen Wilson hosted Booker T. Washington and Mark Twain.

But Julia Grant was careful to also invite common folk to the White House. Frances Cleveland held socials for working women. Although custom dictated that the first lady sit across from the president, this form of protocol was sidestepped by such first ladies as Dolley Madison, who took to sitting at the head of the dining table, and Ida McKinley, who sat next to her husband in the event she experienced an epileptic seizure. Mamie Eisenhower also chose to sit next to her husband. Rosalynn Carter was perhaps one of the most informal hostesses in the White House. Mrs. Carter did away with much of the formal protocol and attempted to save the taxpayers money by employing fewer White House guards, inviting fewer guests, serving less expensive dinners, ending the practice of printing White House menus in French, and creating more family-style functions.

The social hosting duty was never specifically assigned by law to the first lady, but by custom it became her responsibility. Historically, most first ladies held social calendars that involved approximately one or two formal dinners a week, one or two evening or afternoon receptions (sometimes called "levees") or teas a week, and one large party each month. Additionally, by custom, the White House was open to the public for a huge New Year's Day party, and the president and first lady were expected to host a large party each Fourth of July in honor of the nation's independence. Many first ladies excelled at hostessing. Dolley Madison, Louisa Adams, Mary Lincoln, Julia Grant, Mamie Eisenhower, and Nancy Reagan all directly used social events to build political support for their husbands by inviting important guests, strategically timing the events to coincide with important political decisions, and impressing key political allies.

First ladies have accomplished much more than political support for their husbands through their hostessing function. Several first ladies have made the White House into a showcase for national arts and culture, featuring American artists and performers in official White House entertaining, using American recipes and serving American foods, and decorating the building with American paintings and furniture. First Ladies Dolley Madison, Louisa Adams, Edith Roosevelt, Jacqueline Kennedy, Pat Nixon, Rosalynn Carter, and Hillary Clinton all showcased U.S. culture in their social and formal state affairs. Dolley Madison, for instance, served American dishes at meals despite receiving criticism from guests from the courts of Europe not accustomed to such informal, hearty dining. She also solicited recipes from women all across the new nation for use at the White House.

Of course, not all first ladies excelled at hosting. Deeply religious and more interested in politics than parties, Sarah Polk did not serve wine at the White House, did not dance at the inaugural balls, and did not see guests on the Sabbath. The serious and bookish Abigail Fillmore was also not interested in socializing. Moreover, her health was deteriorating while she was in the White House and her bad ankle prohibited her from dancing or standing in long receiving lines. She thus minimized her hostessing functions but still offered receptions on Friday evenings and Tuesday mornings and dinner parties on Thursdays. Abigail is typical of those first ladies who did not give social affairs a high priority: She minimized her social calendar but still obliged the public and White House guests by offering such popular social events.

Symbol of the American Woman

According to Thomas Jefferson, "The tender breasts of ladies were not formed for political convulsions."[22] Whatever the status of women through the ages, it has to a degree been represented in the first ladyship. The first lady simultaneously reflects the status of women and influences the experiences of women in the United States. The office parallels the country's notions about womanhood and has a definite feminine component. The first lady is expected to champion women and women's issues. She also embodies the qualities of femininity and family.

The complexities and difficulties of the office become apparent when the many and changing aspects of womanhood are considered. Women—and thus first ladies—are no longer just wives or mothers. Women run businesses, serve in elected office, write books, and raise children. The first lady faces the challenge of being simultaneously modern and traditional, a concern with which men, including the president, need not contend. She must host a reception for a visiting head of state *and* know the state of U.S. relations with that particular nation. She must appear beside her husband during the campaign *and* be able to respond to questions about his campaign's economic plan. She must find time to champion challenging social problems like homelessness *and* maintain a sense of home for her husband and children in, of all places, the White House.

First ladies have become symbols for much more than womanhood. Martha Washington became a symbol of liberty for the colonies during the American Revolution. Because of the British boycott and supply shortages plaguing General Washington's troops, Martha, through her leadership and deeds, encouraged women to save food for the cause and contribute items like clothing to the army. The wife of the commander-in-chief emerged as a symbol of the Revolution itself, even though she wanted little more than to have her husband home with her and retain a degree of her cherished privacy. Both Mamie Eisenhower and Pat Nixon assumed the symbolic positions of the country's idealized homemaker and wife.

First ladies have also championed women's issues, most notably the employment of women. Several first ladies encouraged their husband's to hire women. Eleanor Roosevelt coerced her husband to appoint the first woman to head a cabinet agency: Secretary of Labor Frances Perkins. As far back as 1877, Lucy Hayes was behind the appointment of women in her husband's administration. First ladies have embraced women's issues and have been in the forefront of such causes. Perhaps the best example of such support is the onstage appearance of First Ladies Lady Bird Johnson, Betty Ford, and Rosalynn Carter at the 1977 International Women's Year Conference in Houston. Betty Ford used the power of the first ladyship and her personal experience with breast cancer to warn women about the disease and encourage regular screenings. Mrs. Ford was also an outspoken advocate for abortion rights, the Equal Rights Amendment, and other women's issues. A decade earlier Lady Bird Johnson hosted "Women Doer Lunches" to highlight women who had achieved special distinction.

Many early first ladies could be considered feminists, and many were active in women's issues. Louisa Adams appears to have embraced such issues as the rights of women and the abolition of slavery.[23] She had read such progressive women writers as Angelina and Sarah Grimke and their book *Letters on the Equality of the Sexes and the Condition of Women* and held unusually modern views for a woman living in the late eighteenth and early nineteenth centuries. Louisa saw the role of women as akin to servitude, because women functioned as sexual and domestic slaves of their husbands. Men, she reasoned, subordinated women out of their own self-interest. She also rejected the subordinate role of women outlined in the Bible.[24] Lucy Hayes was also an enlightened women whose beliefs were well ahead of her time. As a young girl, Lucy became interested in women's rights and even wrote an essay arguing that women were as intelligent as men and that women deserved equality.[25] She also attended a lecture in 1854 by Lucy Stone, a prominent proponent of women's rights. A staunch supporter of the Union during the Civil War, Lucy even boasted that if she and other women were at Fort Sumpter, they would not have surrendered to the Confederates.[26] However, as first lady, Lucy did not fulfill the promise of a new woman; she often deferred to her husband's hesitancy on woman's rights and bypassed opportunities and requests by women's suffrage leaders to participate in the movement.

Abigail Adams remains the prototype of the modern woman. Abigail was well read, intelligent, and functioned as an equal partner to her husband, who is considered by many historians to have been one of the most gifted men of the times.[27] When John and Abigail were apart, she ably ran the family business and plantations. Ironically, it is fortunate for history that John and Abigail spent so much time apart. He was often forced to travel to Philadelphia during the founding days of the Revolutionary period and was later stationed in Europe on diplomatic assignment. In their voluminous correspondence, much of which remains, Abigail expressed her progressive thoughts on the role of women.[28] Abigail was bothered that women, although forced to obey the laws, did not enjoy the rights or protection of these same laws. She noted that women were excluded by the very same legal code from owning property, enjoying opportunities in education, or participating in politics.

Abigail even befriended early women intellectuals and leaders such as the playwright Mercy Otis Warren and exchanged thoughts on these matters with them as well as with her husband. In one of her famous letters to her husband in March 1776, four months before the completion of the Constitution and while John Adams was in the company of the other founding fathers of the nation, Abigail argued for extending legal rights and protections to women. With clarity, logic, and unprecedented candor, Abigail makes her case by arguing the following:

> In the new code of laws which I suppose it will be necessary for you to make, I desire you would remember the ladies, and be more generous to them than your ancestors. Do not put such unlimited power in the hands of husbands. Remember, all men would be tyrants if they could. . . .
> . . . your sex are Naturally Tyrannical is a truth so thoroughly established as to admit of no dispute . . . for whilst you are proclaiming peace and good will to Men, Emancipating all Nations, you insist upon retaining absolute power over Wives.[29]

First ladies have also been role models for women and young girls. Many first ladies have been highly educated, capable individuals and have served as inspirations for young women. Helen Taft was ambitious, wanting to become a lawyer or possibly even the president herself. She was educated at Miami University in Ohio, where she studied German, literature, history, and science. As a young woman Helen was a feminist and supporter of women's equality; her idea of socializing was to establish a political forum for her friends to discuss politics and the issues of the day. Hillary Clinton was an excellent student who was active in student government in both high school and college and went on to graduate from the prestigious Wellesley College and Yale Law School.

White House Manager and Preservationist

The first lady is largely responsible for the White House domestic staff. She hosts the social events held at the White House, has the final word on menus, entertainment, and seating at these events, plans the White House's agenda during holidays, and oversees any renovations to the building. In so many words, she is the manager of the White House and its ample staff and resources. At the time of the nation's founding, the first lady was not formally designated as manager, but the office has evolved to be the principal force in matters affecting the home of the president. It might be that this function was inevitable, given society's assignment of domestic and household duties to women. Regardless of how or why it evolved, the duty is closely affiliated with the first ladyship and requires a high degree of competence. The White House is more than just the official residence of the sitting president; it is also a living history museum, the first home of the U.S. public, and a symbol of the nation.

Many first ladies inherited a White House in dire need of refurbishment. The building, after all, houses dozens of important national offices, is the place of employment for hundreds of individuals, and receives a steady stream of tens of thousands of visitors every year. It is also where the first family lives. Refurbishment of the White House approaches art. It is not entirely accurate to describe most White House renovations as simply redecorations; the task more appropriately involves restorations. Many first ladies have overseen major restoration and renovation projects, including Dolley Madison, Elizabeth Monroe, Julia Tyler, Sarah Polk, Harriet Lane, Mary Lincoln, Julia Grant, Frances Cleveland, Edith Roosevelt, Bess Truman, Jackie Kennedy, Pat Nixon, and Nancy Reagan.

Such renovations or restorations involve repairing the building, replacing furniture, obtaining state china sets, and much more. In overseeing such a restoration, first ladies must act in the capacity of interior decorator, architect, art historian, landscaper, museum curator, and homeowner. Recognizing the poor condition of the White House, Edith Roosevelt wisely enlisted the assistance of the prestigious New York City architectural firm McKim, Mead, and White and lobbied Congress for funding of the restoration project. She was troubled by the irreplaceable loss of history that occurred when old or worn-out White House furnishings were auctioned off and promptly put an end to the practice. To regain a sense of authenticity, Edith procured porcelain, portraits, and china that had been used during former presidencies and attempted to restore the building to its eighteenth-century look. She selected new wallpaper, carpet, and paintings and upgraded the plumbing and lighting. First Lady Edith Roosevelt also oversaw the expansion and modernization of White House offices, the creation of living quarters for the first family separate from the White House office complex, and the practical and long overdue enlargement of the State Dining Room and Cabinet Room. Her actions set a precedent of obtaining the services of experts that has been used by subsequent first ladies attempting to restore the White House to its historical authenticity. Edith

Roosevelt also set the precedent for thinking of the White House as a museum of U.S. history and the presidency.

Perhaps the most famous restoration was accomplished in the early 1960s by First Lady Jackie Kennedy, who recruited experts on history, art, and antiques for the project. The first lady enlisted Clark Clifford, an influential aide to the president and a powerful political figure, to help her establish the White House Historical Association and sought the support of John Walker, the director of the National Gallery of Art, on matters of obtaining antiques and works of art and private funding for the restoration itself. With their assistance, she followed in the footsteps of Edith Roosevelt by collecting furnishings, antiques, and pieces of art to form period collections authentic to the history of the building and the country. Mrs. Kennedy went on to hire the first White House curator, establish a commission to oversee the White House, lobbied for legislation to protect the integrity of the building and its furnishings, and produced a White House guidebook, titled *The White House: An Historical Guide.* Her efforts led to a 1961 act by Congress that classified the White House and its belongings as historical items and forbade presidents from giving away such items to the public or private collectors. Her work was unveiled to the public during a nationally televised tour of the newly restored White House, hosted by the first lady herself on Valentine's Day, 1962. The show later won an Emmy award.

But Jackie Kennedy and Edith Roosevelt weren't the only two first ladies to undertake such important restorations of the White House. Recent first ladies have continued where Mrs. Kennedy left off. Jackie's successor, Lady Bird Johnson, worked with the National Geographic Society to produce *The Living White House,* a guidebook on the history of the building. Pat Nixon added another facet to the first lady's management of the White House by expanding access for the physically handicapped and visually and hearing impaired. Mrs. Nixon also added brochures in foreign languages to the White House tour and expanded the tour to include the White House gardens. Rosalynn Carter published a book on the White House for children, written from the perspective of her young daughter, Amy, titled *The White House . . . It's Your House Too.* Although Mrs. Carter never selected a china pattern for the Carter presidency and did not utilize all the money available to her for renovating the building, she did establish the White House Trust Fund, guaranteeing the availability of sufficient finances for future refurbishments.

Many early first ladies oversaw substantive restorations and improvements. In 1844 and 1845, Julia Tyler attempted to enhance the building's image by purchasing French furniture and serving the best French wines at the White House. This was in contrast to President Tyler's first wife, Letitia, who, because of illness and the lack of congressional funding, presided over a deteriorating building. President Tyler paid for lighting and heating improvements out of his own pocket. Abigail Fillmore, with help from her husband, obtained a congressional appropriation to improve the White House. A bibliophile and former teacher who had helped establish a library in her hometown of Sempronius, New York, Mrs. Fillmore used a congressional grant of $2,000 to procure books to create the first White House library in the second-floor Oval Room. The first lady selected Shakespeare, religious works, biographies, history books, and the writings of one of her personal favorite authors, Charles Dickens, for the new library. In an effort to make the White House a living cultural center, Mrs. Fillmore hosted such literary giants as Dickens, Washington Irving, and William Thackeray. Other first ladies would follow in the footsteps of Abigail Fillmore in opening the White House to cultural and artistic performances. The Fillmores also installed new fixtures, including a bathtub, an iron range in the kitchen, and water pipes.

The onset of the Civil War did not deter Mary Lincoln from making needed improvements to the White House. Mrs. Lincoln was appalled at the broken furniture, old, filthy rugs, and the mismatched china collection she found in the White House. In order to fund her renovations, the first lady relied on private sources, several of which were questionable. Such reliance resulted in a financial scandal for the president. Julia Grant inherited a post–Civil War White House badly in need of improvements. She was successful in obtaining funding from Congress for her redecoration of the East Room and Blue Room and for obtaining a new china collection and new prints for the White House. She also added guards at the White House and gated the grounds around the building. Caroline Harrison, a gifted artist, even lent her own design to the official state china collection.

Mrs. Harrison built support for renovating the White House by giving public tours of the building herself and inviting members of Congress to examine the condition of the building. The first lady believed that the building was near collapse and needed considerable expansion. She cleaned and inventoried all rooms, furniture, and items in the building, enlisted an architect to draw plans for adding an East and a West Wing to the building, and even began planning for the construction of an entirely new building. This new executive mansion became known as "Mrs. Harrison's Place." However, the creation of the new building never came to fruition, but it did set in motion the move that would establish the East and West Wings roughly a decade later. Mrs. Harrison did install new electric lighting and replaced the old, damaged floors in the White House.

By the end of World War II, the White House was a century and a half old and in need of repairs to prevent the building from collapsing. Because of the extensive construction needed to reinforce the structure, columns, and walls of the White House, President and First Lady Truman were forced to vacate the building, living at the nearby Blair House during part of their term.

Each first lady has approached the management of the White House with her own style. Mamie Eisenhower even decorated parts of the living quarters in her favorite color, pink. Departing from the strictures of history, she also eliminated the separate bedrooms for the president and first lady in the upstairs living quarters. Many first ladies' have overseen extensive restoration projects that have helped preserve a sense of history and retain the White House as a living museum for the U.S. public.

Campaigner

Few early presidents actually campaigned for office; presidential campaigns as we know them today are a twentieth-century phenomenon. Campaigning continues to evolve with the advent of television, the mass media, and a growing primary season. The role of the first lady as campaigner has also changed and continues to evolve. Historically, the campaign season for the presidency was extremely brief, barely extending beyond the nominating conventions. Unlike today, most of the positioning for office took place in private. Therefore, early first ladies did not play a significant role in the campaign itself. But this changed as the twentieth century approached. In 1880 Lucretia Garfield campaigned with her husband and assisted him with campaign strategy and decisionmaking. Although she did not enjoy the task, Caroline Harrison was an asset to her husband's 1888 presidential bid during their "front porch" campaign.[30] She endured an endless flow of visitors to their home, which resulted in inappropriate requests for housing, a loss of privacy, damage to the Harrisons' furniture, home, and other belongings, and even the theft of the fence surrounding their property. The campaign of Harrison's opponent—Grover Cleveland—used the image of his popular, young, attractive wife, Frances, on their 1892 campaign paraphernalia, including buttons, cards, and plates. In fact, Mrs. Cleveland's picture appeared above the likeness of the candidate and the candidate's running mate. During William McKinley's 1896 bid for the office, Canton, Ohio, the hometown of McKinley's wife, Ida, organized the Women's McKinley Club and produced campaign buttons with Ida McKinley's picture.[31] The candidate himself was not pictured on the button. That same year the McKinley campaign also produced a biography of the prospective first lady. This was most likely the first time a biographical sketch of a first lady was compiled for the purpose of a campaign. For her part, Mrs. McKinley supported her husband's campaign and took part in the activities. The actions of Caroline Harrison, Frances Cleveland, Ida McKinley, and others during this period mark the beginning of an orchestrated role in campaigning for first ladies.

This campaign role was largely defined by the "front porch" approach to campaigning found in the late 1800s and early 1900s, so named because candidates literally sat on their front porches and invited potential voters to visit them. Candidates of this era, such as James Garfield, Benjamin Harrison, and Warren Harding, all utilized the approach, which allowed the public to meet and talk to the candidates' wives, thus making the spouses part of the campaign. Florence Harding was one of the first spouses to take a prominent and openly public role in her husband's campaign, putting her impressive political skills to work by helping to manage the Harding campaign.[32] Her efforts also mark another historical first for first ladies and for women in the United States. The 1920 presidential campaign was the first election in which women could vote, and Florence took advantage of this by inviting women's political organizations to meet with her in an attempt to enlist their support. A political ad during the race read, "Women! For Your Own Good Vote the Republican Ticket."[33]

Eleanor Roosevelt also proved to be a gifted campaigner. Because of his paralysis, Franklin Roosevelt relied on Eleanor to campaign on his behalf. As early as the 1930s, the first lady began traveling and campaigning for her husband on her own. The rise of campaigning by presidential spouses gave rise to criticism directed at spouses that became part of the opponents' strategy. Eleanor's activism and independence invited criticism from the Republican Party, which used campaign buttons stating, "We don't want Eleanor either."[34] In the 1940s and 1950s, Bess Truman was a visible part of Harry Truman's famous whistle-stop train campaigns, with crowds cheering as much for Bess as for the president.

Not all spouses enjoyed the scrutiny and demands of the long, grueling campaigns. Bess Truman, in particular, did not care for the extensive travel and loss of privacy that accompanied her husband's whistle-stop tours.[35] Mamie Eisenhower, however, seemed to genuinely enjoy campaigning and the large crowds.[36] Despite her husband's enormous popularity owing to his fame as the Supreme Allied Commander during World War II, Mamie was relatively unknown prior to his presidential campaign. But this quickly changed when she hit the campaign trail and proved to be immensely popular. A *New York Times* article even suggested that Mrs. Eisenhower was worth "50 electoral votes" herself.[37] Mamie wrote an article for *Good Housekeeping* magazine during the campaign titled "Vote for My Husband or for Governor Stevenson, but *Please Vote.*" Former journalist Jackie Kennedy penned a newspaper column during the 1960 campaign titled "The Candidate's Wife," describing her experiences and generating considerable positive press for John F. Kennedy's cause. Jackie, however, was pregnant during much of the campaign and was therefore unable to participate in many aspects of it (a fact for which she was thankful). However, her pregnancy was as much an asset for the Kennedy image and campaign as it was a liability.

The televised age created a brand-new dimension to campaigns. Both

Jackie Kennedy's youthful good looks and Mamie Eisenhower's image of a motherly housewife played well on television, assisting their husbands' efforts at winning over the general public. Pat Nixon fulfilled an important role in her husband's campaigns, coming to represent a core theme of the campaign: traditional values and the American family. Richard Nixon and Dwight Eisenhower managed and exploited the traditional image of their wives by producing television ads showcasing their homemaker wives, their children, and their own role as family men, a practice that would be exploited in ensuing years by most candidates for public office.

Regardless of how spouses have been used in campaigns, many have emerged as key players. Lady Bird Johnson did much more than campaign for her husband. Her own donation of $1,000 and her father's contribution of $25,000 helped Lyndon Johnson finance his first political campaign.[38] During the 1960 campaign, the Republican Party developed "Pat for First Lady" campaign paraphernalia and hosted an event called "Pat Week" that was designed to rally female support for Richard Nixon.

This role in campaigning by spouses has not been limited to their husbands' initial quests for the presidency. First ladies often campaign for issues, policies, and public support. A good example of policy campaigning is Lady Bird Johnson's extensive tour aboard an eighteen-car train dubbed the "Lady Bird Special." The whistle-stop tour journeyed throughout the South to build support for her husband among those upset over Lyndon Johnson's backing of the 1964 civil rights bill. It was Lyndon Johnson's idea that his popular wife travel throughout the South to minimize his losses among conservative, segregationist southerners. Followed by a mass of curious journalists, Mrs. Johnson departed on October 5, 1964, from Washington, D.C., and traveled for four days through Virginia, North Carolina, South Carolina, Georgia, Florida, Alabama, Mississippi, and Louisiana on her 1,000-mile tour. Along the way she made forty-seven speeches in as many appearances, calling on southern governors, senators, and representatives in each state. The first lady faced hostile, threatening crowds but held her own.[39] The campaign has been credited with minimizing Republican gains in the region.[40] At other times, first ladies have campaigned for their own issues. First Lady Betty Ford conducted a personal campaign involving speeches, public appearances, and lobbying on behalf of the ratification of the Equal Rights Amendment.

Social Advocate and Champion of Social Causes

First ladies in the modern era have been expected to champion social causes to the extent that most have become identified with their particular social issue. For instance, Barbara Bush was known for her crusade for adult literacy, and Lady Bird Johnson advocated conservation and beautification.

These projects are massive undertakings that employ a staff and expend considerable resources. Even though such projects are expected of first ladies, most first ladies have not hesitated to embrace several social causes and have given freely and generously of their time. Moreover, most have succeeded in advancing the particular cause with which they are identified while making contributions to many other issues.

On a larger level, the first lady can be seen as the nation's "first volunteer." She has become a national symbol of the volunteer sector and devotes a great deal of time and energy to volunteerism. This work on behalf of those in need and humanitarian causes predates the modern era, however. Many earlier first ladies were also very active in volunteer work and in supporting social causes. Lucy Hayes visited numerous prisons, schools, and asylums as part of her efforts to improve the condition of such institutions. She also supported the temperance movement and spent her free time participating in volunteer activities. Frances Cleveland worked with the Needlework Guild of America, an organization that produced clothing for the poor. Several years later, First Lady Edith Roosevelt would also be active in the Needlework Guild. Ida McKinley devoted her energy to making slippers for charities. Caroline Harrison also supported several charities in the capital city and was a benefactor of the Garfield Hospital in Washington, D.C. Helen Taft can be credited for sponsoring the planting of cherry trees throughout the capital city, something for which Washington has become famous. Lou Hoover used her influence and vast wealth to support many needy causes, including the Lyceum Club, Friends of the Poor, the Society of American Women in London, the League of Women Voters, the Campfire Girls, and the Girl Scouts. Mrs. Hoover is also responsible for pushing the legislation that created the National Gallery of Art.

Perhaps the epitome of a social advocate in the office of the first lady was Lady Bird Johnson. No other first lady's social advocacy approaches that of Lady Bird Johnson in terms of the size of the project or the scope of activism. During Mrs. Johnson's campaign travels—in particular, on a trip to the West in 1964 with Interior Secretary Stewart Udall—she developed an appreciation for wildflowers and the natural beauty of the nation.[41] This gave birth to her championship of conservation, wildflowers, and her famous beautification program. Lady Bird recognized the linkage between the human quality of life and the natural and physical environment around us. The first lady's initial program focused on the beautification of the capital city but grew to include removing unsightly billboards, planting wildflowers, preserving scenic rivers, beautifying roadsides, and enhancing national parklands. The first lady was committed to the program and invested in it a considerable amount of time and energy, public speaking, and extensive travel. She wisely hired Sharon Francis, a conservationist with the Department of the Interior, to advise and assist her. Mrs. Johnson also headed the First Lady's Committee for a More Beautiful Capital. This committee organized the improvement of eighty public parks, nine schools, and eight playgrounds in the capital city. She also sponsored the White House Conference on National Beauty, held May 24–25, 1965, bringing experts to the White House to advocate natural improvements to the capital city. The first lady promoted parklands, the planting of cherry tress and flowers, tourism, open spaces, landscaping, and scenic and natural improvements along the Potomac shoreline, Pennsylvania Avenue, and the city's famous Mall.

Lady Bird Johnson was successful in generating public attention to her issues. Donations and volunteers poured into the White House. She took her fight to Congress, and despite criticism from such opponents as U.S. Representative Bob Dole, she was successful in passing the Highway Beautification Act of 1967, known as "Lady Bird's Bill," and advancing a proposal to landscape Capitol Hill in 1967. She supported the Society for a More Beautiful Capital, the Citizens Advisory Committee on Recreation and Natural Beauty, and "Project Pride," a program to expand her efforts to communities all across the country. As a result of her efforts, the president advocated beautification and conservation in his 1965 State of the Union address and submitted a host of proposals to Congress pertaining to beautification and conservation. Her work initiated or at least supported a variety of important natural and environmental policies passed in the late 1960s, including the National Historic Preservation Act, the Clean Rivers Restoration Act, the Air Quality Act, the National Trail Systems Act, and the Wild and Scenic Rivers Act.

Lady Bird Johnson supported much more than beautification and conservation, including her husband's progressive Head Start program and other legislation and programs for children in need. She visited Head Start classes and assisted Sargent Shriver, the president's head of the Office of Economic Opportunity.

Presidential Spokesperson

The first lady serves as a symbol of the president and presidency. Sarah Polk, a well-read, articulate, and outspoken first lady, recognized that, as a woman living in the 1840s, she could not appear to be too outspoken and that she was always representing the president when she spoke. She was thus careful to begin her political comments with the phrase "Mr. Polk believes . . ."[42] Even if the first lady prefers not to function in such a formal capacity, she is nevertheless at all times representing the president and the country. First ladies have actually spoken and appeared at official events on behalf of the president. In 1937 Eleanor Roosevelt delivered on behalf of her husband the keynote speech at a convention on the prospects and causes of the coming war. She spoke again the following year at another such event and officially represented him and spoke for him at the 1940 Democratic National Convention nominating her husband for another term in office. Rosalynn Carter gave hundreds of public speeches during her first ladyship, many of them on behalf of her husband or his policies. Lady Bird Johnson was aware of her role as political spokesperson. In fact, she took a public speaking course with the Capital Speakers Club in 1959 when her husband was serving in Congress. During state visits to France and Spanish-speaking nations such as Mexico and Venezuela, President John Kennedy wisely allowed his wife Jackie, who was fluent in French and Spanish, to prepare and deliver her own remarks.[43] When Grover Cleveland was faced with a tough reelection campaign in 1888 because of personal attacks from the Reverend C. H. Pendleton claiming that the president was a drunk who abused his wife, Frances Cleveland published a personal letter refuting the reverend's charges.[44] This public defense of the president by Mrs. Cleveland was a first for presidential spouses. Although Cleveland lost his bid for reelection, Mrs. Cleveland's presence and her defense appear to have worked. Grover Cleveland was returned to office in 1892, the only president to serve two nonconsecutive terms. In recent years, this practice of the first lady publicly defending the president has grown more common.

In addition to actual speaking engagements, the first lady represents the president through her actions and deeds. For instance, first ladies often attend events such as funerals and marriages of public figures and foreign leaders on behalf of the president. Many first ladies—Eleanor Roosevelt, Barbara Bush, and Mary Todd Lincoln among them—have visited troops in the field and soldiers at hospitals during times of war. First ladies from Sarah Polk to Ellen Wilson to Lady Bird Johnson served as speechwriters and editors for their husbands. Nancy Reagan did even more than that; she was observed many times feeding President Reagan lines when he struggled with reporters' questions. First ladies have even held press conferences. Eleanor Roosevelt held them regularly, and even such traditional first ladies as Mamie Eisenhower and Bess Truman held one press conference each. First ladies have also publicly endorsed presidential policies. Televised documentaries have been produced about the first ladies and their personal projects. An example is the hour-long TV special on November 25, 1965, titled *A Visit to Washington with Mrs. Lyndon B. Johnson on Behalf of a More Beautiful Capital.*

Presidential and Political Party Booster

Dolley Madison's courage during the War of 1812 bolstered a nation still in shock over the burning of the White House and the crushing U.S. defeat at the hands of the British. Her boldness in refusing to leave Washington until the final moment, even as the British invaders marched into the capital city, and her quick thinking that saved priceless White House artifacts from the fires of war boosted the nation's morale.[45] It also enhanced James Madison's image and presidency. Although not often as dramatically as Mrs. Madison, many first ladies have acted as boosters of their husbands, their political party, and the nation. Several first ladies, including Martha Washington and Lou Hoover, adopted the practice of wearing U.S.-made clothing or supporting U.S. products and industries, artists, and institutions. Edith Wilson was a booster of the country, the war effort, and Woodrow Wilson's presidency when she helped sell war bonds and sewed clothing during World War I.

Often boosterism takes the form of political party loyalty. Eleanor Roosevelt was a well-known supporter of the Democratic Party, campaigning for fellow Democrats, leading women's Democratic Party organizations, and editing Democratic Party literature. Rosalynn Carter spoke at fundraisers for Democratic candidates for public office. Popular first ladies like Barbara Bush also appeared at events in support of Republican candidates. Even after their first ladyships, spouses have continued serving as party boosters. Nancy Reagan spoke on behalf of her husband and the Republican Party at the Republican National Convention in 1996, seven years after her husband's presidency ended. In fact, all recent first ladies— even vice presidential spouses—have been expected to speak at their party's presidential nominating conventions.

Boosterism on behalf of the president even comes in the form of a first lady's personality. Such an example would be the warmth and charisma of Dolley Madison, something that James Madison relied on to offset his cold, formal, and noncharismatic demeanor. Her mere presence helped boost his popularity. Lady Bird Johnson's actions inadvertently boosted her husband's and his party's presidential hopes during the 1960 campaign. As the Democratic vice presidential candidate, Lyndon Johnson was campaigning in Dallas, Texas, with his wife when a Republican crowd turned violent and out of control. Nixon supporters began spitting on Lady Bird, and she was hit with a campaign sign. However, showing strength and resolve, she neither complained nor ceased her campaigning. Subsequent press coverage of the incident produced support for Lyndon Johnson and the Democratic ticket.

Diplomat

The first ladies have been called on to serve in a diplomatic capacity, often by accompanying the president on official state visits abroad. The first lady also welcomes visiting foreign dignitaries and heads of state to the White House and thus to the United States. As a diplomat, her role is multifaceted. At times she serves as the official presidential envoy; at other times she acts as a U.S. ambassador of goodwill or simply accompanies the president during his travels. Without advanced training in diplomacy, first ladies have met with many of the most powerful leaders of the world and participated in highly sensitive diplomatic missions. For example, First Lady Nancy Reagan addressed the UN General Assembly and met with Pope John Paul II. (See Box 4.1 for a list of Nancy Reagan's trips abroad from 1981 to 1985.) Pat Nixon accompanied her husband on his historic mission to China.

At times the first lady has been asked to travel without the president, serving as the "first diplomat" or official presidential envoy. In this capacity Mrs. Nixon traveled to Ghana, Liberia, and the Ivory Coast in 1972 and to Peru in 1970 on an earthquake relief mission. Because of her travels, Pat

---

Box 4.1   Nancy Reagan as Diplomat

Mrs. Reagan's International Travels (1981–1985)
State visit to Canada (March 1981)
Royal wedding in England (July 1981)
State visit to Jamaica and Barbados (April 1982)
Economic summit in France (June 1982)
Presidential travel to Italy, Germany, and United Kingdom (June 1982)
Princess Grace's funeral in Monaco (September 1982)
State visit to Japan and Korea (November 1983)
Presidential travel to China (April 1984)
Economic summit in England (June 1984)
D-day celebration in France (June 1984)
State visit to Canada (March 1985)
Economic summit in Germany (May 1985)
First lady travel to Italy (May 1985)
State visit to Spain and Portugal (May 1985)
Earthquake assistance to Mexico (August 1985)
USSR summit in Switzerland (November 1985)

Source: J. Rosebush, *First Lady, Public Wife,* 1987.

Nixon earned the nickname "the President's Ambassador." In 1977 First Lady Rosalynn Carter traveled on behalf of her husband to seven Latin American nations, meeting with heads of state. Mrs. Carter was also sent by her husband to Boston to meet Pope John Paul II, marking the historic occasion of the first papal visit to the United States. The first lady's diplomatic role involved speaking on behalf of the National Cambodian Crisis Committee, advocating international disaster and emergency relief, promoting human rights, and other international and diplomatic issues. First Lady Carter also undertook diplomatic missions to visit Cambodian refugee camps and meet with the King of Thailand and UN Secretary General Kurt Waldheim. In fact, during Mrs. Carter's initial year as first lady she visited sixteen countries.

At other times, the first lady's mere presence has contributed to the cause of U.S. diplomacy. A case in point is President and Mrs. Kennedy's state visit to France. The first lady was adored by the citizens of France and even impressed the not easily impressible Charles de Gaulle, France's powerful leader. For his part, President John Kennedy did little, wisely allowing his wife to charm de Gaulle with her knowledge of French art, culture, and the language.

The role of diplomat is fulfilled in part through the dual role of national hostess. In hosting state dinners and receptions, the first lady contributes as much to diplomacy as she does to the appetites of her guests. A significant degree of White House entertaining is driven by protocol, and most first ladies successfully master the intricacies of social hosting, diplomacy, and state protocol. As first lady, Eleanor Roosevelt did not focus much on the hostessing element of the office, but she did continue the diplomatic function after leaving office when she was selected to serve as U.S. delegate to the UN and to chair the UN Commission on Human Rights.

Political and Presidential Partner

As a political and presidential partner, the first lady engages in a wide array of political activities. Being a political partner implies a significant level of influence and importance. Unlike most senior advisers, first ladies have been with the president throughout his political career and long before his presidency. The partnership is both public and private in nature. First ladies function both behind the scenes and, especially in the modern era, in public. The first lady functions as the president's most trusted confidante and senior political adviser. Even if first ladies do not offer advice on the particulars of policy issues per se, they provide political advice. That is the "political" and "presidential" side of being a presidential partner. The "partner" element of the role involves fulfilling the social obligations of the White House, supporting the president, and continuing to be his wife.

The specific tasks associated with this role are probably too numerous to list. In an effort to understand these tasks, I will present four general types of political activities and three fundamental aspects of public influence in the next two sections of this chapter.

The First Lady as Political Activist:
The Four Ps of Activism

The office of the first lady is inherently political. Despite the lack of formal guidelines, the nature of the office has evolved within and through the political system. The roles of the first lady, as well as almost everything else with which she is involved, have political consequences. To analyze the political activities and political nature of the first ladyship, the political functions of the office may be conceptualized into four basic functions or areas, which I refer to as the "four Ps of political activism": pet projects; public policy participant; political player; pomp and pageantry.

Pet Projects

Recent first ladies have been expected to champion a so-called pet project. Although some of these projects are socially oriented and are purposely selected to be politically safe or conservative, they are nevertheless important and highly political national crusades. As such, the term *pet project* should not detract from the value and politicization of such activism. These projects provide a national voice for important issues and have been used as an instrument of positive media and public relations for both the first lady and the president.[46] They have come in many forms and have varied in their scope and objectives. Some projects, such as those of Hillary Clinton, tend to focus on public policy and have been important causes for the first ladies long before they entered the White House. While serving as first lady of Arkansas, Mrs. Clinton sat on the board of the Arkansas Children's Hospital, chaired the Arkansas Education Standards Committee, founded the Arkansas Advocates for Children and Families, and developed the Home Instruction Program for PreSchool Youngsters. Mrs. Clinton's advocacy of quality, affordable, and accessible health care, education, and the rights and welfare of children has continued through her White House years. Examples of other projects include Edith Wilson's effort to stop Americans from eating meat on Mondays in order to conserve on behalf of aiding the war effort and Lucy Hayes's banning of alcohol in the White

House. Rosalynn Carter was active in mental health reform while serving as first lady of Georgia and continued to advocate this policy cause in the White House.

Some of the projects or causes have not been formally planned by the first lady prior to assuming office. At times, what constitutes activism might simply be a statement made by the first lady on behalf of an issue. Moreover, such activism may be done without invited media coverage. However, in the modern era, the first ladies' projects are more likely to be planned and managed from the White House with considerable attention to polls, public perceptions, and strategic media coverage. These projects have become huge, staged media events, designed to boost the approval ratings for the first couple. They have the attention of a full-time staff assigned to the project and involve travel, public speaking, and appearances. Nancy Reagan's popular "Just Say No" campaign was not an initial theme for the first lady or the president. However, with an eye on public opinion and a finger on the electoral pulse, the White House developed Mrs. Reagan's cause. The first lady's "Just Say No" campaign evolved into a massive undertaking for the White House that involved formal meetings, travel, fundraising, and numerous White House–sponsored events. Nancy Reagan even appeared on prime-time television commercials on behalf of the campaign. Her efforts resulted in an international meeting of first ladies designed to rally support for combating drug abuse, and helped establish many nonprofit antidrug organizations. "Just Say No" became a popular slogan in schools across the country.[47]

Boosterism is a common cause for first ladies. As boosters, first ladies have championed the United States, U.S.-made products, and U.S. cultural, educational, athletic, and artistic endeavors. Martha Washington wore U.S.-made clothing to make a statement on behalf of the young country and to build support for the revolutionary spirit. Lou Hoover wore all-cotton garments to support the cotton industry during the the Great Depression. She also served as national president of the Girl Scouts in 1922 and, the following year, vice president of the National Amateur Athletic Federation. Caroline Harrison served as the first president-general of the Daughters of the American Revolution. Sarah Polk installed new gas lighting in the White House to celebrate that invention, and later Caroline Harrison began using electricity in the White House. Both Polk and Harrison became important boosters and helped legitimize these new products and industries. Perhaps the most popular example of a first lady helping an industry is Eleanor Roosevelt, who through her love of flying and highly publicized, frequent air travel boosted the new commercial air industry.

Irrespective of the degree of political manipulation by the White House of the first ladies' projects, many first ladies have felt deeply about their issues and were successful in rallying national support for their positions. See Box 4.2 for a listing of recent first ladies' pet projects.

Box 4.2   Pet Projects of Recent First Ladies

First Lady   **Project**
Jackie Kennedy   Historic preservation, arts and culture in the
                       White House
Lady Bird Johnson   Conservation and beautification of the capital
                       city and highways
Pat Nixon   Volunteerism
Betty Ford   Handicapped children
Rosalynn Carter   Mental health
Nancy Reagan   "Just Say No" antidrug campaign
Barbara Bush   Literacy
Hillary Clinton   Child advocacy

Public Policy Participant

A few first ladies have chaired task forces or commissions, officially traveled or spoken on behalf of the president, and were responsible for actually
developing public policy or legislation. Ellen Wilson's urban housing bill,
Rosalynn Carter's leadership on mental health, and Hillary Clinton's health
care reform proposals offer vivid examples of public policy activism and
policymaking. Eleanor Roosevelt served in a formal capacity for the president in many areas, from her appointment as a director of civil defense
operations to the site visits and studies she conducted on behalf of prison
and hospital reform to her participation in the early civil rights movement.
In so doing, she functioned as a policy adviser, policy implementor, and
policy evaluator. A few spouses of the president and vice president have
been so identified with a policy issue and recognized as authorities on that
issue that they have been called to formally testify before a congressional
committee (see Table 4.2). This points to these spouses' new role as a participant in policymaking and their power and influence. During testimony,
spouses have generally demonstrated competence in the area and impressed
spectators and committee members.

Activism in substantive policy issues has at times resulted in the office
being a political lightning rod. At other times, the first lady has served as a
key and able player in the policy process. First Lady Helen Taft, for
instance, often attended House and Senate debates and then discussed them
with her husband. She also advised him on his presidential appointments.
Ida McKinley and Mary Lincoln also advised their husbands on appoint-

Table 4.2   Spouses Who Have Testified Before Congress

Spouse	Appearance	Committee
Eleanor Roosevelt	December 10, 1940	House Select Committee to Investigate Migration of Destitute Citizens
	January 14, 1942	House Select Committee Investigating National Defense Migration
Rosalynn Carter	February 7, 1979	Senate Labor and Human Resources Committee
	April 30, 1979	House Science and Technology Committee
Joan Mondale	June 26, 1979	Senate Labor and Human Resources Committee
	September 25, 1979	Senate Governmental Affairs Committee
	February 7, 1980	House Select Committee on Aging
	March 3, 1980	House Education and Labor Committee
Marilyn Quayle	April 23, 1990	House Committee on Energy and Commerce
	May 16, 1990	House Select Committee on Aging
Tipper Gore	May 13, 1993	Senate Labor and Human Resources Committee
Hillary Clinton	1993–1999	House Ways and Means Committee House Education and Labor Committee House Energy and Commerce Committee Senate Finance and Labor Committee Senate Human Resources Committee

Note: From D. C. Diller and S. L. Robertson, *The Presidents, First Ladies, and Vice Presidents,* 1997.

ments. Rosalynn Carter counseled her husband on child immunization, shaping the president's executive order on child immunization. Because of the first lady, the Carter administration established a goal of reaching 100 percent of the United States' children with immunizations and made the inoculation against measles a priority. She was also her husband's top adviser on issues affecting the elderly and Social Security reform. In this capacity the first lady visited homes for senior citizens, chaired the White House Conference on Aging in 1977, and supported the National Council on Aging and the Age Discrimination Act.[48] Rosalynn's role as her husband's policy adviser was perhaps best represented by the issue of mental health policy. The first lady headed the President's Commission on Mental Health, which studied and made 117 recommendations to the president on issues ranging from mental health insurance to community mental health centers to urban and rural mental health needs. With her input, the administration submitted a proposal to Congress in 1979 that ultimately, as a result of Rosalynn's lobbying efforts, became the Mental Health Systems Act of 1980.

Political Player

Several first ladies have demonstrated an impressive grasp of things political and functioned as the president's most trusted political confidante. Others became assets on the campaign trail and boosted the public opinion approval ratings of the president. Several first ladies enjoyed immense popularity, at times even exceeding that of the president's own approval ratings. Jackie Kennedy and Barbara Bush, for example, were very popular first ladies whose popularity was recognized and used by their husbands. So popular was First Lady Dolley Madison that Charles Pinckney, who lost to James Madison in the 1808 presidential race, stated in frustration that he lost because he "was beaten by Mr. *and* Mrs. Madison" and that he "might have had a better chance if I faced Mr. Madison alone."[49]

Although many presidents relied on the political advice of their wives, it appears that First Ladies Abigail Adams, Sarah Polk, Helen Taft, Florence Harding, Eleanor Roosevelt, Rosalynn Carter, Nancy Reagan, and Hillary Clinton were full political partners who appeared to function as their husband's most trusted advisers on major political decisions and issues. There are many manifestations of political support and many first ladies have provided different types of political support to their husbands.

An unusual example involves Julia Tyler, who in an effort to enhance her husband's image instructed the Marine Band to play "Hail to the Chief" whenever the president made a public appearance. The custom initiated by First Lady Julia Tyler has survived from 1844 to the present time. Even Bess Truman, who was well known for her dislike of politics and Washington, D.C., advised her husband on all major decisions and performed clerical work as a paid staffer in his Senate office. Lady Bird Johnson also ran her husband's congressional office while he was away during World War II and, through her letters, kept him abreast of political events stateside. Abigail Adams was a keen political observer and an excellent writer. During John Adams's time spent on diplomatic missions in Europe without his wife, he relied on Abigail's regular letters for his political news and information on the home front. Throughout their long marriage, whether by letter or in person, Abigail and John regularly discussed and debated such political events as presidential politics, the growth of the new country, Adams's political opponents, Congress, and so forth.

In their study of the political influence of first ladies, O'Connor, Nye, and van Assendelft identify a variety of political activities in which spouses have participated and the number of spouses who engaged in each.[50] They find that the first ladies have been a politically active and influential group. In Box 4.3 are examples of the political activity and influence of first ladies.

Pomp and Pageantry

Owing to the nature of White House social ceremonies and events and the public visibility surrounding them, these functions assume a highly political dimension. Many of the ceremonies are, in fact, political events, and formal affairs of state, such as receptions for foreign dignitaries and political VIPs, involve diplomacy and public relations. The first lady has emerged in the U.S. political system as the deputy head of state and White House hostess. Her role might be explained by the lack of division between the offices of head of state and head of government in the United States, but the fact remains that she is in charge of these political duties. In the modern, televised age, many of these state functions are watched or followed by large audiences. Among the first ladies who were especially successful social and political hosts are Julia Grant, who received many celebrities, the politically savvy Dolley Madison, and Jackie Kennedy, who brought arts and culture to the White House.

Box 4.3   Political Activities of First Ladies

Activity	Number Participating
Discuss politics with president	31
Political confidante/adviser to president	26
Have an identifiable political issue	17
Lobby president	17
Make policy preferences known to president	15
Influence appointments	14
Travel officially with the president	12
Travel alone on behalf of president	9
Publicly state policy views	8
Attend White House meetings	7
Influence policy decisions	5
Lobby congress	3

Source: O'Connor, Nye, and Van Assendelft, *Presidential Studies Quarterly,* 1997.

First ladies oversee the White House Easter egg roll, preside over the lighting of the White House Christmas tree, ride down Pennsylvania Avenue with their husbands during the inaugural festivities, and stand beside the president as he takes the oath of office. There are numerous ceremonies in which the first lady must participate that have the potential to impact public policy and the president's political standing.

The First Lady as Woman of Influence: The Three Ps of Influence

First ladies wield political influence in and out of the White House. They have influenced their husband's decisions, presidential politics, and public opinion. A model of the first lady's influence is offered by scholar Barbara Burrell, who identifies four types of influence.[51] The first type of influence comes from directing her spouse's career. First ladies exert influence politically through actions that are not inherently political but are often private. Many future first ladies such as Nancy Reagan and Florence Harding were instrumental in supporting and even guiding their husbands into and throughout their political careers. This type of influence could even involve protecting the health and welfare of their spouses in the demanding world of politics. A second type of influence is derived from controlling the social affairs of the White House and the capital. First ladies have become the nation's hostess and leading social figure in the White House. Many of the social facets of the White House are quite political and provide first ladies with an avenue of influence. This type of influence can even involve personnel matters and interpersonal relations. A third type of influence derives from the first lady's role as the president's personal political adviser, through which she has enormous influence over a wide array of matters. The first lady's actions may not be overtly political; her advice to the president and her interest in his political health might be better explained by her own interest in what is best for her spouse. The final type of influence is found in the first lady's interest in public policy. Some first ladies, like Rosalynn Carter and Hillary Clinton, have become policymaking partners, taking an active role in the policy process or a particular issue. The first ladies' influence may be understood conceptually as existing in three spheres: political, "pillow," and public.

Political Sphere of Influence

The political sphere of influence encompasses such formal political activities as speechwriting and speech editing, policy advising and advocacy, lobbying, selecting or endorsing presidential appointments, and campaigning. It is important to distinguish here between influence and power. The first lady's influence is through her relationship with the president or through her popularity. Power usually derives through a formal office or expertise on a particular subject. Several first ladies have played a very active role in politics and have also been highly influential forces in the politics and policy decisions of the White House. Thus the political sphere of influence identifies one avenue—politics—by which the first lady both influences the president and extends her own influence within and beyond the White House. Many first ladies influenced their husbands on political matters. Abigail Fillmore talked her husband into ending the practice of flogging in the U.S. Navy.[52] Campaign buttons proclaiming "Vote for Betty's Husband" and "Elect Betty's Husband—Keep Betty in the White House" are examples of Mrs. Ford's influence with the electorate. Among the most politically influential first ladies are Sarah Polk, Helen Taft, Florence Harding, Eleanor Roosevelt, Rosalynn Carter, Nancy Reagan, and Hillary Clinton.

"Pillow" Sphere of Influence

This apolitical and informal sphere of influence includes behind-the-scenes influence that might come simply from being the president's longtime partner, wife, and confidante. The home and family life, social interests, and moral beliefs of the first ladies have influenced the president. This type of influence probably cannot be measured but should not be ignored by scholars studying the presidency or presidential spouses. The pillow sphere of influence identifies the direct effect first ladies have on the day-to-day lives of the presidents and, as a result, the indirect impact they have on presidential decisionmaking. This notion is at the core of the partnership model of the presidency.

Eliza Johnson stood by her husband during the crisis of his impeachment, bolstering his resolve. A century later, Pat Nixon demonstrated the same kind of support as her husband contemplated resignation and impeachment. Edith Roosevelt used to joke that the president was her "fifth child" (the Roosevelts had four children) and that she was the only one who could control him. Other first ladies who were especially influential in the president's personal life include such full partners as Abigail Adams, Dolley Madison, Hannah Van Buren, Sarah Polk, Abigail Fillmore, Lucretia Garfield, Ellen Arthur, Ida McKinley, Helen Taft, Florence Harding, Lou Hoover, Bess Truman, Rosalynn Carter, Nancy Reagan, and Hillary Clinton.

Public Sphere of Influence

Many first ladies have been among the most well known and popular Americans of their time.[53] The first ladyship is a highly public institution, one that both reflects and shapes societal attitudes toward women. In their formal capacity, first ladies have hosted foreign dignitaries and entertained thousands of visitors to the White House, campaigned in public for their husbands, traveled around the nation and world, and spoken to or appeared before huge audiences. Through these efforts the first ladyship has become an inherently public institution, one that could be said to belong to the U.S. people. Accordingly, it is also an institution with considerable influence among the larger U.S. public.

Some first ladies who were especially well known public figures and possibly among the best known women of their day and age are Martha Washington, Dolley Madison, Elizabeth Monroe, Julia Tyler, Mary Lincoln, Julia Grant, Frances Cleveland, Edith Roosevelt, Edith Wilson, Lou Hoover, Eleanor Roosevelt, Mamie Eisenhower, Jackie Kennedy, Lady Bird Johnson, Betty Ford, Nancy Reagan, Barbara Bush, and Hillary Clinton. Lou Hoover was awarded the Cross Chevalier, Order of Leopold, from Belgium's King Leopold. Louisa Adams was so beloved that, when she died on May 15, 1852, Congress adjourned for the day, the first time a woman had been thus honored.

Most recent first ladies have appeared on television. Nancy Reagan made a guest appearance on the popular TV sitcom *Diff'rent Strokes* playing herself. Hillary Clinton and Barbara Bush made several nationally televised appearances on a variety of news shows and network news channels. Even Bess Truman, a reclusive first lady who shunned the public eye, appeared in 1955 on the popular Edward R. Murrow show *Person to Person.*

The First Lady as Human Rights Advocate

A History of Advocacy

Women have always been on the front lines of the human rights battlefield. In the nineteenth century, the early leaders in women's suffrage such as Elizabeth Cady Stanton, Lucretia Mott, and Susan B. Anthony were also supporters of the rights of African Americans. Similarly, the ranks of the "Garrisonians," the northern abolition organization named for its leader William Lloyd Garrison, were filled with women. History repeated itself a century later during the civil rights movement of the 1950s and 1960s.

Although they were not always the visible leaders of the movement, women were the civil rights foot soldiers. Women marched, organized, and performed the clerical work. Many volunteered with the Congress of Racial Equality, Student Non-violent Coordinating Committee, and other leading civil rights groups active in voter registration drives, literacy training, and health clinics across the South. It was Rosa Parks's refusal to give her seat up for a white man on December 1, 1955, that started Martin Luther King's Montgomery Improvement Association, the famous boycott of segregated city buses in Alabama. This boycott was a key event initiating the civil rights movement.

Women have always been the leaders in children's rights crusades. The spokesperson for the new Mississippi Freedom Democratic Party at the 1964 Democratic National Convention, who addressed a nationally televised audience, was Fannie Lou Hamer, a poor black woman from rural Mississippi. Leaders have also been found in the White House, but not always in the office of the presidency. First ladies have championed civil rights, fought for the welfare of children, embraced the cause of peace, and come to the aid of the poor, hungry, and disenfranchised.[54] For example, peace advocate First Lady Ida McKinley opposed the Spanish-American War, Rosalynn Carter is a recognized spokesperson for international human rights, and Edith Roosevelt deserves recognition for her efforts on behalf of the cause of peace. Edith assisted President Teddy Roosevelt with negotiations during the close of the Russo-Japanese War by meeting with diplomats and decoding sensitive messages. For his part, Teddy Roosevelt was awarded the Nobel Peace Prize. More recently, in 1999, when the Clinton administration announced a huge disaster relief package for the earthquake and hurricane victims in Latin America, it was First Lady Hillary Clinton who announced the aid relief plan to the nation.

One issue common among first ladies was their assistance to disabled veterans and wounded or hospitalized soldiers. Caroline Harrison joined her officer husband at his camps in Kentucky and Tennessee during the Civil War, where she worked mending uniforms and doing chores. Back at home, she continued her efforts by tending to wounded soldiers at hospitals and organizing public drives for food, clothing, and medicine to aid the war effort and troops. She also worked with the Ladies Patriotic Association and Ladies Sanitary Committee to help soldiers. Another common campaign for first ladies has been the improvement of the status of women in U.S. society. Most first ladies contributed to some extent to this issue, but most notable among the contributors are Abigail Adams, Helen Taft, Florence Harding, Lou Hoover, Eleanor Roosevelt, Betty Ford, Rosalynn Carter, and Hillary Clinton.

Some first ladies have used their pet projects to champion human rights. Dolley Madison supported orphaned children. Harriet Lane was interested in the rights of American Indians and advocated Indian education. Lady Bird Johnson used her popular beautification and conservation program to rebuild black neighborhoods, and Barbara Bush embraced the need for universal literacy. Others devoted their lives to the issue. Grace Coolidge was a teacher of the deaf before becoming first lady and returned to that cause after her White House years. Much of Hillary Clinton's pre–White House career was devoted to child advocacy; she had worked with the Children's Defense Fund and the famous children's activist Marian Wright Edelman. In the White House the first lady continued her commitment to the issue by writing a best-selling book on the welfare of children, *It Takes a Village.*

Frances Cleveland showed some interest in civil rights, attempting to create a charitable organization dedicated to helping orphaned and poor black children. Unfortunately, her efforts failed to find sufficient public enthusiasm and the charity was never realized. But Frances did make a difference as a member of the Colored Christmas Club, an organization in the capital that donated money for blacks in need during the holiday season. Mrs. Cleveland also opened White House reception areas and her Saturday receptions to blacks and was possibly the first presidential spouse to integrate the White House in this manner.

In the twentieth century the visibility of first ladies as human rights advocates increased with the advent of mass circulation newspapers and television. Lou Hoover created quite a stir in the southern press in 1929 when she hosted the wife of Illinois representative Oscar DePriest for tea at the White House. Mrs. Jessie DePriest happened to be an African American. The Texas state legislature even symbolically censured Mrs. Hoover. The press followed closely the "Lady Bird Special," Lady Bird Johnson's personal train used for campaigning for her husband in the South. The first lady was sent by the president on a whistle-stop tour through the South on a mission to minimize white hostility to his support of the 1964 civil rights bill. Lady Bird faced hostile mobs and threats from the Ku Klux Klan in the unrepentant South, along with severe public criticism from the ultraconservative John Birch Society. The first lady stood her ground and earned praise in more objective journalistic circles. Media attention to such activism by the first ladies provided the cause of civil rights with necessary public awareness.

Some first ladies took the fight to the streets the old-fashioned way— through direct action. Ellen Wilson made slum clearance her mission, lobbying members of Congress and personally taking them to observe the poor conditions under which many blacks in the nation's capital lived. Through her actions and those of the District of Columbia National Civic Federation, to which she belonged, the first lady brought attention to the plight of "alley dwellers" and succeeded in getting Congress to pass legislation on the matter, known as "Ellen Wilson's Bill," or the Clearance Act of 1914. The measure passed on the day of her untimely death. Interestingly, Ellen Wilson's crusading was partially due to her belief in Christian responsibility and partially due to her feeling of personal responsibility because she was descended from a slave-owning southern family.[55] At the time, Washington, D.C., was a border city, more southern than northern in character despite its location outside the deep South. Thus, the so-called Jim Crow segregation laws extended into Washington. Although Ellen Wilson was not able to overturn any of these laws, she was opposed to them.

In the latter twentieth century, the first ladies' activism on behalf of human rights spread beyond the national borders and took on many new dimensions. Both First Ladies Pat Nixon and Hillary Clinton participated in symbolic visits to Africa, Pat without her husband in 1972 and Hillary with her family in 1998. First Ladies Lady Bird Johnson, Betty Ford, and Rosalynn Carter appeared at the International Women's Year Conference in 1977. Roughly two decades later, Hillary Clinton gave a keynote speech at a similar meeting in China. Betty Ford was an outspoken advocate of women's rights, including the controversial Equal Rights Amendment. The first lady even lobbied Congress to support the measure. Rosalynn Carter championed mental health in the governor's mansion in Georgia and in the White House, where she played a leading role in drafting legislation on behalf of the mentally disabled while serving as honorary chair of the presidentially commissioned task force on mental health. Growing up in rural, segregated Georgia, Rosalynn had witnessed the evils of racism and responded by criticizing white Baptist preachers for disallowing blacks into their churches. Later in life, the first lady was the recipient of an honorary degree from a black college. Barbara Bush added another dimension to the first lady's civil rights activism by serving as the commencement speaker at Bennett College, a black college in Greensboro, North Carolina. Another first for Mrs. Bush was the appointment of the first ethnic minority to a senior position in the first lady's staff, in this case her press secretary, Anna Perez.[56]

The Proving Grounds of the Civil War

The key human rights event for the nation was the Civil War, where the ideals put forth by the framers of the Constitution met the reality of the inhumane practice of slavery in the South. The slavery question proved to be one of the earliest testing grounds for first ladies. The prevailing social norm of the times prohibited first ladies from being active or speaking out on any political issue, let alone such a sensitive, divisive subject as slavery. Relatedly, ladies of the age were not supposed to be interested in such issues or have opinions on the matter. However, several first ladies held firm opinions on the issue, some spoke out against slavery, and a few followed their words with actions. The institution of slavery and the Civil War proved to be one of the initial forays into politics and one of the first rallying points for activism of the office.

Although she was from a prominent, slave-owning southern family, the first lady during the Civil War, Mary Todd Lincoln, spoke out against slavery and in support of the efforts of the Union army. Attacks from both the northern and southern press and many politicians and citizens of both regions of the nation did not silence Mary. The South considered her a traitor, the North did not trust her, and there were even accusations of treason leveled against the first lady. In many ways the war and the issue of slavery were very personal for Mrs. Lincoln. Several of her family members fought and died for the Confederacy, which devastated Mary. She was also proud that her maternal grandmother actually helped enslaved blacks escape to the North through the infamous Underground Railroad.[57] During her first ladyship Mary befriended Elizabeth Keckley, a free black who became Mary's intimate confidante and personal assistant. Although Mary and Elizabeth would eventually have a falling-out, Mary stood by Elizabeth despite criticism of their relationship. Keckley herself was an outspoken abolitionist and supporter of assistance for freed blacks. Perhaps because of Keckley's influence, Mary supported the Contraband Relief Association, an organization devoted to raising funds and support for freed slaves, by speaking in favor of assistance to blacks, and both raising and donating money to the relief effort. Mary favored emancipation and hosted Frederick Douglass, the most prominent black in the country, in the White House. Mary also invited other blacks to the White House long before it was politically acceptable to do so. In fact, she did this roughly three-quarters of a century before Eleanor Roosevelt would do the same thing, yet Eleanor was simultaneously brutally criticized for her actions and applauded for being so bold.

Abigail Fillmore and Jane Pierce also opposed slavery. These first ladies were upset with their husbands' (both of whom were from the North) susceptibility to arguments from southern politicians and accommodation of the southern delegation in Congress. First Lady Fillmore even opposed the Fugitive Slave Bill her husband reluctantly supported, which allowed for federal assistance in returning run-away slaves to slavery. Even as early as the eighteenth century Abigail Adams stated her opposition to slavery.[58] Although Abigail once owned slaves, she taught them to read and write and then offered her family's slaves their freedom. Another Adams, daughter-in-law Louisa, also abhorred slavery and publicly supported abolition. She followed the Garrisonians, perhaps the country's most prominent antislavery society, read their paper *The Liberator,* and even participated in antislavery petitions in the capital city. Louisa also supported her husband's postpresidential career in the House of Representatives, where he emerged as an abolitionist and human rights leader. Louisa circulated antislavery petitions and supported his position against "Indian removal" and the annexation of Texas.

Lucy Hayes begged her husband, an officer for the Union during the Civil War, not to allow his soldiers to return slaves to the South. In fact, Mrs. Hayes became an identifiable figure in the abolition movement and supported the rights for former and freed enslaved individuals. She has even been credited for influencing her husband's opposition to slavery.[59] On a personal level, Mrs. Hayes appears to have practiced what she preached, teaching a former slave by the name of Eliza Jane Burrell to read and write and befriending another former slave by the name of Winnie Monroe, who was hired by the first lady to be a cook in the White House.

Of course, not all first ladies have been leaders in civil rights or, specifically, in opposing slavery. Some never discussed the issue. Other first ladies such as Tennessean Sarah Polk utilized slaves in the White House. Later, Sarah was neutral on the question of the Civil War but did use slaves to run a family-owned cotton plantation in Mississippi after leaving the White House. She also failed to free her slaves after her husband's death, even though James Polk's will suggested doing just that. Margaret Taylor of Maryland and Martha Washington of Virginia also owned slaves. Ellen Arthur's family owned slaves and fought for the South during the Civil War. Perhaps the biggest blemish in the first ladies otherwise respectable record on the slavery question was Julia Tyler's support of slavery. Despite being from the North (New York), Mrs. Tyler staunchly supported her southern husband's pro-slavery and pro-Confederacy politics. Even after her husband's death, she supported southern secession. When British women organized a campaign to appeal to southerners to end the horrific practice of slavery, Julia responded to the appeal with a firm "no" written in the form of an open letter and published in the *Southern Literary Messenger.* She also sent letters to the *New York Herald* and *Richmond Inquirer* defending slavery. In her letter of rebuttal, Julia claimed that slave owners were kind, referred to the southern cause as "Holy," and attacked the North's efforts as "fiendish."[60] Mrs. Tyler did not stop there. She participated in the Civil War by distributing anti-Lincoln literature, refusing to take the Union oath of loyalty to the nation, sending money to Confederate soldiers in Union prisons, and flying the southern rebel flag at her home.

The First Lady of Human Rights

Although the office has a long and impressive record of advocating human rights, one first lady stands out among the rest. Indeed, Eleanor Roosevelt was one of the country's leading crusaders for human rights from 1933 to her death in 1962. Moreover, her activism on behalf of human rights transcended the nation's borders, earning her the nickname "First Lady of the World." She could also be described as the leading advocate for human rights in the history of the White House.

As did several other first ladies, Eleanor faced hostility in the South and in southern papers for inviting African Americans to the White House. But Eleanor did much more to earn that resentment: She worked to oppose job discrimination against blacks, she pushed for the desegregation of the U.S. military, and she brought to the country's attention the inequalities in pay experienced by ethnic minorities. As first lady, she pushed her husband and key members of his administration to support antilynching laws, a very sensitive issue at the time. President Roosevelt was unwilling to fully embrace an antilynching law because of opposition from powerful southern politicians. As a politician, he felt he needed the support from these key southerners. Eleanor, however, was less the politician than she was the idealistic crusader.

In addition to the many human rights issues she backed, First Lady Roosevelt also participated in numerous civil rights activities and organizations. She joined sit-ins at restaurants, invited black entertainers to perform in the White House, served on the board of directors of the National Association for the Advancement of Colored People, the leading black civil rights organization in the country, and was named an honorary member of the National Council of Negro Women. When traveling in the South, the first lady refused to follow the segregation codes and adopted the practice of sitting in the "colored only" sections of public facilities or moving her seat to a neutral location between the black and white seating areas. Eleanor gave her support to blacks in political office. For example, she was instrumental in getting her good friend Mary McLeod Bethune named to head the Negro Affairs Division of the National Youth Administration. To demonstrate her support of and confidence in the black airmen of Tuskegee, the first lady personally traveled to Alabama to take a ride in the plane of a black pilot. At the time there was public and political concern about the fitness of blacks to serve as pilots in World War II. In part because of the first lady's action, the Tuskegee airmen and other black pilots eventually flew combat missions in the war.

Eleanor Roosevelt's human rights activism was not limited to civil rights for African Americans. She also took an interest in the rights of miners and laborers, the poor, women, those in prisons and mental health institutions, and nearly anyone she deemed to be at a disadvantage. The first lady toured institutions, making reports of the conditions she encountered, fought for housing and public assistance for the poor, and was instrumental in getting her husband to appoint the first woman ever to head a federal cabinet: Secretary of Labor Frances Perkins.

Eleanor held weekly press conferences that were open only to female reporters, providing opportunities and credibility for women journalists. (Previously, female reporters routinely found themselves omitted from the serious political, White House, or news beats.) One of the first lady's most memorable and visible acts on behalf of human rights was her resignation from the Daughters of the American Revolution. Traditionally, first ladies often served in an honorary capacity with the well-known group. But in 1939, when the DAR refused to allow black singer Marian Anderson to perform in Constitution Hall, a building owned by the organization, the first lady resigned from the group. Mrs. Roosevelt's actions were covered in the press and she was criticized in certain circles. However, she arranged for Marian Anderson to perform at a free public concert at the Lincoln Memorial near the Capitol. Fittingly, the concert was scheduled on Easter Sunday and attended by 75,000 people.[61]

Eleanor Roosevelt was nominated for the American Peace Award for her work on behalf of human rights. Her work continued after her first ladyship when she was selected as a U.S. delegate to the UN and chaired the UN Commission on Human Rights, which produced the famous UN Universal Declaration of Human Rights.

Office and Staff

The East Wing of the White House is the first lady's domain. Since its construction during Franklin Roosevelt's administration, first ladies have had offices and staff located in the East Wing. The West Wing was built to house the president's office and staff and was first occupied by Teddy Roosevelt in 1902. Before the East Wing was established, first ladies relied on makeshift arrangements to carry out their duties. For instance, Lou Hoover worked out of her upstairs bedroom. (Even though the East Wing was available, Mamie Eisenhower also used her upstairs bedroom as an office.) Grace Coolidge enjoyed using a small sitting room in the White House, and Florence Harding used what is now the Yellow Oval Room as an office. Throughout the presidencies of the late twentieth century, about 100 employees were working in the East Wing at any one time.[62] The East Wing sometimes houses other offices in addition to the first lady's office, including the office of the presidential military attaché, the White House visitor's office, and some of the president's legislative staff, but the East Wing has often been defined by the first lady's presence. The West Wing of the White House serves as the command center for the president, housing most of the senior presidential offices. Breaking with tradition and reflecting her influence within her husband's administration, in 1993 Hillary Clinton moved her office to the West Wing. This move is symbolic of the evolving power of the office of first lady.

Not surprisingly, Mrs. Clinton received a lot of criticism for her move to the West Wing. However, the critics failed to recognize that this move is not entirely without precedent. During the Polk presidency (1845–1849), long before there even was a West or an East Wing, First Lady Sarah Polk had an office beside her husband's. Edith Roosevelt wanted an office next to the president's office so that she and her husband could talk and see each other during the day. She also scheduled an hour each morning for a private meeting between them. Florence Harding often worked with her husband in his West Wing office, and first ladies have regularly visited the West Wing and Oval Office. Moreover, although she has moved her business office to the West Wing of the White House, Mrs. Clinton retains a social office in the East Wing. She also keeps an office in the nearby Old Executive Office Building. Likewise, there have been exceptions to the use of the East Wing as the social wing. During the World War II, Franklin Roosevelt, who oversaw the construction of the East Wing, used much of it as a military command center. His wife, Eleanor, preferred to work out of a two-bedroom suite near the living quarters on the second floor of the White House. And the East Wing was too busy and distracting for First Lady Jackie Kennedy, who usually escaped to the Treaty Room to work.

To assist in meeting the many demands of her position, the first lady has an office staff. The White House also employs a butler, a curator, a chef and kitchen staff, a chief usher, and other individuals. These staffers often work with or directly for the first lady because such tasks as White House management, renovation, and entertaining are largely the responsibilities of the first lady. The office of first lady has grown dramatically in size and importance, as have the scope and magnitude of the functional areas for which the first lady is responsible. Her staff has evolved alongside this growth and has become an essential part of the modern first ladyship. For instance, the first lady must often select and order official White House china and furniture, is responsible for overseeing renovations to the executive mansion, must attempt to answer thousands of pieces of mail each year, and organizes and selects the menu and entertainment for official state dinners. In order to accomplish these tasks, the first lady requires considerable clerical support, specific expertise in diplomatic protocol, organizational resources, and communication systems.

Public Law 95-570, passed in 1978, granted legal authority for the establishment of funds to manage the White House. Part of this act provided for "assistance and services" for the president's spouse in connection with the discharge of the president's duties. Prior to this act, the first lady obtained funds for staff support, travel, hosting, and so forth on an item-by-item and as-needed basis from a White House general budget. Since 1978 the funding process is more efficient and reflects the institutionalization of the office.

The first lady's staff has grown incrementally in response to new duties and responsibilities of the office. As the volume of mail and public requests for appearances grew under First Ladies Mamie Eisenhower and Jackie Kennedy, the need for clerical support became obvious. At the same time, these two first ladies entertained more than their predecessors had and hosted larger and more formal social affairs. As many as forty employees worked for Jackie Kennedy at any one time, a higher number than for any other first lady.[63] However, only as recently as Rosalynn Carter's term did this staff emerge as a coherent, organized entity with distinct lines of authority, jurisdictional areas of responsibility, and professional requirements. It is now similar in organization to, albeit significantly smaller than, the office staff of the president.

The administration of Theodore Roosevelt (1901–1909) was the first to utilize nondomestic staff to assist First Lady Edith Roosevelt with all the mail she received. In 1902, Isabella Hagner James, a clerk in the Department of War, was reassigned to be Mrs. Roosevelt's assistant, thus becoming the first permanent staffer working directly for the first lady. She was paid $1,600 a year. Theodore Roosevelt's presidency was one of the first to receive daily, personal press coverage, owing in part to the president's' charisma, his attractive, young family, and a changing style of journalism developing around the time of his presidency. Consequently, the Roosevelts received more mail and requests from the public than had any previous president or presidential family.

Historically, first ladies often befriended members of the president's cabinet or senior advisers and, accordingly, received assistance and advice from them from time to time. First ladies were not above using such relationships to protect their husband, forward his political agenda, or advance their own ideas in a behind-the-scenes manner. This tactic of using key presidential aides to intervene with the president on behalf of the first lady is nearly as old as the office itself. What comes around, goes around, and senior presidential advisers now routinely enlist the support of the first lady so as to get their messages and preferences to the president. Edith Roosevelt's use of staff was not completely without precedent, but it signaled the start of formally assigning staff to work exclusively for the first lady.

The growth of the first lady's staff has been shaped to a degree by the need to work with the press. Edith Roosevelt had her secretary talk to the press on her behalf, a practice that would later be used by presidents and first ladies alike through the advent of press secretaries and spokespersons. But Julia Tyler, back in the early 1840s, hired perhaps the first public relations agent to ensure positive press coverage of her first ladyship. The position of a press secretary to the first lady was later formally initiated under Jackie Kennedy, in part because of her enormous popularity and in part because of the growing public and media demands on the first lady. First ladies appeared to start talking directly with the press shortly after Edith Roosevelt's first ladyship in the early 1900s. Florence Harding was the first spouse to speak on a regular basis with the press, although both Ellen and Edith Wilson did occasionally talk to reporters and answer questions. At times Dolley Madison also talked with reporters and answered their questions.

Several first ladies have been quite skilled at handling the press. Florence Harding, who had helped manage her husband's paper the *Marion Star* before becoming first lady, was up to the task of working with the press. Florence also helped women journalists by agreeing to interviews, allowing female reporters access to herself and the White House, and supporting their work. Florence Harding and Eleanor Roosevelt often discussed matters beyond social affairs such as current political issues, thus helping the female reporters by giving them angles on those stories that were typically covered by male journalists. Today a first lady not only must deal directly and regularly with the press but is expected to understand the issues. She is often asked questions about politics and current events by both the press and public while making public appearances, attending charitable events, and hosting official functions.

Following Jackie Kennedy's addition of a press secretary to the office of first lady, most subsequent first ladies have added vital staff positions to the office. Lady Bird Johnson was the first to employ a full-time projects manager for her massive, nationwide beautification and conservation program. The important advance and scheduling office was created under Pat Nixon, a first lady who traveled extensively. The effort to modernize and formalize the first lady's office staff became necessary by the time of Rosalynn Carter. Offices and staff positions had been added on an as-needed basis without much thought to the larger issue of the organizational structure, efficiency, and nature of the first lady's office. Rosalynn Carter wisely and impressively employed the services of management consultants to assist her in organizing her staff into a formal office of the first lady. The reorganization was long overdue, much needed, and proved to be a success. Subsequent first ladies have benefited from Mrs. Carter's reforms. Interestingly, however, Rosalynn was not able to complete her vision for the office because her requests for additional staff were denied by her husband. Jimmy Carter, mindful of budgetary pressures, even cut the size of his wife's staff.

To help her accomplish her demanding schedule as an activist first lady and presidential surrogate, Rosalynn Carter did what early first ladies did: She utilized professional staffers from various executive agencies. Mrs. Carter's reorganization helped create a model for today's modern office of the first lady. This organizational configuration has been the basis for first ladies serving since the Carter years and includes roughly 20 to 28 full-time paid employees.[64] Betty Ford had an office of approximately 26 employees, Rosalynn Carter had roughly 21 to 24 employees at any given time,[65] and Nancy Reagan had 18 to 22 employees plus the use of clerical staffers drawn from the White House.[66] Barbara Bush's staff was smaller than that of her immediate predecessors, but her first ladyship was also less active. Modern first ladies continue to use staff from the president's office, including speechwriters, schedulers, and policy experts. (See Box 4.4 for a breakdown of staff offices of recent first ladies.)

Box 4.4   Staff Offices of Recent First Ladies

Rosalynn Carter (24)

Staff Director for the First Lady	Director of Projects
Administrative Assistant to the Staff Director	Assistant to Director of Projects
Research Assistant	Director of Scheduling
	Director of Advance
Personal Assistant to the First Lady	Assistant to Director of Scheduling
Personal Secretary to the First Lady	Scheduling and Advance Assistant
Administrative Assistant to the First Lady	Assistant to Director of Advance
Press Secretary	Social Secretary
Deputy Press Secretary	Assistant Social Secretary
Assistant Press Secretary	Assistant to the Social Secretary (2)
Press Aide	Calligrapher (3)

Nancy Reagan (22)

Deputy Assistant to the President	Deputy Press Secretary
	Executive Assistant
Administrative Assistant	Social Secretary
Personal Assistant to the First Lady	Assistant Social Secretary
	Executive Assistant
Press Secretary	

(Box 4.4 continues)

Box 4.4 Continued

Nancy Reagan (continued)

Director, Graphics and Calligraphy

Graphics Assistant

Staff Assistant

Calligrapher (2)

Director, Projects and Correspondence

Executive Assistant to Director, Projects and Correspondence

Deputy Director, Projects and Correspondence

Staff Assistant

Director, Scheduling and Advance for the First Lady

Deputy Press Secretary for Communications

Secretary

Assistant Chief, Arrangements

Barbara Bush (12)

Deputy Assistant to the President/ Chief of Staff to the First Lady

Staff Assistant to the Chief of Staff

Press Secretary

Deputy Press Secretary (2)

Social Secretary

Deputy Social Secretary

Director of Projects

Director of Scheduling

Director of Correspondence

Special Assistant to the First Lady

Director of Advance for the First Lady

Hillary Clinton (15)

Assistant to the President/ Chief of Staff to the First Lady

Executive Assistant to the Chief of Staff

Deputy Assistant to the President/Deputy Chief of Staff to the First Lady

Deputy Assistant to the President/Press Secretary to the First Lady

Deputy Press Secretary (2)

Special Assistant to the First Lady

Special Assistant to the President/Social Secretary to the First Lady

Deputy Social Secretary

Assistant to the Social Secretary

Special Assistant to the Social Secretary

Director, First Lady's Correspondence

Counselor to the First Lady

Assistant to the Counselor to the First Lady

Special Assistant to the Counselor to the First Lady

Prior to Rosalynn Carter's first ladyship, the position of chief of staff for the first lady was not a full-time post. It often was a task that was fulfilled by the first lady's press secretary or social secretary. With a full-time chief of staff and her own press office, the first lady no longer must rely solely on the president's press secretary and schedulers. The East and West Wings do, however, work together because the first ladyship has become an integral part of the presidency. The White House social affairs office, for example, is located in the East Wing, and most recent presidents have delegated at least one member of their correspondence office to the first lady's staff. According to James Rosebush, former chief of staff to Nancy Reagan, such assistance was vital to the first lady, who received an average of 4,000 letters per month during her service.[67] Presidents and presidential advisers recognize that the first lady affects public perceptions and public opinion about the president, and they value her role as a leading campaigner and spokesperson for the president.

The organization of the office of the first lady varies slightly from occupant to occupant, of course, but most staff functions can be categorized into three primary areas: social affairs, press relations, and policy issues. The primary positions are chief of staff, press secretary, director of special projects and policy, director of scheduling and advance, and social secretary.

The chief of staff is usually the most important and senior member of the first lady's team; this staff member's functions include managing the office, assisting in hiring and other personnel matters, allocating or reallocating resources, and serving as the first lady's senior adviser. Management of the media and public affairs falls to the press secretary, who is often the second most important and senior member of the first lady's office. The press secretary works with the media, providing press releases, scheduling meetings with the press, preparing the first lady for her interviews, and all other forms of press management. With the rise of the modern first ladyship, the director of special projects has become increasingly important. The director coordinates the first lady's political and policy activities and manages her social projects, which often involve considerable staff and resources, travel, and public appearances. This office must brief the first lady on the issue at hand, work with the press office to ensure positive media coverage of the issue, and monitor the progress of the first lady's cause.

First ladies now travel throughout the United States and around the world. The first lady's days are filled with meetings, events, and activities. The scheduling and advance office makes sure these demands are met yet are not too overwhelming for the first lady. The final main position within the office of the first lady is the social secretary. Social secretaries have been used for a variety of tasks, and the job often takes on different dimensions for different first ladies. The office could entail everything from managing the first lady's mail, dealing with clerical and office management tasks, overseeing the busy social functions for which the first lady is responsible, and even functioning as a personal assistant to the first lady. Each of the primary units or areas within the first lady's office is usually headed by an individual and has at least one executive assistant, along with several volunteers. Examples of this structure can be found in Boxes 4.5 and 4.6, which show, respectively, the organizational structure of Nancy Reagan's office and the full-time, paid employees working in Hillary Clinton's office.

It is interesting to note that the first ladyship has become a part of the plural presidency and that the first ladyship itself has become a pluralist institution, comprising many offices, staffers, and external entities that, together, make up the office. Because the office has become an institution, the first lady's office can be expected to retain these core functional areas. As new responsibilities emerge or innovative first ladies take office, these core areas will remain but new staff positions matching the new first ladyship might emerge.

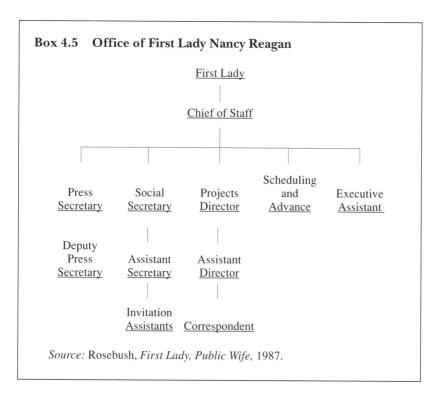

Box 4.5   Office of First Lady Nancy Reagan

First Lady

Chief of Staff

| Press Secretary | Social Secretary | Projects Director | Scheduling and Advance | Executive Assistant |

| Deputy Press Secretary | Assistant Secretary | Assistant Director |

| Invitation Assistants | Correspondent |

Source: Rosebush, *First Lady, Public Wife,* 1987.

Box 4.6   Office of First Lady Hillary Clinton, 1997

Position (Staff Member)
Counselor to the First Lady (Margaret Williams)
Assistant to the Counselor to the First Lady (Peggy Lewis)
Special Assistant to the Counselor to the First Lady (Evan Ryan)
Assistant to the President and Chief of Staff to the First Lady
    (Melanne Verveer)
Assistant to the Chief of Staff to the First Lady (Katherine Button)
Deputy Chief of Staff to the First Lady (Ellen Lovell)
Deputy Assistant to the President and Director of Communications to
    the First Lady (Marsha Berry)
Special Assistant to the President and Press Secretary to the First
    Lady (Neel Lattimore)
Deputy Press Secretary to the First Lady (Steve Cohen)
Deputy Press Secretary to the First Lady (Karen Finney)
Special Assistant to the First Lady (Capricia Marshall)
Executive Assistant (Pamela Cicetti)
Staff Assistant (Eric Hothem)
Director of Correspondence for the First Lady (Alice Pushkar)
Special Assistant to the President and Social Secretary (Ann Stock)
Deputy Social Secretary (Robyn Dickey)
Special Assistant to the Social Secretary (Tracy LaBrecque)
Executive Assistant (Kim Widdess)

Source: White House Office of the First Lady.

Notes

1. President Jimmy Carter did not appoint his wife, Rosalynn, to head his Presidential Task Force on Mental Health Reform because of the possible legal concerns surrounding the appointment. However, he fulfilled his wish to have her lead the effort by naming her the "honorary" director of the task force. That title bypassed any legal concerns that might be raised by the first lady's work. Also, as has been mentioned throughout the book, the first ladies have wielded influence in many ways without formally serving for government.

2. Hillary Clinton had a long history of heading her husband's policy initiatives, dating back to when Bill Clinton served as governor of Arkansas. While governor, Bill Clinton asked his wife to take the lead on several education reform initiatives, for example.

3. Throughout 1993 and even into 1994, several prominent newsmagazines,

such as *Time* and *Newsweek,* and the leading newspapers and political talk shows reported that Hillary Clinton was generally receiving positive reviews for her work on health care reform, despite the controversy surrounding her appointment as head of the task force.

4. The court case in question was *The Association of American Physicians and Surgeons, Inc., et al. v. Hillary Rodham Clinton et al.,* 997 F. 2nd 898, 904 (U.S. App. DC, 22 June 1993), also 813 F. Supp. 90 (D.D.C. 1993).

5. Ibid.

6. I conducted a survey/interview with former first lady Barbara Bush on February 18, 1997, through Mrs. Bush's aide Quincy Hicks.

7. Ibid.

8. See Chapter 5 for a more comprehensive discussion of internal and external factors that influence the roles and functions of the first lady.

9. The new first ladies exhibit focuses on the public and political roles of the first ladies and is housed at the Smithsonian Institution's Museum of American History, Washington, D.C. The old exhibit contains the first ladies' inaugural gowns.

10. M. Gutin, *The President's Partner,* 1989.

11. J. S. Rosebush, *First Lady, Public Wife,* 1987.

12. K. O'Connor, B. Nye, and L. Van Assendelft, "Wives in the White House," 1997.

13. I conducted a survey/interview with former first lady Rosalynn Carter on February 25, 1997, through Mrs. Carter's aide Deanna Congileo.

14. Hillary Clinton appeared on national television immediately following the 1992 Superbowl and defended her husband, their relationship, and the marital troubles they had worked through. This is widely credited as saving Bill Clinton's presidential campaign amid the rumors of his alleged affair with Gennifer Flowers.

15. Barbara Bush revealed her views in Barbara Bush, *Memoir,* 1994, and in an interview conducted by Quincy Hicks, aide to Mrs. Bush, February 18, 1997.

16. See Nancy Reagan's autobiography *My Turn,* 1989.

17. See the chapters on Mamie Eisenhower in C. S. Anthony, *Saga,* 1990; and L. Gould, *First Ladies,* 1996. An account of Ike and Mamie's life together is offered in L. David and I. David, *Ike and Mamie,* 1981.

18. Quote appears in the chapter on Mamie Eisenhower in Gould, 1996.

19. I conducted a survey/interview with Barbara Bush on February 18, 1997, through Mrs. Bush's aide Quincy Hicks.

20. The Gallup organization conducts an annual poll of most admired women. See "The Women We Admire," 1989, and "Who Best as First Lady?" 1996.

21. See E. S. Arnett, *Mrs. James Madison,* 1972; M. B. Klapthor, *The First Ladies,* 1994; Rosebush, 1987.

22. E. M. Betts and J. A. Bear, *Family Letters,* 1966.

23. Louisa Adams held personal views that could be considered progressive for the time. She wrote two books that provide insights into her beliefs: *Record of a Life* (also called *My Story*) in 1825 and *Adventures of a Nobody,* 1840. The former is more helpful. See also P. C. Nagel, *The Adams Women,* 1987. This offers a good study of two of the most progressive women of U.S. history.

24. Ibid.

25. Lucy Hayes's school essay on women is discussed in the chapters on Mrs. Hayes in Anthony, 1990; and Gould, 1996. It is also presented in E. A. Geer, *First Lady,* 1984.

26. The battle at Fort Sumpter was fought on April, 12, 1861, in South

Carolina and was a key event that started the Civil War. The Union ended up surrendering the fort to the Confederate forces.

27. See L. H. Butterfield, Marc Friedlaender, and Mary-Jo Kline, eds., *The Book of Abigail and John,* 1975.

28. Abigail's progressive thoughts and political views are discussed in P. L. Leven, *Abigail Adams,* 1987; Nagel, 1987; J. Whitney, *Abigail Adams,* 1947; L. Withey, *Dearest Friend,* 1981. The best source is Abigail's own writings. See S. Mitchell, *New Letters,* 1947.

29. Butterfield et al., 1975.

30. See H. J. Sievers, *Benjamin Harrison,* 1969.

31. First ladies exhibit at the Smithsonian Institution's National Museum of American History, Washington, D.C.

32. See the helpful discussion of Mrs. Harding in Anthony, 1990.

33. First ladies exhibit at the Smithsonian Institution's National Museum of American History, Washington, D.C.

34. Ibid.

35. See M. Truman, 1996 and 1968.

36. Although Mamie Eisenhower, a warm, "people-oriented" person, did not play any overtly political role in the campaign or in her husband's presidency, she enjoyed the social aspect of campaigning. See D. Brandon, *Mamie Doud Eisenhower,* 1954.

37. See the chapter on Mamie Eisenhower in Gould, 1996.

38. See Gutin, 1989. Gutin offers an excellent discussion of Lady Bird Johnson's public speaking and campaigning abilities, including her contributions to her husband's campaigns and political career.

39. See H. Fuller, "The Powerful Persuaders," 1964; N. Robertson, "First Lady Booed in South Carolina," 1964; N. Robertson, "First Lady Is Torched in the South," 1964.

40. N. Robertson, "First Lady Is Torched in the South," 1964.

41. Lady Bird's love of the environment was also sparked by her father's interest in the natural world and his being a naturalist and outdoorsman. See R. Montgomery, *Mrs. LBJ,* 1964. See also H. Middleton, *Lady Bird Johnson,* 1992, which provides a photographic collection (with some discussion) of her life and her love of nature. Lady Bird herself discusses her environmental views in her book (with Carlton Lees) *Wildflowers Across America,* 1988. She was also influenced by her trip to the American West. Mrs. Johnson's conservation and beautification programs are discussed in C. S. Anthony, *Saga,* 1991; B. B. Caroli, *First Ladies,* 1987; Gould, 1996; and M. Truman, 1996.

42. The discussion appears in M. Means, *Women,* 1963.

43. See Gutin, 1989. Also, numerous books on Jackie Kennedy discuss this, including C. D. Heymann, *A Woman Named Jackie,* 1990; and M. Van Renssalaer Thayer, *Jacqueline Kennedy,* 1967.

44. A discussion of her defense of her husband and contribution to his campaign appears in the books of A. Nevins, *Grover Cleveland,* 1932; and A. Nevins, *Letters,* 1933–1934. See also the chapters on Mrs. Cleveland in Anthony, 1990; Gould, 1996; M. Truman, 1995.

45. For a discussion of the event, see Arnett, 1972; N. B. Gerson, *The Velvet Glove,* 1975. See also Anthony, 1990; Gould, 1996; and M. Truman, 1996. These books provide chapters on Dolley that discuss her actions during the War of 1812.

46. Rosebush, 1987.

47. Ibid.

48. R. Carter, *First Lady from Plains,* 1984.

49. Gerson, 1975.

50. O'Connor, Nye, and Van Assendelft, 1997.

51. B. Burrell, *Public Opinion,* 1997.

52. See F. H. Severence, *Millard Fillmore Papers,* 1907; and Gutin, 1989.

53. See "Who Best as First Lady?" 1996, and "The Women We Admire," 1989.

54. For an excellent discussion of the first ladies and the issue of civil rights, see C. S. Anthony, "Skirting the Issue," 1992. I feel that first ladies were more aggressive in their commitment to human rights and civil rights, especially given the day and age when many served and the social constraints limiting a woman's ability to be politically active.

55. See the Ellen Wilson chapter in Gould, 1996.

56. B. Bush, *Barbara Bush,* 1994.

57. See Anthony, 1992, 1990.

58. See C. W. Akers, *Abigail Adams,* 1980; Anthony, 1990; Leven, 1987; M. Truman, 1996.

59. See Anthony, 1990; Gould, 1996.

60. Julia Tyler's pro-slave letter was titled "To the Duchess of Sutherland and the Ladies of England." It was printed in the *Southern Literary Messenger* in the February (Vol. 19) issue of 1853.

61. A. M. Black, "Championing and Champion," 1990.

62. Rosebush, 1987. Information can also be obtained from the White House Information Office and Office of the First Lady.

63. See Rosebush, 1987.

64. D. C. Diller and S. L. Robertson, *The Presidents,* 1997.

65. I surveyed/interviewed former first lady Rosalynn Carter on February 25, 1997, through the public affairs office of the Carter Center.

66. Rosebush, 1987.

67. Ibid.

Eleanor Roosevelt testifies before the Senate Foreign Relations Committee on the importance of the UN (April 22, 1955). Several first ladies have taken an active role in politics, even testifying before Congress as expert witnesses (collection of the Library of Congress).

5

Approaches to the Office

The public expects the first lady to fulfill a multitude of roles flaw-
lessly, and there is criticism at any departure from perceived stan-
dards.

—Lewis L. Gould

As it is with the presidency, the nature of the office of the first lady varies from first lady to first lady. As each first lady determines how she will approach her first ladyship, she must consider a host of external and internal forces acting on the office. The many external forces that guide the development of the office include public opinion, key historical events, and the period in time in which the first lady serves. Thus the nature of the office is partly determined by forces outside the immediate control of the first lady or even the president. There are also forces that influence the organization of the institution of the presidency and thus the institution of the office of the first lady that are within the control of the first lady and president. Such internal forces include the president's perception of and objectives for the first ladyship, the nature of the presidential marriage, and the first ladies' own talents, dispositions, ambitions, and visions for the office. It is within these many complex external and internal factors that first ladies function and determine their particular approach to the office.

Multidimensional Office, Multiple Approaches

External Factors

Whatever the actual nature and scope of the first lady's roles and responsi-bilities, these functions appear to have evolved in large measure from his-torical precedent and custom. These historical, cultural, and political forces that have fashioned the first ladyship as an institution have also shaped the various approaches of particular first ladies. Each first lady enters the office with a vision and a plan for her first ladyship; however, she is not free to carve out functions for her office completely on her own.

She must consider, for instance, public opinion. Public opinion plays a role in setting the parameters of what activities are deemed acceptable or tolerable for presidential spouses by the electorate as well as what is expected of a first lady. Unfortunately, public opinion on the first lady reveals a wide degree of fluctuation and variance from first lady to first lady. Such fickle perspectives pose great challenges.

The media fascination with the first lady has grown throughout the country's history. Press coverage has significantly increased with the advent of the modern, mass media era. Early first ladies were very private and shunned public attention. Moreover, the prevailing social customs of the time precluded any serious discussion of women in the press. However, there were exceptions to this rule. Dolley Madison and Julia Tyler, through their sheer charisma, attracted a considerable public following. The press reported on their activities and White House socials, and Dolley- and Julia-watching became a rage in the first half of the nineteenth century. The Civil War brought an increase in press coverage of the White House and of First Lady Mary Lincoln. In 1902, because of the volume of mail she received, First Lady Edith Roosevelt felt compelled to hire a social secretary, thus creating an office to deal with public relations and the press. The advent of mass circulation newspapers and, later, television further increased the first lady's visibility and required presidential spouses to pay attention to the power of the mass media.

Another external factor that influences the first lady's approach to the office is the period in which she serves as well as the key events of the day. Eleanor Roosevelt, for example, was spared from performing some of the first lady's time-consuming and demanding social hostessing responsibilities because of the Great Depression and World War II. Eleanor was glad this burden was lightened because it allowed her more time to pursue her political and policy interests. However, there have been first ladies who have been politically and socially active regardless of the times or events. Of course, more recent first ladies have had more opportunities to express themselves and carve out their own approach to the office. Although the times and the events of the day do factor into individual first ladies' approaches to the office, they are not the sole factors or even necessarily the most important factors shaping the office.

Internal Factors

Barbara Bush's first ladyship of the late 1980s and early 1990s was not nearly as progressive as was Eleanor Roosevelt's first ladyship roughly six decades earlier. Nor was Mrs. Bush as assertive as Mrs. Clinton, even though the two served during the same decade. It might be that Mrs. Bush, raised during World War II, was a product of a different generation than Mrs. Clinton, who grew up in the postwar period and came of age in the 1960s. Perhaps the events and the time of the first lady's formative years influence her approach to the office. Another possible explanation would be that internal factors such as the first lady's personality and view of the office play a more powerful role than external factors in shaping the nature of the office. Thus the president's expectations for the office of the first lady, together with the first lady's personal perspective toward the office, would be the primary internal forces shaping approaches to the first lady-ship. More than anyone else working in the White House, the first lady derives her power and legitimacy through the president, and thus the approach to the office is to a large measure controlled by the president.

Consider the presidencies of Jimmy Carter and Richard Nixon. Despite the fact that both men served in the 1970s and had highly capable spouses, each president had a different vision for the office of the first lady. Whereas Carter saw his wife, Rosalynn, as a full partner whose advice was not only valued but sought after on every presidential decision, Nixon did not encourage his wife, Pat, to become involved in any aspect of his presidency. In fact, he limited her ability to function as first lady and framed the office so that it would reflect traditional values onto his presidency.

The aptitude, character, and interests of the particular first lady in office also influence the extent to which she is active and the types of functions with which she is involved. First ladies have had varying levels of ambition, intelligence, charisma, and talent, and they have also viewed the office differently. Some served only out of a sense of civic duty or out of obligation to their husbands; others embraced the idea of using the office to accomplish personal and political objectives. First Lady Hillary Clinton was an Ivy League law school graduate with an agenda of goals she wanted to pursue and a strong desire to effect a change in the country and the political process. Barbara Bush was a homemaker prior to her husband's presidency with little interest in anything other than continuing in her role as supportive wife in the White House.

No One Best Way

The first ladyship is a multidimensional office, with many duties and responsibilities. Each first lady must determine, within a complex political environment and amid other external factors acting on the office, what duties or elements of the office she will prioritize. As was presented in Chapter 4, ten general duties of the first lady can be identified, including serving as presidential spokesperson, cocampaigner, champion of social causes, and White House hostess, along with the basic role of serving as presidential partner. These duties cover a wide spectrum of roles and responsibilities and each one poses a challenge to the occupant of the office.

Considering the many external and internal forces shaping the office and the many duties for which first ladies are responsible, it is not surprising that there have been many different approaches to the office of first lady. Some first ladies, such as Mamie Eisenhower and Julia Grant, seemed to approach the office from a social hosting perspective and prioritized that particular role to a degree that it defined their first ladyships. Others, like Rosalynn Carter and Eleanor Roosevelt, largely ignored this aspect of the office and focused their White House years on politics and policy activities. In recent years, first ladies have been expected to be both competent White House hostesses and knowledgeable political advisers. A dual approach has come to define the modern office.

It appears that there has been even more variance in conceptual approaches to the office of the first lady than there have been approaches to the presidency. This may be due to the lack of constitutional guidelines for the first lady and the changing role of women in society. It might also be explained by the fact that the electorate plays little direct role in the first lady's mandate for the office and that the political party exerts less influence over the first lady than it does over the president. Another explanation may be that the first ladyship is technically not a formal office; it lacks pay and constitutional precedence, is neither elected, appointed, nor confirmed by the Senate, and, until recently, it did not have the staff, office space, and budgetary support necessary to fulfill a viable public role.

So how does one write a job description for or identify approaches to a job that is not even a job per se? It is not an easy task. In this chapter I will examine the types of approaches to the office used by the first ladies.

The Fallacy of a Two-Dimensional Office

When discussing the different approaches to the office of the first lady, the media, public, and scholarly literature tend to dichotomize the office: First ladies are categorized as either traditional or modern in their approach. However, I have attempted to present the office as much more complex and multidimensional and thus caution against thinking of the office in such an either/or manner.

The notion of the modern presidency often begins with or immediately after the administration of Franklin Roosevelt (1933–1945). The same can be said of the first ladyship. However, the dichotomy between modern and traditional first ladies suggests more than the era of service; it also implies a difference in duties and responsibilities. The notion of a traditional first lady emphasizes her role as wife and conceptualizes the office in a nonpublic and apolitical manner. The modern first lady is cast in terms of a feminist partner and the office is that of an activist, political, and highly public approach. Of course, these narrow conceptualizations of the office are not entirely accurate or even appropriate. Many earlier first ladies have approached the office as a political partner and in a highly public way, and a few first ladies of the modern era did not emerge as political activists.

Ironically, traditional elements of the office such as social hostessing have been performed under intense public scrutiny and in a highly political fashion, revealing the linkage between social entertaining and presidential politics. Dolley Madison enjoyed a considerable amount of public attention and was a huge political asset to President James Madison, even though she was known almost exclusively for her social hostessing acumen. But it was through her hostessing skills that she emerged as a political player in Madison's presidency, by gaining fame and therefore political support and by mixing politics with social hostessing.[1] This has remained true in recent years. Barbara Bush had a very public profile, even though her actions and approach to the office appeared to be very traditional. Her popularity was tied to her traditional image and proved to be an asset to her husband's presidency. Many seemingly traditional first ladies have been quite active, influential, and political, but in a behind-the-scenes manner. Therefore, it is not accurate to identify such first ladies as traditional simply because they did not overtly or publicly participate in politics; they were powerful political forces in private. Because of the enormous social constraints on the role of women in society for most of the nation's history, first ladies were forced to exercise any form of power or influence they had in a behind-the-scenes manner.

Models for Studying the Office of the First Lady

Communicator Approach

Myra Gutin offers a conceptual model for studying the first lady that centers on her role as communicator.[2] The various approaches to the office are thus based on communication activities; secondary consideration is given to such communication-related activities as public speaking, press relations and the first lady's use of the media, her role as spokesperson for the president, and her advocacy of issues. Such communication roles are among the primary functions or responsibilities of the office. Most first ladies serving since the year 1900, and a few prior to the twentieth century, have been active public communicators. Gutin offers three basic categorizations:

1. Housekeepers, social hostesses, and ceremonial presences (Florence Harding, Grace Coolidge, Bess Truman, Mamie Eisenhower)
2. Emerging spokeswomen (Lou Hoover, Jackie Kennedy, Pat Nixon)
3. Political surrogates and independent advocates (Eleanor Roosevelt, Lady Bird Johnson, Betty Ford, Rosalynn Carter)

Although her work is an important contribution to first lady scholarship, Gutin limits her analysis to first ladies in the twentieth century and to only the communication functions of the job. Betty Boyd Caroli also classifies first ladies according to their approach to the office, focusing on the public dimension of the office.[3] She rejects the notion that pre-twentieth-century first ladies were inactive and traditional by identifying such exceptions to conventional wisdom as Mary Todd Lincoln, Sarah Polk, and Julia Grant. Caroli believes that each of these spouses achieved prominence as a public figure. She also identifies those early and modern first ladies who approached the office as activists.

The first lady has been a visible and public member of the office of the president. Part of this public role has required that she serve as presidential communicator. Consider, for example, such duties of the office as presidential spokesperson, presidential booster and political party booster, campaigner, social advocate, diplomat, symbol of the American woman, and public figure. These are highly public activities that require the first lady to be a good communicator and to have a positive public image and press relations. To perform these public duties, the first lady does not have the full power and support of the federal government, the legitimacy of elected or appointed office, the assurance of having been elected by a sizable percentage of the public, or the backing of the Constitution. In many ways, the public dimension and duties of the first ladyship are more challenging than those confronting the president. She is required to rely almost exclusively on her ability as a public communicator. But there is a parallel to this challenge. Much of the president's power does not derive from the Constitution or other formal sources. Rather, the president often leads, builds support, enhances his power, and indeed governs through the use of the "bully pulpit."[4]

The "White Glove Pulpit" Approach

Presidents have sought direct public support for themselves and their programs, thereby both bypassing the often hostile, cumbersome legislative channels and gaining the ally of a public that puts pressure on legislators on behalf of the president. The president is in a unique position to use the bully pulpit because of the intense media coverage devoted to the institution and because the president, unlike Congress, can speak with one voice rather than a plurality of voices. The president is recognized and has an attentive national (and international) audience. The advent of mass communication technologies has also enabled him to utilize an instantaneous global pulpit.

The president has always had and used the bully pulpit approach to the office. Presidents have served as moral leaders and national figureheads, transcending the political combat of partisan legislative politics. They have used the media to enhance their image and popularity and advanced their policy agenda by going directly to the people. Theodore Roosevelt is credited for "inventing" the presidential bully pulpit.[5] Much as a preacher uses the power of persuasion from the pulpit, President Roosevelt bypassed the legislature and used his powers of persuasion to make direct appeals to the U.S. public. He was successful in using the media to create and exploit his "Rough Rider" war hero image, his charisma, and his active, young family. Roosevelt managed public opinion and the press. Later presidents attempted with varying degrees of success to replicate Teddy's bully pulpit. Franklin Roosevelt's famous "fireside chats" proved enormously popular and were listened to by a large audience. These radio addresses built support for the president and for his policies. In the modern era, four presidents are generally identified as having successfully mastered the media and used their speaking prowess and charisma in a manner that aided their popularity and ultimately their presidencies: Franklin Roosevelt, John Kennedy, Ronald Reagan, and Bill Clinton.[6] But many presidents have not been able harness the power of the bully pulpit.

An entire institution within the White House has evolved to deal with the media, public relations, and public opinion, and, ultimately, to assist the president in using the bully pulpit. In a sense, the bully pulpit has become institutionalized in the presidency and is a primary tool used by modern presidents to govern. The White House contains a buzzing press office, public relations masters, presidential spokespersons, speechwriters, pollsters, and image handlers. Many presidential scholars now agree that image management and public speaking abilities are important elements in presidential success. In the era of mass communications, the bully pulpit has become an integral part of contemporary leadership and the presidency.

Vestiges of the bully pulpit are found in the first ladyship. The office of the first lady is also a highly public institution, where image and public speaking competence are important. Because the first lady is without formal constitutional powers, she, even more than the president, must rely on her "white glove pulpit." She derives her credibility through the presidential marriage only and must stand on her own two feet in the public arena, assisted only by her affiliation with the president. Not surprisingly, first ladies have used their own pulpit to benefit themselves, their causes, and the president's image and popularity. First Ladies Eleanor Roosevelt and

Hillary Clinton wrote syndicated newspaper columns while serving as first lady. Jackie Kennedy penned a column titled "Campaign Wife" for the Democratic Party during her husband's bid for the presidency in 1960. The first lady employs a white glove version of the bully pulpit also through her public appearances, public relations, public speaking, and social hostessing.

The difference between the bully pulpit and the white glove pulpit is that the latter has a definite feminine quality and involves advancing the image of the first lady and the president through social functions like teas, receptions, and state dinners. New dimensions to the office of the first lady have expanded the ways in which first ladies employ this pulpit, including campaigning, speaking publicly, and advocating social issues. When speaking publicly, first ladies use this pulpit, but the nature of the first ladyship and the white glove pulpit restricts them from attacking opponents, openly engaging in policy debates, and celebrating their own accomplishments or records. In many ways, the white glove pulpit approximates the type of pulpit used by the monarchs of Europe. The parameters of the white glove pulpit are limited, but it is still an effective means to promote oneself and one's agenda.

The modern presidential partnership has added yet another dimension to the white glove pulpit. Increasingly, as first ladies offer policy advice, campaign independently, and discuss current issues, the white glove pulpit has begun to encompass some elements of the bully pulpit. As the office of the first lady joins both the political responsibilities of a presidential partnership with the social and hostessing responsibilities of a chief of state, a hybrid approach is evolving that encompasses elements of both pulpits.

Political Party Approaches

Another approach to the office of the first lady is political party affiliation. The question then arises as to whether a difference exists in the approach to the office between Democratic and Republican first ladies. Moreover, studying the political party approach for pre-twentieth-century first ladies presents a problem. The ideological orientation and policy positions of today's Democratic and Republican parties, as well as the leading political issues, are unlike those of the major political parties prior to the twentieth century. Moreover, early parties such as the Federalists and the Whigs are now defunct. Therefore, in comparing first ladies of different political parties, it would bias the comparison to consider first ladies serving prior to the year 1900.

Recent Democratic first ladies, such as Hillary Clinton and Rosalynn Carter, were extremely politically active and powerful members of their husbands' administrations. Each of these wives attended cabinet meetings, were briefed on the issues, and openly functioned as the president's chief political adviser. They traveled on behalf of their husbands and gave speeches on political and policy topics. They also headed major policy task forces: Hillary led the president's health care reform initiative, and Rosalynn headed her husband's mental health reforms. In contrast, recent Republican first ladies Nancy Reagan and Barbara Bush, although influential members of their husbands' administrations, were less inclined to exercise their influence, activities, or opinions in public than their Democratic cohorts. Both Mrs. Reagan and Mrs. Bush functioned and nurtured public images as loyal, apolitical wives. When they exercised power, it was in a behind-the-scenes manner and rarely involved public policy matters.

The examples from the last two and a half decades of the twentieth century might lead one to conclude that there are different approaches to the first ladyship by political party. Democratic first ladies appear to be more active in public, more concerned with public policy, and wield their influence and power both privately and publicly. Republican first ladies, though also powerful, exercise their power only in private, are less active publicly, are unconcerned with public policy, and function largely in the role of wife. But such conclusions are based on only four first ladies. Are such approaches found among the other first ladies of the twentieth century?

Other Democratic first ladies, including Lady Bird Johnson (1963–1969) and Eleanor Roosevelt (1933–1945), appear to conform to this "Democratic model" of first ladies. They were powerful advisers who involved themselves in many political and policy concerns and were highly visible public figures. Likewise, Republican first ladies of the latter half of the twentieth century, such as Pat Nixon (1969–1974) and Mamie Eisenhower (1953–1961), are good examples of the "Republican model" of first ladies: They were not politically active, did not involve themselves in public policy matters, and were seen almost exclusively as wives of the president. Democratic first lady Bess Truman (1945–1952) and Jackie Kennedy (1961–1963) did not conform to the Democratic model or approach. Bess was President Harry Truman's most trusted political confidante, but she was neither active in public nor interested in public policy. Mrs. Kennedy could not be considered a public policy player or political adviser, although at times she did offer her husband valuable advice on public speaking, his image, and other political matters. She was not a powerful political force in the White House outside the realm of social hostessing and renovating the Executive Building. Republican first lady Betty Ford (1974–1977) also fails to reflect the Republican approach to the first ladyship as demonstrated by First Ladies Eisenhower, Nixon, Reagan, and Bush. Mrs. Ford was outspoken, active in controversial political issues such as the Equal Rights Amendment, and even disagreed with some of the policy positions taken by her husband. She fits the Democratic model better than the Republican model.

The first lady alone does not define the duties and responsibilities of the office; there are many external factors that shape the nature of and approach to the office. The particular approach of first ladies therefore might be part of the political agenda of the political party in the White House. For instance, the Republican Party's support of a more traditional notion of family values and role for women in society might pressure the first lady to function as the party's vision for womanhood. In such a capacity, the first lady would be a figurehead or symbol of the party's vision of U.S. womanhood. The agenda of the Republican Party and the Republican president might be better served, or at least appear more consistent, if the first lady was a reflection of those values. Republican first ladies would thus function largely as loyal wives and remain inactive in politics, uninterested in public policy, and unwilling to exercise power in public. Thus a Republican model of the first ladyship might be more a part of the Republican Party's national platform or approach to the presidency than it is a model by Republican first ladies. Democratic first ladies, backed by the party's position on women's rights and feminism, would function more as political partners and have an active and strong profile in public.

In order to further examine whether a Democratic or Republican archetype exists in the approach to the first ladyship, it is useful to consider polls and studies of the first ladies' approaches to the office. In 1995 I developed a list of women serving in senior positions in the Clinton administration, women in Congress, women governors, individuals making *Washingtonian* magazine's ranking of the most powerful women in the nation's capital city, and so on in an effort to identify women of influence and women leaders in politics in the United States.[7] From this list, 200 individuals were randomly selected and polled about their views of the first ladies. These individuals were asked about the differences or perceived differences between Democratic first ladies and Republican first ladies. The survey respondents did perceive differences in a first lady's approach to office depending on her political party affiliation. Exactly one-third of the poll respondents had no opinion on the matter, one-third stated that the party affiliation of a first lady did not factor into her approach to the office, and another one-third believed that party affiliation was a factor in her approach.

As with so much public opinion polling on the first ladies (see Chapter 6 for a further discussion of this), the polls seem to be defined by a lack of consensus rather than any single finding. The public is undecided about what it wants or expects from the first lady. The findings in this poll suggest that the same thing is true of the survey respondents. Another explanation could be that the respondents, despite being well-known women in public life, know little about the first ladies or that there is a great deal of disagreement on the issue. Interestingly, however, of the one-third of respondents saying that there was a difference between Democratic and Republican first ladies, every such respondent viewed Democratic first ladies as more independent, active, and political than Republican first ladies. The respondents described Democratic first ladies as more "progressive," more "their own persons," and "more active" than Republican spouses. The same respondents described Republican first ladies as "more traditional" or "functioning only as the adoring wife," and other similar kinds of comments.

Another way of comparing first ladies by political party is to consider the party affiliation of first ladies who were involved in political activities. For example, as of 1998, there have been three first ladies and three vice presidential spouses, or "second ladies," who have testified before congressional committees on policy matters. Of this group, all three first ladies have been Democrats (Eleanor Roosevelt, Rosalynn Carter, Hillary Clinton) and two of the three second ladies have been Democrats (Joan Mondale, Tipper Gore). Marilyn Quayle, the wife of Republican vice president Dan Quayle, also testified before a congressional committee. (See Table 4.2 in Chapter 4 for a list of these testimonies.) According to these appearances before Congress, it would appear that Democratic first ladies are more politically active, but congressional appearances alone are not a comprehensive means of examining political and active approaches to the first ladyship.

First ladies of both political parties have functioned as full political partners in their husband's political careers. This includes Republicans such as Helen Taft, Florence Harding, and Lou Hoover. Thus political party affiliation may not play a major role in the first lady's approach to her office; her approach may be more a product of the state of the presidential marriage or particular inclinations of the president and first lady. There might be some evidence, however, that recent Democratic wives are somewhat more likely than Republican wives to approach the office in the capacity of a political partner.

There have been only a handful of polls ranking or rating the first ladies, because of the challenges of doing such and the lack of attention given to the first ladies. However, in the few rankings that do exist (Siena Research Institute polls; my own poll),[8] it appears that in general Democratic first ladies have been perceived as more effective and more popular than Republican first ladies. A total of seven Democratic first ladies from the twentieth century tend to appear in the top-ten lists. Four, in particular, appear in more than one ranking: Eleanor Roosevelt, Hillary Clinton, Jackie Kennedy, and Lady Bird Johnson. Only two Republican first ladies made at least one appearance in the top ten: Betty Ford and Barbara Bush. Of those first ladies listed in at least one of the polls of the ten worst first ladies, Republicans occupy five of the spots: Ida McKinley, Helen Taft, Florence Harding, Mamie Eisenhower, and Nancy Reagan. No Democrat from the twentieth century appears at the bottom of the lists. This might suggest that Democrats or some Democratic approach to the first ladyship has been more popular or successful, at least with those scholars who rank first ladies.

There is also evidence that both Democratic and Republican first ladies have been popular or successful. For instance, first ladies of both parties have made the Gallup organization's annual list of "most admired women."[9] Several first ladies have even earned the top spot in the Gallup poll, which has been conducted almost every year since 1948. Those appearing at the top of the poll include Democrats Eleanor Roosevelt (13 times), Jackie Kennedy (5 times), Rosalynn Carter (3 times), and Hillary Clinton (4 times) and Republicans Mamie Eisenhower (2 times), Pat Nixon (1 time), Betty Ford (1 time), Nancy Reagan (3 times), and Barbara Bush (2 times). Thus a Democratic first lady has led the Gallup poll a total of 25 times and a Republican has headed the list a total of 9 times. However, from 1948 to 1998, Democratic first ladies have appeared within the top ten spots on the list a total of 67 times, and Republican first ladies have made the top ten list a total of 77 times. Of course, such a listing is not the only way to measure a first lady's popularity, and there are a variety of limitations in such a measure, including the field of competition from year to year and the number of presidential terms served by either party since the poll's commencement. In the latter case, there is an even split: There have been five Republican first ladies since 1948 (Eisenhower, Nixon, Ford, Reagan, Bush) and five Democratic first ladies since 1948 (Truman, Kennedy, Johnson, Carter, Clinton).

Some of the measures presented indicate that Democratic first ladies tend to be slightly more popular, successful, active, political, and influential than Republican first ladies. This might indicate the existence of a different and possibly more successful approach to the first ladyship by Democrats. However, it is difficult to determine whether the first lady's approach, popularity, or activism is a matter entirely up to the particular first lady. Moreover, both Democratic and Republican first ladies have been, on the whole, popular and admired.

The First Lady Character Approach

One of the most popular ways of assessing the various presidential approaches to the office is the "presidential character" model forwarded by James David Barber.[10] Barber reasons that when the public votes for a president there is a degree of uncertainty about the voting decision and in many ways the voting decision is a prediction that one candidate will perform better than another candidate. The president's personality and character are believed to influence presidential performance and thus become part of the voter's decision process. Barber believes that presidential character allows one to predict, or at least explain, presidential performance.[11] His model has also been used to assess various approaches to the presidency.

Using criteria such as a president's personality, worldview, style, and power situation, Barber identifies four fundamental types of presidential character. He places presidents into one of these four character types using two baselines for assessment: active-passive and positive-negative orientation. Using the first baseline measure of active-passive, Barber determines the president's activism or passivism by considering whether the president worked all day, was eager to make a change, or approached the office and challenges with energy. In this analysis, presidents such as Lyndon Johnson and Jimmy Carter would be considered active because they put in very long hours at the White House and devoted great amounts of energy to their work. Presidents Calvin Coolidge and Ronald Reagan would be considered passive because they were not actively involved in many of the decisions and facets of the office, had short workdays at the White House, enjoyed napping, and generally did not work hard while in office. For the second baseline measurement of positive-negative, Barber considers the president's feelings about his activities, people, and the office and his experience of political and public life—whether he genuinely enjoyed, just tolerated, or was burdened by the office. In this analysis, President Franklin Roosevelt appeared to enjoy making decisions and having power, whereas President Dwight Eisenhower tried to avoid making decisions and did not enjoy many aspects of the presidency.

Barber combines these two baseline measures to form the four fundamental types of presidential character: active-positive, active-negative, passive-positive, and passive-negative. Type 1, the active-positive personality, is active and tends to enjoy politics, the presidency, and the challenges that accompany the office, such as working with the public. Barber has found that active-positives have high self-esteem, value productiveness, establish high goals, and want to achieve results. This type of personality uses many styles to govern or accomplish goals and is flexible and adaptable. Type 2, the active-negative personality, shows intense effort but experiences a low level of emotional rewards for such activism. Type 2 presidents tend to display anxiety about their work and struggle with the office, power, and problems. Barber has found that these presidents desire power and are ambitious. They work hard to obtain and then keep power, but they are also aggressive and are often perfectionists. The third type of personality, the passive-positive character, is often receptive to others and to new ideas and is overly compliant, often to the point of becoming a liability. In fact, this type of president is rarely personally assertive and sometimes suffers from low self-esteem. According to Barber, these presidents seek affection and support and like rewards. They are agreeable, motivated by cooperation, and are optimistic but do not always have a burning desire to work or to accomplish specific goals. The passive-negative personality, Barber's final character type, neither attempts much nor enjoys what he does attempt. These presidents do not enjoy politics and usually serve out of a sense of dutiful service. Passive-negative presidents don't like the uncertainty of politics and constant demands of the office. They withdraw from conflict and, when they do act, tend to act procedurally.

Box 5.1 provides an example of Barber's character types for selected twentieth-century presidents. In his categorization Barber examines each president serving since Teddy Roosevelt (1901–1909) and also the first four presidents. Barber feels that the first four presidents portray each of the four character types or approaches to the office: Jefferson as the active-positive, Adams as the active-negative, Madison as the passive-positive, and Washington as the passive-negative.

Barber's presidential character model can be adopted and used to assess various approaches to the office by first ladies. The same four approaches or personalities of presidents serve as the basis for identifying the "First Lady Character." It is more difficult to assess the first lady's character and approach to her office than it is to determine presidential

---

Box 5.1   Presidential Character Model

Active-positive
    F. D. Roosevelt, Truman, Kennedy
    (Jefferson)
Active-negative
    Wilson, Hoover, L. B. Johnson
    (J. Adams)
Passive-positive
    Reagan, Harding, Taft
    (Madison)
Passive-negative
    Coolidge, Eisenhower
    (Washington)

Source: J. D. Barber, *The Presidential Character,* 1985.

character because first ladies do not govern. However, they do make important decisions, assist the president as his political partner, and function as a public figure.

Just as the first four presidents provided useful examples of Barber's four presidential character types, the wives of those first presidents illustrate the range of character types of first ladies. First Lady Dolley Madison was active and enthusiastic about serving, wholeheartedly enjoyed the social affairs of the White House, and became the center of Washington social life and the Madison White House. Her style was outgoing, pleasant, and engaging. Dolley Madison is a good example of Barber's first character type: the active-positive personality. Martha Washington, although serving ably and competently, did so only out of a sense of dutiful service to her husband and the country, characteristics that resemble Barber's passive-negative character type. Lady Washington's husband, George, also exhibited this character type. Abigail Adams, the second presidential spouse, also exhibited some of the same characteristics as her husband. Both Mr. and Mrs. Adams were hardworking but demonstrated some anxiety about the office and struggled with power and public life. Abigail was very active and influential in her husband's public life and during her first ladyship. Both Abigail and John Adams are examples of Barber's active-negative type. The spouse of Thomas Jefferson, the third president, died many years prior to his presidency and thus is not categorized. However, from the little that is known about her, she appears to have conformed to the passive-positive personality type.

First ladies serving since Teddy and Edith Roosevelt (1901–1909) are categorized in Box 5.2 according to their character type and approach, as are the spouses of the first four presidents.

One of the potential problems in determining the first lady's character is that her actions in the White House are, to a degree, influenced by the president. An example of this is First Lady Pat Nixon. Although Mrs. Nixon was a talented, hardworking person, she was deterred from activism in the White House by her husband. Consequently, she was at times uninspiring when discussing her personal cause of volunteerism.

Another difficulty in categorizing the first ladies is that some personalities do not fit neatly into one of the four character types. For instance, Barbara Bush resembles both the passive-negative and passive-positive character types. Compared with other recent occupants of the office, Mrs. Bush was not an active first lady and she did not appear to have a desire to advance an agenda in office. She wanted only to support her husband and avoid becoming a liability for his presidency. In the process of doing this, she showed both positive and negative traits. On the one hand, the first lady had a playful sense of humor and could be quite charming. She was widely admired and viewed as a warm, caring person. On the other hand, Mrs.

Box 5.2   First Lady Character Model

Active-positive
  Ellen Wilson, Lou Hoover, Eleanor Roosevelt, Lady Bird Johnson,
  Betty Ford
  (Dolley Madison)
Active-negative
  Helen Taft, Edith Wilson, Florence Harding, Rosalynn Carter,
  Nancy Reagan, Hillary Clinton
  (Abigail Adams)
Passive-positive
  Grace Coolidge, Mamie Eisenhower
  (Martha Jefferson)[a]
Passive-negative
  Bess Truman, Jackie Kennedy, Pat Nixon[b]
  (Martha Washington)

  a. Martha Jefferson died prior to her husband's presidency.
  b. Part of Pat Nixon's passive-negative character and approach to the first
ladyship appears to be a result of her husband limiting her roles and influence.
  Note: Barbara Bush displays a mixture of passive-positive and passive-
negative.

Bush could be vindictive toward those people she considered political enemies of her husband. She also suffered from a lack of self-confidence
throughout her life and was prone to depression, self-pity, and feelings of
inadequacy.

Most first ladies, however, can be firmly identified with one of the four
character types identified. One such first lady is the active-positive Lou
Hoover. Mrs. Hoover's life and first ladyship were marked by decisiveness
and strength. She was a full partner with her husband, traveling with him
during his many international ventures. She held up well during the Boxer
Rebellion while they were living in China, and she endured the challenges
of the Great Depression in the White House. Lou Hoover willingly accepted many roles and new projects. She enjoyed working with others, which is
evident in the many charitable and volunteer endeavors she undertook. She
was confident and flexible and took a personal interest in a wide array of
issues. Ellen Wilson is also identified as having an active-positive character. Woodrow Wilson's first wife was actively engaged in his career and
presidency. She advised him with his speeches and cabinet appointments.
Ellen enjoyed political life and her time spent in the White House. In her

personal life, Ellen promoted a variety of causes, appears to have liked working with people, and was a happy person with many hobbies, including painting.

Among the active-negative first ladies is Helen Taft. Mrs. Taft was always an active, ambitious individual. In fact, as a young woman she dreamt of becoming a lawyer or even the president. She was a hard worker but at times was overly sensitive to criticism, could be critical of herself, tended to focus on the minuscule, and micromanaged details of her husband's political career. Helen Taft attempted to control everything she encountered and was a demanding first lady who expected too much of the White House staff and was quick to fire those who disappointed her. In fact, the first lady worked to the point of collapsing. At times Mrs. Taft could be petty and cold to those she perceived as enemies. Florence Harding also fits this personality type. First Lady Harding was decisive and actively engaged in her husband's political career. But she became overwhelmed with the challenges of the White House, in part from her own doing. Florence had a tendency to be rude and demanding and acted in a petty and revengeful manner toward those she perceived as her enemies. Edith Wilson is also another example of the active-negative typology. She was successful in business prior to her White House years and fulfilled many of the functions of the president while her husband was incapacitated by a stroke. She offered the president advice, took an interest in political and policy issues, and participated in many social causes. However, she regularly let her personal bias cloud her political decisions. For instance, she would not let Senator Henry Cabot Lodge attend Woodrow Wilson's funeral because Lodge had differed with Wilson on political issues. She was notoriously critical of the president's aides, often bad-mouthed public figures, and was vindictive to a fault. Edith was also controlling and had an unforgiving demeanor.

The Presidential Partnership Approach

The central argument in this book is that the first ladies function as political and presidential partners. This partnership is a dominant approach to the office, and other scholars such as Caroli, Gutin, and Troy classify many twentieth-century first ladies as partners.[12] Likewise, in their study of the first ladies O'Connor, Nye, and Van Assendelft attempt to measure the influence of first ladies by tallying types of viable political activities in which the first ladies participated.[13] They find that the great majority of first ladies have functioned as the president's confidante or adviser. However, there are differing degrees of a partnership and variations of the partnership relationship. Some first ladies could be considered full political partners because they publicly and fully shared in all political facets of the presidency and their husbands' political careers. Other first ladies exhibited characteristics of this partnership but could not be classified as full partners. They only participated in some political matters and may not have been the president's top adviser. Other first ladies were not interested in being partners or in participating in the presidency, and still others were presidential partners, but in a more domestic, private, or social capacity.

Several first ladies approached their White House years as full presidential partners. Whether or not this was primarily due to the first lady's particular talents or disposition or the president's view of his spouse's role remains unclear. However, the answer is probably a combination of explanations. As a partner, first ladies have served as presidential adviser and confidante. The partnership often predates the first couple's White House years, existing throughout their marriage and the president's career. Many first ladies—most notably Helen Taft—persuaded their husbands to run for the presidency. The partnership also has varying political, social, and personal manifestations. First ladies have fulfilled elements of both the traditional and modern notions of the first ladyship, serving as influential advisers in both the social and professional affairs of the presidency.

First Lady Julia Grant was a partner in her husband's career, actively supporting him through the Civil War, his business failures, and his presidency. She visited him and his troops during the war, discussed battlefield tactics with him, and served as an important sounding board for decisions regarding Confederate prisoners, the key battle of Vicksburg, and problems the general encountered with his officers.[14] Although Mrs. Grant would not be considered a full political partner, she did occupy an important role in her husband's presidency through her highly successful social affairs. She was also a constant source of support for him throughout their married life. Sarah Polk was a full political and presidential partner in every sense of the term. She encouraged her husband to pursue higher elected offices throughout his long political career. She was his political partner and leading political adviser. Mrs. Polk edited her husband's speeches, discussed politics with him, campaigned with him, was his constant traveling partner, and, as an avid reader of newspapers, even briefed him on current events. The Polk partnership was well known. Samuel H. Laughlin, a newspaper editor from Nashville, even referred to Sarah as "Membress of Congress," and President Andrew Jackson so liked Sarah that he encouraged his young political protégé James Polk to marry her.[15]

In my study of presidential scholars conducted in 1996, the different approaches to the first ladyship were conceptualized according to the degree of partnership existing in the presidential marriage. In a questionnaire, five basic types of partners or partnership approaches were listed, and presidential scholars were instructed to identify each first lady with one of the five partnership approaches.[16]

Box 5.3 lists the five different partnership approaches to the first lady-ship. Though they are not mutually exclusive or exhaustive, these approaches do provide a starting point for developing theory and building an understanding of the approaches to the office of first lady and the existence of a presidential partnership. The classifications range from 1 to 5; a Type 1 partner is a full partner and a Type 5 is not a partner in any aspect of the presidency.

First ladies were classified as one of the five types of partners by the respondents of the poll of presidential scholars. Scholars were asked to consider the relevance of the day and age within which first ladies served. (For example, nineteenth-century first ladies were obviously much more constrained in terms of public activism and influence than contemporary first ladies.) The method used to classify the first ladies into one of the five categories involved simply selecting the particular partnership approach or category receiving the most responses from the survey respondents. That is, if 50 percent or more of the survey respondents listed a particular first lady as a Type 4 partner, then she was classified as this type. If no single type or partnership approach received over 50 percent of the votes, the first lady was assigned to the type for which she received the most votes, provided she received at least one-third of the total votes for a particular type or approach. In the case of a tie between types, whereby a particular first lady received an equal amount of responses for two or more of the types, or if no single type was selected by at least one-third of the respondents, the average (mean) overall score was computed (the responses were totaled and divided by the total number of responses). Scores in the 1.0 to 1.5 range correspond to Type 1, scores in the 1.51 to 2.5 range correspond to Type 2, scores in the 2.51 to 3.5 range correspond to Type 3, scores in the 3.51 to 4.5 range correspond to Type 4, and scores above 4.51 correspond to Type 5. (This approach to classification was used only when a single type did not receive a significant number of the respondent's votes.) The first ladies are classified in Table 5.1 according to their partnership approach to the office.

It is possible that presidential scholars know little about the first ladies. For example, numerous respondents failed to fill in a partnership type for some of the first ladies. Moreover, there was much disagreement by the scholars as to the particular classification to which each first lady belonged. This is evident in the percentages listed for a few of the first ladies. Also, many of the first ladies received at least one vote for each of the five available types. But there was also a fair amount of consensus among respondents. In the case of some first ladies such as Julia Grant, all but one schol-

Box 5.3   Partnership Types

Type 1: The Full Partner
- Very active in politics
- Top presidential adviser
- Active and influential both publicly and privately
- Active in social issues and White House social affairs

This type of first lady is very active in politics and takes an interest in her spouse's speeches, appointments, and policies not only by supporting him in these areas but through assisting and advising the president on political and administrative matters. She is the president's top adviser and confidante. This first lady is knowledgeable of the issues and enjoys politics. Full political partners were also active in their spouses' careers and campaigns prior to the presidency. This type of first lady is active behind the scenes, but her activism often carries over into the public realm of the presidency. Full partners also participate in social issues and the hosting duties of the office.

Type 2: The Partial Partner
- Somewhat active in politics
- Serves as a presidential adviser
- Somewhat active/influential publicly
- Participates in social issues and White House social affairs

This type of first lady is somewhat active in politics and shows some interest in and support of her spouse's political activities. She may even assist the president with his speeches, appointments, and so forth, although she is not the major adviser in such affairs. This first lady displays some interest in the issues and has been supportive of her spouse's career and campaigns prior to the presidency but has not been the major force in such matters. The partial partner plays a role away from the public eye and at times is even a visible force in public. She also participates in the social duties of the office.

Type 3: The Behind-the-Scenes Partner
- Active in politics, but behind the scenes
- Advises the president in private
- Activism and influence not conducted in public
- Participates in social issues and White House social affairs

(Box 5.3 continues)

Box 5.3 Continued

This type of first lady is active and supportive of her spouse's political activities, but she is not a public participant in political or presidential affairs. Rather, this first lady's partnership is private and personal in nature. By definition, she is not as visible, active, and political as the first type of partner and is therefore not a full partner. But away from the public, she is a powerful, influential force in the White House. She also participates in White House social affairs.

Type 4: The Partner in Marriage
- Not active in politics
- A personal adviser, not a political adviser
- Activism and influence limited to social and personal affairs
- Participates in social issues and White House social affairs

This type of first lady is not identified as a political partner. The first lady's more traditional duties of being a supportive wife and social hostess define her approach to the first ladyship because she does not participate in politics or take an active role in the political elements of the office. The partner-in-marriage first lady might also be known as "White House wife and hostess." These first ladies dedicate themselves to their role as wives and to hostessing. Often, these first ladies do not enjoy politics.

Type 5: The Nonpartner
- Not active in politics
- Not a political adviser; might advise in private and personal matters
- Not interested in political activities or influence
- Not interested in White House social affairs

Not only is this type of first lady not active, supportive, or influential in the political and policy affairs of the presidency, but she is also not an active participant in the more traditional social and hostessing roles of the first lady. She might be seen as "the inactive first lady." This type of first lady shows little interest in being a first lady, no interest in being a partner in the presidency, and no interest in politics or policy. She is not active in any of the public dimensions of the office.

Table 5.1   Types of First Ladies

First Lady	Percentage of Votes	Average Score
Type 1: The Full Partner		
Hillary Clinton	97.2	1.1
Eleanor Roosevelt	91.4	1.1
Rosalynn Carter	52.1	1.5
Edith Wilson	61.4	1.6
Type 2: The Partial Partner		
Abigail Adams	45.9	2.1
Nancy Reagan	33.3	2.1
Lady Bird Johnson	46.6	2.4
Dolley Madison	37.9	2.4
Helen Taft	33.4	2.6
Betty Ford	44.9	2.7
Type 3: The Behind-the-Scenes Partner		
Elizabeth Monroe	60.0	2.8
Barbara Bush	40.0	3.0
Edith Roosevelt	50.0	3.1
Jackie Kennedy	33.3	3.1
Florence Harding	33.3	3.2
Mary Lincoln	43.6	3.3
Lou Hoover	33.3	3.3
Sarah Polk	57.1	3.6
Type 4: The Partner in Marriage		
Francis Cleveland	57.1	3.3
Julia Tyler	50.0	3.3
Harriet Lane	75.0	3.5[a]
Louisa Adams	66.7	3.5
Pat Nixon	43.7	3.6
Grace Coolidge	61.1	3.7
Ellen Wilson	58.3	3.7
Martha Washington	51.7	3.7
Lucy Hayes	50.0	3.7
Caroline Harrison	83.3	3.8
Lucretia Garfield	75.0	3.8
Bess Truman	50.0	3.8
Julia Grant	85.7	3.9
Mamie Eisenhower	71.2	3.9
Ida McKinley	42.9	3.9
Type 5: The Nonpartner		
Eliza Johnson	28.6	3.7
Abigail Fillmore	50.0	4.3
Jane Pierce	75.0	4.5
Margaret Taylor	75.0	4.5
Anna Harrison	66.7	4.7

a. Harriet Lane was not married to the president.

Notes: First ladies dying prior to White House years were not rated. No single type emerged for Letitia Tyler. Half the respondents selected Type 2 and half selected Type 4.

ar classified her as a Type 4 first lady, which she most definitely was. Moreover, the findings provide a starting point for further study attempting to assess the various conceptual approaches to the office

For Mary Todd Lincoln, only 43 percent of respondents listed her as a Type 2 with the remaining 57 percent split between all other remaining clarifications. Bess Truman was listed as a Type 4, which she was in many ways, as she demonstrated little interest in the presidency, the first ladyship, or politics. However, Bess was also very influential behind the scenes in all of her husband's decisions. She would better match a Type 3 first lady.

Taking into account the possibility that presidential scholars responding to the survey might not know a lot about the first ladies, another classification is offered. Box 5.4 lists my categorization of the first ladies according to their type of partnership.

Box 5.4   Watson's Types of First Ladies

Type 1: Full Partner
Abigail Adams, Sarah Polk, Helen Taft, Florence Harding,
Eleanor Roosevelt, Rosalynn Carter, Hillary Clinton

Type 2: Partial Partner
Dolley Madison, Julia Tyler, Mary Lincoln, Frances
Cleveland, Caroline Harrison, Ellen Wilson, Edith Wilson,
Lou Hoover, Lady Bird Johnson, Betty Ford

Type 3: Behind-the-Scenes Partner
Martha Washington, Louisa Adams, Abigail Fillmore, Eliza Johnson,
Lucy Hayes, Lucretia Garfield, Ida McKinley, Edith Roosevelt,
Bess Truman, Jackie Kennedy, Nancy Reagan, Barbara Bush

Type 4: Partner in Marriage
Elizabeth Monroe, Anna Harrison, Margaret Taylor,
Julia Grant, Grace Coolidge, Mamie Eisenhower, Pat Nixon

Type 5: Nonpartner
Letitia Tyler, Jane Pierce

Note: Martha Jefferson, Rachel Jackson, Hannah Van Buren, and Ellen Arthur died prior to their husband's presidency. Harriet Lane was not a first lady.

Presidential Liabilities

In the 1990s Greek premier Andreas Papandreou's wife proved to be less than an asset to his presidency. There had been charges by Papandreou's opponents that the seventy-six-year-old head of the Socialist Party was being manipulated by his politically ambitious forty-year-old wife, who had presided over cabinet meetings. In 1995 the Greek newspaper *Avriani* began a crusade to ask Dimitra Papandreou to discontinue her involvement in politics. *Avriani* ran a series of nude photographs of the first lady of Greece that appeared in color on the front page of the newspaper.[17] As if that were not damaging enough, one of the photographs depicted Mrs. Papandreou sitting naked on the beach in a sexual act with another woman. Although there have been scandalous and sensationalized stories involving U.S. first ladies, none have been as unsavory as the Papandreou scandal. However, at times the first ladies have become political liabilities for their husbands.

One example is Nancy Reagan, with her poor sense of timing and excessive tastes in clothing and socializing. At the same time President Reagan was pushing cuts in the school lunch program, and asking the Department of Agriculture to reclassify ketchup as a vegetable in order to justify his cuts in nutrition and food supports, his wife announced the acquisition of a new White House china collection costing $200,000. After the president's inaugural address challenging the country to rid itself of excessive governmental spending, the first lady appeared at the inaugural balls wearing a gown and accessories worth $25,000.

Margaret Taylor opposed her husband's election to the presidency and, for a variety of reasons, one of which was her poor health, did not even attend his inauguration. Moreover, she ignored presidential custom by snubbing an invitation from the outgoing first family—the Polks—to meet with them before the inauguration.[18] First Lady Eliza Johnson, who suffered from poor health, turned down numerous requests and invitations and consequently earned the wrath of the Washington social crowd.[19] She appeared in public only twice, at a children's ball in December 1868 and during an August 1866 White House visit by Hawaii's Queen Emma.

Jane Pierce rarely functioned in the capacity of first lady, and the Pierce administration was criticized for its depressing mood and lack of social events. The first lady, even as a young woman, never enjoyed politics. She came from a serious, subdued New England family. Her father was a strict, pious Congregationalist minister, and her mother never approved of politics or of her husband, Franklin. Jane disliked politics, her husband's career, and Washington, D.C. She not only failed to support any of her husband's efforts but even attempted to get Franklin to abandon his successful career in politics. To that end, she was somewhat successful, talking Franklin into giving up his U.S. Senate seat in 1842 after his first term ended. Later, back in retirement in Concord, New Hampshire, she forced him to decline lucrative offers to run for governor of New Hampshire, to reclaim his old senate seat, and to become President James K. Polk's attorney general.

Throughout her life Jane was also ill and depressed and was described as "frail, nervous, and sensitive."[20] Her somber, reclusive mood was in part the result of suffering from tragedies, including the death of her father when she was only thirteen years old and the death of two of her three sons, one in infancy and the other at the age of four. After a brief retirement and over her protests, Franklin Pierce again became active in politics and was elected president. However, Jane refused to appear during the campaign and even prayed that he would lose the election. Shortly after his election, the Pierces' only remaining son was tragically killed in a train wreck. The wreck occurred on January 6, 1853, only two months prior to Franklin Pierce's presidential inauguration. Jane went into deep mourning and blamed her husband, convincing him that the wreck was God's revenge on him for his political career. Needless to say, the mood of the Pierce White House was heavy. Jane failed to attend her husband's inauguration on March 4, 1853. As first lady, she held a minimal, spartan social calendar, declined public appearances and invitations to meet guests, remained confined to the second floor of the White House, and held no receptions. About the only thing Jane Pierce did as first lady was attend church services and read her son's Bible.

Mary Todd Lincoln also became a liability for her husband. Her vanity, insecurity, and impulsiveness, including public outbursts of jealousy, continually proved problematic for the president.[21] One such embarrassment occurred in March 1865 while the president was reviewing the Union troops. When the first lady found out that the wife of one of the officers was invited to join Lincoln and his officers during the review but that she herself had not been invited, she became frantic and loud. Mary also became enraged when she saw Abe speaking to General Edward Ord's attractive wife. There were many other occasions when Mrs. Lincoln embarrassed the president in public with her fits of jealousy. Abe Lincoln also had to contend with Mary's migraine headaches. During these regular attacks, Mary demanded her husband's full attention and became uncontrollable, even if the attack occurred in public. The first lady came from a prominent Kentucky family, many of whom supported and even fought for the Confederacy during the Civil War. As if this were not enough of an embarrassment for the author of the Emancipation Proclamation, Mary invited some of her pro-slavery relatives to visit her in the White House. Charges of espionage were fueled when Mary's relatives actually moved into the White House.

Perhaps the biggest problem caused by the first lady, however, was her penchant for spending money the Lincolns did not have. Mary's tastes were excessive and she routinely went on lavish shopping trips to buy dresses and redecorate the White House. These "flub-a-dub" bills, as Abe called them, caused controversy because of the public austerity necessitated by the Civil War. One of Mary's shopping sprees resulted in a new 190-piece French china set for the White House and a matching set for her private use. An added problem arose when Mary borrowed money from questionable sources or manipulated the White House budget to cover the bills she attempted to hide from the president.[22] She later fired the commissioner who oversaw White House expenditures and enlisted the help of John Watt, the White House gardener, and Benjamin French, the new commissioner for capitol buildings, to help her with the many creditors demanding payment. She opened herself and the president up to charges of corruption and financial illegalities.

In all fairness to Mrs. Lincoln, she had suffered setbacks: She had lost her eleven-year-old son, Willie, in 1862, she had endured criticism from both the North and the South throughout the war, and several relatives of hers died during the war. To console herself, Mary sought out the help of spiritualists and took to conducting seances in the White House, behaviors that were judged as inappropriate for a first lady. Her problems continued after her White House years. Mary continued to spend too much money, had delusions of plots to assassinate her, and lost two more children. In 1875 she was ultimately placed in a home for the insane in Illinois by her sole remaining child, Robert. The former first lady appears to have been wrongly accused by her son and the judge sentencing her. She was released one year later. However, Mary is remembered largely for the embarrassments she caused her husband.

Perhaps the spouse who proved to be the biggest liability to her husband was Rachel Donelson Jackson. As a young girl Rachel Donelson was outgoing and well liked. At the age of seventeen she married Lewis Robards of Virginia. Her husband, however, turned out to be extremely jealous and violent and their marriage soon deteriorated into quarrels and unhappiness. Rachel initiated a separation, moved back home with her mother, and asked Robards for a divorce. Soon afterward, she met Andrew Jackson and the two became romantically involved. Both Rachel and Andrew Jackson demanded that Robards grant Rachel a divorce because women could not legally divorce at the time. Robards failed to act on the request and, in turn, threatened to take Rachel away, to sue her, and to not grant her the divorce. Eventually Andrew Jackson's powers of persuasion and threats of physical violence led Robards to grant Rachel the divorce. Rachel and Andrew Jackson were thus married in October 1791 but soon learned that the bride's first husband had never completed the formalities for the divorce. Although Robards eventually did initiate the divorce on September 27, 1793, and Rachel and Andrew were remarried during a second ceremony in January 1794, rumors of adultery plagued the couple.[23] Newspapers and the courts demanded answers to the allegations and the story became ammunition for Jackson's political enemies. Although Rachel and Andrew appeared to have been happy together, as Jackson's political career advanced, stories of adultery advanced along with it. Rachel became depressed, gained an unhealthy amount of weight, and lost much of her will to live.

The constant attacks from the press, his political enemies, and Washington society along with rumors that Rachel was an adulterer made her a liability to Jackson's political career. Rachel was not well read, was not particularly fashionable, had little interest in politics, and had had a rural, frontier upbringing. These qualities produced another line of scandal, and Rachel was attacked in the press and in social circles as a potential embarrassment to the White House because she was "ignorant" and "unsophisticated." For her part, Rachel appears to have been judgmental. Highly religious, she was often critical of the communities that she and her husband visited as part of his political and military duties. While Andrew Jackson was being celebrated as a hero in New Orleans, Rachel condemned the city. She also spoke disparagingly of other places where his career took them, such as Alabama and the town of Pensacola, Florida. She was appalled by the mix of races she encountered and the lack of whites and Protestant clergy living in the communities.

As her husband's political star rose, Rachel grew to dread the first ladyship and the scandalous attacks awaiting her. This was never to be. Shortly after Jackson's election, Rachel died.

Notes

1. E. S. Arnett, *Mrs. James Madison,* 1972.
2. M. G. Gutin, *The President's Partner,* 1989.
3. B. B. Caroli, *First Ladies,* 1987.
4. Many texts on the presidency discuss the bully pulpit and its centrality to the modern presidency. See, for instance, T. E. Cronin and M. A. Genovese, *The Paradoxes,* 1997. See also the section on Teddy Roosevelt in M. Nelson, *The Presidency,* 1996.
5. Nelson, 1996.
6. See essay by M. Rozell in J. P. Pfiffner and R. H. Davidson, *Understanding the Presidency,* 1997. This essay, the statements of which echo many other presidential scholars' words, recognizes the importance of mastering television and being an effective communicator in the modern presidency. Presidents who used the media well and who were effective communicators include Teddy Roosevelt, Franklin Roosevelt, John Kennedy, Ronald Reagan, and Bill Clinton.

7. In 1995 and 1996 I surveyed 200 women who were recognized as influential women in public service. The questions in the survey instrument focused on perceptions of first ladies and identifying those first ladies the respondents perceived as failures and successes.

8. The Siena Research Institute at Siena College polls presidential scholars in an attempt to rank or rate first ladies.

9. The Gallup organization also conducts polls on the first ladies' popularity and annual polls to determine the most admired women, the latter of which the first ladies usually dominate. A number of other organizations, including most of the major media polling organizations, now conduct a variety of polls on the first lady. See, for instance, B. Burrell, *Public Opinion,* 1997; D. W. Moore, "Public Uncertain over First Lady's Role," 1994); "Public Portraits," 1989; "The Women We Admire," 1989.

10. J. D. Barber, *The Presidential Character,* 1985. A number of scholars use Barber's model in their studies of the presidency and it is often discussed in leading textbooks on the presidency. See, for instance, G. C. Edwards and S. J. Wayne, *Presidential Leadership,* 1994. Barber's approach using presidential character and personality has influenced other related models for studying the presidency. See, for instance, A. L. George and J. L. George, *Presidential Personality and Performance,* 1998.

11. Barber, 1985.

12. Many scholars of the first lady appear to have recognized the existence of a political partnership between the president and first lady, including Caroli, 1987; Gutin, 1989; and G. Troy, *Affairs of State,* 1997.

13. See K. O'Connor, B. Nye, and L. Van Assendelf, "Wives in the White House," 1997.

14. See Gutin, 1989.

15. See the chapter on Sarah Polk in L. L. Gould, *First Ladies,* 1996. This is also discussed in C. G. Sellars, *James K. Polk,* 1957.

16. In 1996 I polled presidential scholars in an effort to rank the first ladies. Two hundred surveys were mailed out; the response rate was 87. The survey asked scholars to rate first ladies and identify each first lady as belonging to one of five basic types or approaches to the office. The survey furnished scholars with a list of the first ladies and encouraged them to forgo rating those first ladies with whom they were unfamiliar.

17. An AP wire report by Nikos Konstandaras appeared on the Internet/World Wide Web on October 20, 1995, discussing the scandal.

18. See the chapters devoted to Margaret Taylor in C. S. Anthony, *Saga,* 1990; Gould, 1996.

19. See the chapter in Gould, 1996, on Eliza Johnson.

20. Gould, 1996, p. 66.

21. Examples of Mary Todd Lincoln's jealousy and public outbursts can be found in Anthony, 1990; Caroli, 1987; Gould, 1996; and M. Truman, *First Ladies,* 1996. For interesting insights into the private life of Mary and her personality, see W. H. Crook, *Memories of the White House,* 1911 (Crook worked in the White House); E. Keckley, *Behind the Scenes,* 1868 (Keckley was Mary's friend and seamstress).

22. Ibid.

23. Gould, 1996; M. Truman, 1996.

6

Public Opinion and the First Lady

Being first lady requires a woman to act . . . as a mixture of queen, club woman, and starlet.

—Lewis L. Gould

New scholarship on the first lady is slowly changing the way we view what is arguably one of the most difficult and demanding jobs in the country. Considering that the job of first lady is technically unofficial and it is neither elected, appointed, nor paid, and considering the historic and social forces that have limited a woman's involvement in politics and public life, it is remarkable that the first ladies have been the subject of intense curiosity and interest by the public and the press. But the public image and visibility of the first lady are only beginning to be studied. One of the reasons for the lack of scholarly interest in the first lady's high public profile is that, in many ways, the institution evolved in a behind-the-scenes manner and thus many of the accomplishments of early first ladies were realized outside the purview of public inspection. With a few exceptions, the majority of the duties and responsibilities associated with the modern office have not always been performed in public. Therefore the public has been aware of the first ladies but largely unaware of the power and influence inherent in the office. The first ladies and presidents themselves downplayed the first lady's influence and power. Indeed, the prevailing social etiquette prior to the twentieth century dictated that women should neither appear in newspapers nor be discussed in public. Although this has not been the case in the twentieth century, the previous social taboos were replaced by the belief that first ladies should not wield serious power or be too active in political affairs.

Be that as it may, even early first ladies were in fact public figures. The first lady has always been one of the most well known women in the country, all first ladies have appeared in public, and all of them have faced public criticism. There has always been a public element to the office, and first ladies have always been responsible for the social affairs of the White House. But it has only been in the twentieth century that the office has become a highly visible and overtly public institution. In recent times, the public nature of the office has grown. For example, the first family now monopolizes national and local news coverage around the time of presidential elections and inaugurations, and the first lady is better known than members of the president's cabinet, members of Congress, and the vice president. The first lady has found herself in the public limelight for most of the nation's history.

First Ladies in the Spotlight

Even in the early days of the country, newspapers covered the social functions of such first ladies as Martha Washington, Dolley Madison, and Julia Tyler. However, the scope and nature of the coverage devoted to today's first ladies is unlike anything early first ladies could have ever imagined. The contemporary modern media fixation on the first lady is the natural progression of mass media reporting that has become increasingly personalized, sensationalized, probing, intrusive, and saturated. First ladies must now be proficient public speakers, are expected to make numerous public appearances, and must be prepared to forfeit their privacy. The roots of the media coverage of the first family date to developments in the later part of the nineteenth century that made possible a mass media society, including the advent and improvement of the telegraph, the electronic printing press, the quality of wood pulp paper, and growing literacy rates nationwide. By the end of the nineteenth century, the small, local newspapers with partisan journalism were being brushed aside by huge profit-driven newspapers with a vast circulation and national political coverage often involving personal, sensationalized reporting known as yellow journalism. In the pursuit of profits through higher circulation, papers reduced their cost, enticing a new cross-section of the country to begin reading the papers. This was known as the penny press. The president and the presidential family were newsworthy and boosted readership.

Key events like the Spanish-American War and World War I also expanded circulation, the scope of coverage, and a growing interest in national politics. From 1901 to 1909 President Teddy Roosevelt forever changed the way the media and the nation viewed the first family. With his magnetic personality and attractive young family, Roosevelt proved to be refreshingly newsworthy and coverage of the first family sold newspapers. Unlike his predecessors, Roosevelt recognized the value of media coverage. Indeed, he invited the press's interest in him so as to promote himself and enhance his popularity with the U.S. people and, in so doing, advance his policy agenda as well.[1] The Roosevelts set a precedent for human interest reporting on the presidency (including the president's wife), and media coverage of the White House would never be the same again.

Today media coverage of the first lady is assisted by a White House that is concerned with public opinion ratings and values the boost in approval and visibility a popular first lady can bring to the presidency. Presidents and presidential advisers do not allow public opinion to proceed unchecked; rather, the White House actively attempts to guide or manipulate public opinion in a favorable manner. It does so by controlling media coverage, seeking favorable coverage, staging and timing public appearances, and the like. The modern White House contains an entire bureaucracy devoted to image and the media, including a press office, press secretary, pollsters, speechwriters, communications directors, and media advisers whose job is to ensure favorable coverage of the president (and first lady). Such advisers plan regular presidential press briefings and photo opportunities staged for the media along with an occasional strategic press leak. The press has responded with year-around, twenty-four-hour-a-day coverage of the institution. The public knows what the first family eats, where they vacation, how they spend their leisure time, and even the name of their pets. Even what presidents (and first ladies) do not do is now deemed newsworthy. The White House press corps is the name given to these elite reporters and multinational news outlets who are offered intimate access within the White House. All of the main media organizations have Washington correspondents and reporters covering the White House beat. Those invited to the restricted press conferences include newspaper giants like the *Washington Post* and *New York Times,* United Press International and the Associated Press, such leading weekly newsmagazines as *Time* and *Newsweek,* and the biggest newspaper chains, including Gannett, Knight-Ridder, and Scripps-Howard. It is inevitable that the first lady has become an internationally known public figure.

Still, little is known about the first lady's public opinion approval ratings, the first lady's image, and her relations with the media. Examining such issues will help us explore other important subjects, including how the White House manages the image of the first lady and the extent to which public perceptions guide the development of the first lady's roles and responsibilities. It benefits our understanding of this complex and evolving office to examine both mass and elite public opinion concerning the first lady's image and influence.

Public Opinion Polling and the First Lady

Historically, first ladies have been of only minor interest to pollsters. The rise of first lady polling mirrors the advent of scientific polling. Although a few unscientific attempts at polling predated the twentieth century, political polls are a product of the latter half of this century. The first national poll involving a first lady appears to have been performed by the Gallup organization in 1939, when it asked the public its opinion of Eleanor Roosevelt.[2] It was around this time that public opinion polling began to employ the scientific standards of the social sciences, such as sampling techniques, and accordingly, public opinion research became a more reliable and accurate endeavor.[3] As a media and political tool, it gained popularity in the ensuing years, but it appears that little polling was done on the first ladyships of Bess Truman and Mamie Eisenhower during the late 1940s and 1950s. However, when Jackie Kennedy took office in 1961, Gallup again polled the public about its view of the new first lady.

Paralleling the growth of political polling on the subject, public interest in the first lady grew in the 1970s with Pat Nixon and the controversy surrounding Betty Ford's outspokenness and open support of women's rights. But it was not until Nancy Reagan in the 1980s that regular, systematic use of questions on or about the first lady occurred. This may seem ironic in that Nancy was not a feminist and did not have a liberal or (overtly) active policy agenda. Yet it is clear that she wielded power, although often in private and from the perspective of a concerned spouse. By the 1980s polls on the first ladies began resembling those taken of the presidents. First lady polls took on another new dimension with the first ladyship of Hillary Clinton, who has become a regular subject for the pollsters.[4] The entire range of political polling was directed at Mrs. Clinton, from approval ratings to public perceptions of her duties and activities to her perceived influence on the president. All the major polling organizations conducted opinion research on Mrs. Clinton, and the results were carried by all the major television networks and leading print media. In this respect, Mrs. Clinton is without precedent. Only three first ladies prior to Hillary Clinton also caused pollsters to focus on the first lady's power or influence with the president: Rosalynn Carter, Nancy Reagan, and Eleanor Roosevelt. Mrs. Clinton is also unique in that she has become the focus of pollsters who examine her as an individual, independent of her husband or his presidency.

Barbara Burrell, in her comprehensive study of public opinion on Hillary Clinton, found that four of the main polling organizations (Yankelovich/Time/CNN; NBC/Wall Street Journal; Gallup/USA Today/CNN; CBS/New York Times) performed a total of 63 polls on Mrs. Clinton's approval rating during the first two years of her service, from 1993 to 1994.[5] Yankelovich/Time/CNN conducted 9 in 1993 alone and another 9 in 1994; NBC/Wall Street Journal conducted 8 polls in 1993 and another 8 in 1994; Gallup/USA Today/CNN performed 7 polls in both 1993 and 1994; and CBS/New York Times performed 8 polls in 1993 and 7 in 1994. Many other polls were conducted by a variety of less well known newspapers, TV stations, and magazines during the same period.

By the 1988 presidential race, polls were even being taken on the prospective first ladies. Just one month prior to the presidential elections in October, NBC polled the public concerning its views toward the candidates' wives, Barbara Bush and Kitty Dukakis. The poll demonstrated some support for the spouses, but much uncertainty and an apparent lack of information about them. For example, in the 1988 poll Mrs. Bush received a 48 percent favorable rating and Mrs. Dukakis a 42 percent favorable rating, but a sizeable 41 percent and 47 percent, respectively, indicated that they were uncertain about the spouses. Both prospective first ladies enjoyed remarkably low unfavorable ratings of 11 percent.[6] The public now knew the candidates' wives, but perhaps they did not know the particular beliefs or plans of first ladies. Until this time, the press had largely focused any campaign coverage devoted to the prospective first ladies on their roles as supportive wives. But this focus has changed. Increasingly, spouses not only accompany the presidential hopefuls everywhere but regularly speak out during campaigns, address the issues, and answer personal and policy questions. First lady forums and debates between the candidates' spouses have even been proposed during recent presidential campaigns. In 1992 the famous and widely followed American National Election Study conducted by the University of Michigan included for the first time questions about the first ladies alongside the usual questions on the candidates and political issues. The first ladyship has become institutionalized within the practice of political polling.

Polling has emerged as an everyday facet of White House political operations; the two major political party committees and the president employ professional pollsters, spend huge budgets on polls, and regularly conduct polls, some of which now include the first lady. Still, public opinion is not an exact science and what the public says in polls is not always consistent or coherent.[7] For instance, polls point out very clearly that the public wants the federal budget to be balanced, yet the same polls also clearly show that when asked about solutions for doing just that, such as increasing taxes or cutting domestic spending or programs, the public does not support such actions. Poll results can also be manipulated through the timing of the commissioning, or the release, of the polls and through the wording selected for questions. For instance, polls consistently reveal that a majority of the public favors "public support for the poor." Yet when the question is phrased differently, polls show the opposite result, with a majority opposing "welfare spending." Public opinion research has shown that the public may not always know the specifics of the issues and that such factors as the intensity and saliency of issues—the degree or level of importance and whether the issue holds in importance over time—are important to understanding public opinion.[8]

It can be assumed that such general shortcomings of public opinion polling also apply to polls on the first ladies. As with polls on presidential approval, questions remain as to whether such polls of the first lady report the public's approval of personality or policy, style or substance, or other factors. But because public opinion polling on the first lady is such a new practice, there may be additional problems inherent in the endeavor. An obvious concern is that there is no defined or written role for the first lady. The first ladyship is not a job and no agreed-upon criteria exist for how she should be assessed. Moreover, functioning in the capacity of a political partner, the first lady is responsible for seemingly contradictory duties. She must serve as both hostess and political confidante. She must appear in public and be active in causes; but she cannot be perceived as being too powerful or too active and such activism must remain confined to vague and shifting parameters. She must appear to be traditional and embody the virtues of womanhood, even if such concepts are difficult if not impossible to define in the present era. And she must support her spouse politically but not cross some ill-defined line of political activism.

Many public opinion polls have been devoted to the first lady's approval rating. The Democratic and Republican National Committees and also the White House conduct polls regarding approval of the first lady. Similarly, "political horse race" polls, assessing who is winning or who has more support, are performed during campaigns for prospective first ladies. In order to examine approval of the first lady not only by the masses but also by elites, and in an effort to compare and contrast the views of these two audiences, I conducted two elite polls. One such poll examined the perceptions and approval of the first lady by influential political women; the second poll surveyed presidential scholars about their opinions on the first ladies.[9]

Several generalizations emerge from the body of opinion polling. The discussion of polls and their findings are divided into four areas focusing on public opinion and image: (1) approval ratings; (2) influence and importance; (3) media attention; and (4) duties and roles.

The First Lady's Approval Ratings

The first national poll taken of the public's approval of the first lady was performed by the Gallup organization in 1939; its subject was Eleanor Roosevelt (her first ladyship began in 1933). In this poll, the Gallup organization asked, "Do you approve of the way Mrs. Roosevelt has conducted herself as 'First Lady'?" Sixty-seven percent of those polled answered yes to this question and 33 percent of the respondents answered no. The Gallup poll also revealed that Eleanor's approval rating surpassed that of the president's, which was listed at 58 percent in the same poll. Furthermore, the poll identified women as generally being more likely to approve of the first lady than men, and the first lady's fellow Democrats were more likely to approve of her conduct than were Republicans.[10] Such findings of support for first ladies within their political party and among women has generally held true to the present day.

The next major poll of the approval of a first lady does not appear to have been taken until the Kennedy administration, over two decades later.[11] In June 1961, Gallup asked a national sample of people, "What are your impressions of Jacqueline Kennedy?" It was found that 59 percent had a favorable view, only 13 percent had an unfavorable view, 6 percent listed mixed, and another 22 percent had no opinion on the matter. Since the time of Mrs. Kennedy's first ladyship, most public opinion polling on the first ladies has focused on public approval ratings. Table 6.1 lists sample approval ratings of first ladies from Pat Nixon to Hillary Clinton.

Generally, approval ratings of a particular first lady vary over her term in the White House, sometimes varying a great deal from year to year, and approval ratings vary from one first lady to another first lady. This is also the case with presidential approval ratings. However, unlike the general trend with presidents, first lady approval ratings do not decline as much over the course of their term in the White House or do not decline at all. Most presidents have found that their approval rating deteriorates over time in office.[12] There may also be a "honeymoon" period for first ladies when they initially get to the White House, as conventional wisdom suggests exists for new presidents. New first ladies have very low unfavorable ratings or negative ratings. But, polls of first ladies taken at the outset of their tenure also indicate very high uncertainty levels, something that might also explain the low negatives new first ladies experience. Perhaps most interestingly, approval ratings of first ladies tend to be higher than the corresponding ratings for their spouses. Based on the small sample of first ladies available for which approval ratings exist, first ladies generally enjoy a fairly high amount of public support.

First ladies from the time of Rosalynn Carter have generally had approval ratings in the in the range of 50–60 percent, and often even higher. As with presidents, it has been found that different groups exhibit varying levels of approval of different first ladies. Approval ratings of Hillary Clinton, for instance, vary along gender, party, race, geography, and ideological lines.[13] Research has shown that such groups as women, Democrats, liberals, blacks, and those living in the Northeast and in urban areas are more likely to approve of Mrs. Clinton's performance than such groups as

Table 6.1   Public Approval Ratings of First Ladies

Pat Nixon

Approve:	54%	Very/somewhat favorable:	85%
Disapprove:	6%	Very/somewhat unfavorable:	14%
No opinion:	40%	*Source:* Gallup, 1973.	

Source: Gallup, 1969.

Betty Ford

Very/somewhat favorable:	93%
Very/somewhat unfavorable:	6%

Source: Gallup, 1976.

Rosalynn Carter

All in all, how would you rate the job Mrs. Carter has been doing as the first lady?		Do you generally approve or disapprove of the way Mrs. Jimmy Carter is handling her role as first lady?			
Excellent/pretty good:	68%	Approve:	59%	Favorable:	46%
Only fair/poor:	21%	Disapprove:	19%	Unfavorable:	9%
Not sure:	11%	No opinion:	22%	Undecided:	45%
Source: Harris, 1977.		*Source:* Gallup, 1979.		*Source:* CBS/NYT, 1980.	

Nancy Reagan

Do you generally approve or disapprove of the way Nancy Reagan is handling her responsibility as first lady?

Approve:	57%	Approve:	58%	Approve:	53%
Disapprove:	26%	Disapprove:	23%	Disapprove:	31%
Don't know:	17%	Don't know:	19%	Don't know:	16%
Source: Gallup, 1981.		*Source:* Gallup, 1987.		*Source:* Gallup, 1988.	

Barbara Bush

In general, do you have a favorable or unfavorable opinion of Barbara Bush?

Favorable:	58%	Favorable:	38%	Favorable:	85%
Unfavorable:	9%	Unfavorable:	3%	Unfavorable:	9%
Not sure:	33%	Undecided:	59%	Undecided:	6%
Source: NBC/WSJ, 1989.		*Source:* CBS/NYT, 1989		*Source:* Gallup, 1992.	

Hillary Clinton

Do you approve or disapprove of the way Hillary Rodham Clinton is handling her job as First Lady?

Approve:	55%	Approve:	54%	Approve:	47%
Disapprove:	40%	Disapprove:	40%	Disapprove:	48%
No opinion:	5%	No opinion:	6%	No opinion:	5%
Source: Gallup, 1994.		*Source:* Gallup, 1995.		*Source:* Gallup, 1996.	

men, Republicans, conservatives, and southerners. In fact, gender and political party affiliation appear to be the most important factors in explaining or predicting approval ratings of first ladies.[14] Because the approval ratings of so few first ladies have been studied, it cannot be assumed that such findings would hold true for first ladies other than Hillary Clinton. Additionally, there are such extreme differences in the approach to the office by first ladies that what holds true for the base of support for one first lady might not be the case for another first lady.[15]

Influence and Importance

Recent polls have highlighted the public concern over the first lady having too much influence and power. For example, Gallup polls have reported that over one-half of poll respondents believe Hillary Clinton has too much influence in the Clinton administration.[16] However, many respondents recognize Mrs. Clinton's influence but feel that it has been positive.[17] These contradictory opinions highlight the paradox that exists concerning the influence of the first lady. First ladies must not give the appearance of influence and power and are forced to exercise such influence behind the scenes.[18]

In recent years, polls show that the public recognizes the influence first ladies have in the White House. For instance, NBC/Wall Street Journal polls in 1985 and 1987 asked the question: "How much influence do you think Nancy Reagan has on her husband's official presidential policies and decisions—a great deal, some, not very much, or none at all?" The findings show that in the 1985 poll, 64 percent (81 percent in 1987) of respondents indicated either "a great deal" or "some," 29 percent (16 percent in 1987) indicated "not very much" or "none," and only 7 percent (3 percent in 1987) reported that they "didn't know."

In 1987 another NBC/Wall Street Journal poll asked the question: "How much influence do you think Nancy Reagan should have on her husband's official presidential policies and decisions?" As with so many issues pertaining to the first lady, they found a mixed response. Fifty percent stated "a great deal" or "some" and 48 percent indicated either "not very much" or "none at all."[19]

In 1995 Gallup polled the public on the issue of influence, asking: "Do you think Hillary Clinton's influence has been generally positive or generally negative on the Clinton administration?" The findings were similar to the 1987 poll, with 47 percent stating "generally positive," 48 percent stating "generally negative," and only 3 percent seeing a "mixed" influence.

The public recognizes the influence of first ladies and is generally concerned by this influence, but it has mixed views on the nature of the influence or its desirability. As Table 6.2 reveals, the group of influential women in public life whom I polled perceived the first lady to be very important and influential. Over one-half of the respondents in this poll "strongly agree" that the first lady is important to the success of the president and exactly one-half felt that she also fulfills an important role in the political

Table 6.2   Importance of the First Lady

The First Lady is important to the success of a president.

Category	Percentage
Strongly agree	55.7
Agree	34.3
Neutral	7.1
Disagree	2.9
Strongly disagree	0

Candidates' wives play an important role in campaigning.

Category	Percentage
Strongly agree	50.0
Agree	41.4
Neutral	7.1
Disagree	1.4
Strongly disagree	0

Source: R. P. Watson, Women in Public Life Poll, 1995–1996.
Note: The sum of scores may not total 100 because of rounding and nonresponse.

campaigns. Moreover, not a single respondent indicated that she would "strongly disagree" that the first lady is important. This view of the first lady as influential and an important component of presidential success is echoed in the recent scholarly studies on the first lady.[20]

Another dimension for assessing the perceived influence of the first lady is the factors determining citizen voting choices in presidential elections. Table 6.3 reveals that presidential scholars do not appear to view the first lady as influential in an individual's voting decision in presidential elections. She is likewise unimportant regarding other political issues that may factor into the voter's decisionmaking. Further research and mass opinion polls should be conducted on this issue to clarify the parameters of the first lady's perceived importance.

Even though presidential scholars do not feel the first lady is considered in a citizen's voting decision in presidential elections, some research supports the notion that first ladies can benefit a president's or presidential candidate's approval rating. For instance, even though she is considered controversial, Hillary Clinton is believed to have contributed to a slight increase in her husband's overall public approval rating.[21] Such findings point to the influence and importance of first ladies. Presidential wives also appear to be an asset to presidents in that their favorability ratings usually

Table 6.3   Voting and the First Lady

The public considers the First Lady when voting for President:

Category	Percentage
Strongly agree	1.1
Agree	4.6
Neutral	10.3
Disagree	42.5
Strongly disagree	33.3

Relative importance of First Lady in the public's Presidential voting decision (in percent)

Compared to:	(less than) 1	2	(about same) 3	4	(more than) 5
Current issues	74.7	12.6	1.1	1.1	0
Political party	72.4	12.6	3.4	1.4	0
Candidate's character	60.9	19.5	6.9	3.4	0
VP candidate	50.6	26.4	11.5	2.3	0
Nation's economy	81.6	4.6	1.1	1.1	1.1

Source: R. P. Watson, Presidential Scholar Poll, 1996–1997.
Note: The sum of scores may not total 100 because of rounding and nonresponse.

surpass those of the presidents. Approval ratings taken of first ladies from Eleanor Roosevelt to Hillary Clinton depict a solid level of public support. Also, most first ladies who have been studied were found to have low unfavorable or negative ratings.

Media Coverage of the First Lady

It is important to note the relationship the first lady has with the media. The media is the avenue by which first ladies shape their image, and in turn, the media shapes the nature of the office. The media has certainly contributed to the institutionalization of the first lady in the modern era, because it has been through the media that modern first ladies have established the power of the white glove pulpit. My poll of women in public life revealed somewhat mixed views on the degree of media attention given to the first lady: 41.4 percent of the poll's respondents felt that the amount of attention was about right and 47.2 percent believed that there was too much interest in the first lady by the media. Only 1.4 percent strongly disagreed with the statement that there was too much media coverage of the first lady. The

Table 6.4   Media and the First Lady

There is too much media attention on the First Lady.

Category	Percentage
Strongly agree	18.6
Agree	28.6
Neutral/about right	41.4
Disagree	5.7
Strongly disagree	1.4

The media focuses largely on traditional roles of First Lady.

Category	Percentage
Strongly agree	25.7
Agree	31.4
Neutral	14.3
Disagree	27.1
Strongly disagree	1.4

Source: R. P. Watson, Women in Public Life Poll, 1995–1996.
Note: The sum of scores may not total 100 because of rounding and nonresponse.

majority of respondents also saw the media as focusing mostly on the more traditional roles of the first lady.

First Lady's Duties and Responsibilities

Given the level of media scrutiny of the first lady and the recent increase in public opinion polls devoted to the wife of the president, it would appear that public opinion plays a role in determining the duties and responsibilities of the first lady. A first lady involved in unpopular activities risks negatively affecting presidential approval ratings and thus public and political support for the president. Thus the public's perceptions toward the various duties and responsibilities of the first lady are watched closely by presidential advisers. It benefits the study of the first lady to consider the possible relationship between public opinion and a first lady's public roles. (See Chapter 4 for a discussion of the first lady's duties.)

Unfortunately, this question is more easily asked than answered. Not surprisingly, public opinion polls reveal much disagreement regarding the proper or even desired roles and responsibilities of the first lady. For example, a 1995 Gallup poll asked the question: "In the next two years, do you think Hillary Clinton should play a more traditional role as First Lady, like the roles other First Ladies have filled; or should she continue to be more publicly involved in policy matters than other First Ladies were?" The public response to this poll reveals the division over the issue: 49 percent said the first lady should "play a traditional role," 48 percent preferred that she "be involved in policy," and 3 percent had "no opinion" on the matter.[22] This poll is indicative of most public opinion polling on the first lady: It shows a high level of uncertainty about the office in general and the first lady's role in particular. Such polls and findings also highlight the activist-traditionist rift or duality that exists concerning her role.

A few additional points are worth mentioning. The first problem is that the poll is biased in three possible ways. The first bias is that the poll assumes that "the roles other First Ladies have filled" have been traditional. The phrasing of the question also treats such supposed traditional roles as opposite to (and possibly even mutually exclusive of) those that are "more publicly involved in policy matters." This is, of course, not completely true. Although many early first ladies were not as visible in public or active in substantive policy matters, some were visible and active in policy. As to what constitutes a role in policy matters, it is vague and ever changing. It may not cover policy activism that occurs behind the scenes.

Second, the poll assumes that Hillary Clinton has been involved in policy matters in a way in which other or traditional first ladies were not involved. The poll conceptualizes Mrs. Clinton as a new type of first lady, a conceptualization that is not entirely true. She is a modern and active first lady who has carved out new dimensions to the office, but she is not the first to be active in policy or political manners.

A third problem with such questions is that there is no differentiation between those respondents who feel that Hillary Clinton should not play a public role because they are opposed to such a role for first ladies in general and those who feel that she should not play a public role because they are opposed to Hillary Clinton (no matter what role she plays). It is also possible that some respondents felt that Hillary Clinton should not play a public role because the press and U.S. public can be quite critical of such roles, even though the particular respondent might personally prefer such a role for first ladies in general or for Hillary in particular. So one is left to guess why respondents opposed such a role.

Such questions—which are raised by most public opinion polls about first ladies—dichotomize the nature of the office of the first lady into two polar approaches: one a nonpublic, nonpolicy, traditional role and the other a public, policy-engaged, activist role. This dichotomization is unrealistic, especially in the modern era when all first ladies fulfill both roles. The public expects first ladies to fill multiple roles, and, ironically, first ladies are forced into a highly public role by an intrusive media, the curious U.S. public, and the nature of presidential politics. This dichotomization is also inaccurate because it ignores the reality that several early first ladies, such as Martha Washington, Dolley Madison, Julia Tyler, and Mary Todd Lincoln, were public celebrities in their time, whereas other early first ladies, such as Abigail Adams and Sarah Polk, were active policy advisers for their husbands.

This type of dichotomization oversimplifies the complex office and creates a no-win situation for the presidential spouses, at least in the arena of public opinion polling, where the public is forced to choose between one or the other and the first lady is criticized whatever she does. If a first lady is an activist, she is subject to criticism, and if she is inactive, she is subject to criticism. If she gains the support of those preferring the activist approach, she loses the support of those preferring the traditionalist approach. It can only be hoped that the public is willing to accept the dual nature (with multiple approaches) of the office that it seems to demand of first ladies. Much of the alleged hostility toward first ladies or rejection of the partnership approach to the office thus might be the product of the way in which such concepts are measured in opinion polls, whose questions are designed to produce such findings. Assuming the example of the 1995 Gallup poll is marginally accurate, the U.S. public appears divided over the proper role of the first lady. It is hard to determine, however, how much of this split might be attributed to the phrasing of the poll's questions or the inherent nature of the office, which is complex, uncertain, and misunderstood.

Another example of mixed public reaction comes from a 1977 Harris poll conducted in response to the controversy generated by First Lady Rosalynn Carter's trip to Latin America and the Caribbean. During this trip Mrs. Carter traveled on behalf of the president to meet with the leaders of Jamaica, Costa Rica, Ecuador, Peru, Brazil, Colombia, and Venezuela. The response to the trip by the public, media, and political leaders in the United States and abroad was mixed. The poll asked whether "a first lady should or should not officially represent the United States in talks with other countries." The response was split, with 55 percent saying a first lady should represent the United States, 33 percent saying she should not, 7 percent stating that "it depends who the first lady is," and another 5 percent indicating they didn't know.[23] The response "it depends who the first lady is" seems to highlight the uncertainty over the office and its highly personalized nature. This response also raises the question of whether or not the particular duties of the first lady should depend on the particular first lady. Another poll concerning Mrs. Carter's trip to Latin America revealed a great deal of support for her diplomatic role. Fully 70 percent of the respondents viewed the trip as either excellent or good.[24]

Some polls of the first lady's role seek to compare the roles and approaches of first ladies. In their polling about First Lady Rosalynn

Carter, the Harris organization also included the following statement, to which the public was asked to agree or disagree: "Mrs. Carter is trying to be the kind of first lady Mrs. Roosevelt was and such a role is questionable for a first lady." Harris found that 26 percent agreed, 39 percent disagreed, and 35 percent were unsure. Again, the poll is consistent with other polls in that it depicts little consensus among the respondents about the first lady-ship. The high percentage of respondents who were unsure may again point to the apparent widespread uncertainty over the proper role of the office. But it might also be explained in part by the bias in the question. First, there were two First Lady Roosevelts, Edith and Eleanor (and three *Mrs.* Roosevelts, but Alice died before Theodore's presidency). The question's wording might lead the respondent into the response, depending upon the respondent's view of Eleanor Roosevelt. For instance, the wording "such a role is questionable" is very leading, especially to respondents uncertain about the office or about Mrs. Roosevelt's tenure as first lady. At best it implies controversy and uncertainty; at worst it deters individuals from agreeing altogether.

As with Mrs. Carter's trip to Latin America, polls have focused on specific actions of first ladies. Nancy Reagan's first ladyship brought questions about the first lady's proper role in response to allegations that Mrs. Reagan ran the show behind the scenes and was responsible for firing members of the Reagan administration. This general perception of excessive power in the office of the first lady, along with an image of a first lady who lived an extravagant lifestyle, resulted in the media's use of nicknames like "Queen Nancy" and "Dragon Lady" for the first lady.

In the first year of the Reagan presidency, Gallup even conducted a poll (December 1981) attempting to assess this image. Gallup found that 62 percent of those polled felt that "Nancy Reagan puts too much emphasis on style and elegance during a time of federal budget cuts and economic hardships." Another 30 percent disagreed, stating they felt Nancy Reagan "brought more style and elegance to the White House." Of course, the wording "during a time of federal budget cuts and economic hardships" biases responses by leading respondents into seeing a problem with Nancy Reagan's actions. The poll also creates hostility toward the first lady through her association with the president because the president is often blamed for economic hardships. A poll finding that respondents demonstrated hostility toward the first lady could simply be measuring the public's hostility toward her husband or toward the state of the economy. Somewhat relatedly, the poll also found that 61 percent of the public believed Nancy Reagan was less sympathetic to the needs and problems of the underprivileged and poor than other first ladies had been. Only 16 percent saw Mrs. Reagan as more sympathetic than other first ladies to such problems, 9 percent indicated that she was the same, and 14 percent were unsure about the issue.[25] This may point to a rejection of Mrs. Reagan's approach to the office and her roles, but the fact that this question accompanied the previous question might bias responses. After all, the previous question already establishes that economic hard times are at hand, and it implies that the first lady is preoccupied with "style and elegance," a pursuit potentially at odds with that of working with the poor.

The polls of the 1970s concentrated on a specific aspect of the first lady's role, for example, Betty Ford's so-called "outspokenness" on controversial issues. Mrs. Ford publicly expressed and demonstrated her support for women's rights, and she also was open and honest in answering sensitive personal questions regarding her family and taboo social issues of sex and drug use. Apparently, the U.S. public of the 1970s was not yet ready for a candid, frank discussion from a first lady about teen sex, drug use, and women's rights. Table 6.5 contains a sampling of the public opinion polling on First Lady Betty Ford's outspokenness during the time of Gerald Ford's presidency.

To further examine the issue of public opinion and the duties of first ladies, my polls of two groups of experts (women in public life and presidential scholars) on the subject can be considered. So that the findings

Table 6.5   Betty Ford's "Outspokenness"

Do you tend to agree or disagree with Mrs. Betty Ford when she said . . .
   she favors passage of the Equal Rights Amendment on women's rights?
              Agree: 70%   Disagree: 15%   Not sure: 15%
Do you tend to agree or disagree with Mrs. Betty Ford when she said . . .
   she would not be surprised if her daughter had an affair?
              Agree: 60%   Disagree: 27%   Not sure: 13%
Let me read you some statements that have been made about Betty Ford.
For each, tell me if you tend to agree or disagree:
   A. She ought to keep more of her opinions to herself and let her husband
   take stands on the issues.
              Agree: 39%   Disagree: 52%   Not sure: 9%
   B. She is brave and courageous, such as when she had her operation for
   breast cancer and when she said a prayer for a Jewish leader who just
   had a heart attack.
              Agree: 86%   Disagree: 5%   Not sure: 9%
   C. She has stood up firmly for women's rights, and that is good.
              Agree: 73%   Disagree: 14%   Not sure: 13%
   D. She was wrong to talk about what she would do if her daughter
   were having an affair.
              Agree: 42%   Disagree: 48%   Not sure: 10%
   E. She is too active in her husband's political campaign and
   should stay more behind the scenes.
              Agree: 23%   Disagree: 67%   Not sure: 10%

Source: Gallup and Harris Polls, 1975 and 1976.

might be compared, the Watson polls asked questions about the first lady's duties that are similar to those asked of the public by such prominent polling organizations as Gallup, Harris, and Roper. Even though there is some concern about such terms as *traditional,* I chose to incorporate them into the poll questions because the purpose of my polls was to compare them with mass polls that regularly use such terminology. According to my poll of women in politics, the respondents generally perceive that the U.S. public is neither ready for nor supportive of a politically active first lady. I should note that the questions do not ask respondents to indicate their preference, but merely their perception of the public's preference.

In Table 6.6, for instance, the vast majority of survey respondents felt the public held an unfavorable view of "nontraditional" first ladies.[26] This finding appears to mirror the arguments of critics of active first ladies who feel the approach creates controversy and has been rejected by the public.[27] However, the experts' perceptions of the public do not appear to match mass polls of the public, such as those examined earlier in this chapter. The mass polls, though they do not necessarily point to high levels of public support for so-called nontraditional first ladies, do reflect a somewhat even split between approval and disapproval for politically active first ladies. The data in Table 6.6 do not appear to correspond to the findings of Gallup's annual "most admired women" polls, wherein activist first ladies like Eleanor Roosevelt, Rosalynn Carter, and Hillary Clinton appeared at the top of the lists, often more than once. These first ladies were found by the Gallup organization to be the most admired women in the world, even though some critics and some polls state that the public disapproves of such first ladies. It is true that first ladies are generally found in such popularity polls, and even top them, yet the fact remains that several nontraditional, activist first ladies are among those topping the lists. Interestingly, several

Table 6.6   Perceptions of Politically Active First Ladies

How does the American public view politically active, "non-traditional" First Ladies?

Category	Percentage
Very favorably	0
Somewhat favorably	14.3
Neutral	1.4
Somewhat unfavorably	64.3
Very unfavorably	15.7

Source: R. P. Watson, Women in Public Life Poll, 1995–1996.
Note: The sum of scores may not total 100 because of rounding and nonresponse.

of these activist first ladies tended to do better in the Gallup polls than more traditional first ladies such as Bess Truman, Mamie Eisenhower, and Pat Nixon, who also made the lists.

When the women in public life were asked about what roles or duties they envisioned for the first lady, there was again disagreement among the respondents. Interestingly, the category of "loyal/supportive wife" was overwhelmingly selected as the primary role of the first lady. The only other role designated as important is that of "ambassador to the world," a vague term allowing for a number of possible roles and duties, both political and social. Table 6.7 lists the most and least important roles for the first lady according to respondents of the author's poll of women in public life.

Table 6.7   Most and Least Important Roles of the First Lady

Role	Most Important (percentage)	Least Important (percentage)
White House preservationist	0	12.9
Advocate of social causes	10.0	1.4
Symbol of the American woman	12.9	1.4
Ambassador to the world	24.3	2.9
Loyal/supportive wife	40.0	2.9
Lady of the White House	1.4	20.0
Social hostess	0	25.7
Presidential adviser	4.3	12.9

Source: R. P. Watson, Women in Public Life Poll, 1995–1996.
Note: Sum of scores may not total 100 because of rounding and nonresponse.

Not one respondent in the poll highlighted in Table 6.7 felt that the category of "social hostess" was the primary role for first ladies, yet historically that has been one of the most important and most visible duties of the office. In fact, over 25 percent of the respondents indicated that hostessing was the least important task, perhaps signifying a major change in the nature of the office. However, this does not mean that women in politics reject traditional roles for the first lady; such a conclusion is refuted by the large amount of support for the role of "loyal/supportive wife." Moreover, only 2.9 percent found that particular duty to be the least important. This might indicate that women in politics envision a strong private role with the possibility of a strong but nonthreatening public role. Still, this poll reflects, as do mass public opinion polls, a lack of consensus concerning the roles and duties of a first lady.

As shown in Table 6.8, presidential scholars were found to be supportive of a first lady traveling on behalf of a president. However, they were less supportive of a first lady's activism in the policy process and generally less supportive of this role than were the women in politics who were polled on the matter. Presidential scholars were also less supportive of a first lady's activism than the general public, as indicated in the Gallup and Harris polls presented earlier in this chapter. So it might be said that presidential scholars do see political duties for the first lady (traveling on behalf of the president) but differentiate between types of political roles. This finding is interesting given that travel might be part of the policy role, and such differentiations are not clearly definable. The results again point to the uncertainty surrounding the duties of the first lady.

Table 6.8   Policy Roles of the First Lady

	Percentage
A First Lady traveling on formal affairs of state is overstepping her role.	
Strongly agree	2.3
Agree	0
Neutral	6.9
Disagree	26.4
Strongly disagree	57.5
A First Lady active in public policy is overstepping her role.	
Strongly agree	3.4
Agree	11.5
Neutral	17.2
Disagree	29.9
Strongly disagree	31.0

Source: R. P. Watson, Presidential Scholars Poll, 1996–1997.
Note: Sum of scores may not total 100 because of rounding and nonresponse.

The results of these two elite polls and the mass opinion polls reveal much disagreement and uncertainty about the roles of the first lady. There are some similarities and some differences between the mass and elite polls, and generally different perceptions of the nature of the institution of the first lady. It may be the variety and the range of views of the office that define public opinion on the first ladies more than any other statement or finding. It appears that public opinion on the first lady is contingent on who is being asked and the particular first lady under consideration. Women, for instance, are generally more approving of first ladies than are men. Democrats are more supportive of Democratic spouses and Republicans are more supportive of Republican spouses. Some support exists for active first ladies, as long as that activism is not directly perceived to be related to politics. It may also be wise for first ladies to restrict their activism and power to the private realm, away from scrutiny by the public or press. The partnership approach to the office sparks controversy and criticism, but a base of support exists for first ladies who function as partners, something that is usually not discussed and is overshadowed by criticism. In light of feminist analysis of gender power, perhaps such findings are not surprising. Women must still be careful with how they use power. And we have yet to decide what we expect of first ladies.

Notes

1. Teddy Roosevelt's use of the media is discussed in M. Nelson, *The Presidency,* 1996.

2. See B. Burrell, *Public Opinion,* 1997.

3. See B. Ginsberg, *The Captive Public,* 1986. This book includes a discussion about George Gallup and the advent of mass public opinion polling.

4. Burrell, 1997.

5. Ibid.

6. Ibid.

7. All major textbooks on research methods and public opinion polling concede the bias present in flawed public opinion polls and inherent difficulties in measuring public opinion. For a good discussion of the shortcomings of public opinion research and bias in political polls, see R. A. Seltzer, *Mistakes,* 1996. The journals *Gallup Poll Monthly* and *Public Opinion* are good sources for studying polling research.

8. Ibid.

9. My poll of women in public life assesses the perceptions of the first lady in a variety of areas, such as approval, roles, and perceptions. A short questionnaire was mailed to 200 leading women in public and political life in the United States in 1995. The total number of responses for this study is 78, which is a response rate of 39 percent. The sample of women in politics and public life included a random selection of (1) women in the Clinton administration in senior political and administrative positions; (2) female members of the U.S. House and Senate; (3) women on the Supreme Court; (4) female governors; (5) wives of married, male governors; and (6) women listed in the *Washingtonian* magazine's list of the most powerful women in Washington who were not members of any of the previous groups.

My second elite poll focused on presidential scholars. A questionnaire was mailed in 1996 to a random list of 200 political scientists and historians deemed to be presidential scholars because of their inclusion in the American Political Science Association's (APSA) "presidency research" section or their identification of the subject area of the presidency as an area of academic specialization and expertise. This information was available in APSA's biographical directory. The total number of responses was 87, for a response rate of 43.5 percent. Both polls were pretested on professors.

10. Burrell, 1997.

11. Ibid.

12. Most major textbooks on the presidency discuss this phenomenon. See, for instance, T. E. Cronin and M. A. Genovese, *The Paradoxes,* 1997 (chapter 3).

13. Burrell, 1997.

14. Burrell, 1997; L. McAneny, "'First Lady' Contest," 1996; McAneny, "President Clinton," 1995.

15. Burrell, 1997; McAneny, 1995, 1996; D. W. Moore, "Public Uncertain," 1994.

16. See the Gallup polls taken from 1994–1996, *The Gallup Poll Monthly;* McAneny, 1996.

17. McAneny, 1996.

18. B. B. Caroli, *First Ladies,* 1987; M. G. Gutin, *The President's Partner,* 1989; K. O'Connor, B. Nye, and L. Van Assendelft, "Wives in the White House," 1997.

19. "Public Portraits," 1989; "The Women We Admire," 1989.

20. Caroli, 1987; L. L. Gould, *First Ladies,* 1996; Gutin, 1989.

21. Burrell, 1997; K. Cocoran, "Pilloried Clinton," 1993; A. Moughan and B. C. Burden, "The Candidates' Wives," 1995.

22. See *Gallup Poll Monthly,* 1995.

23. K. B. Smith, "The First Lady Represents America," 1997.

24. F. L. Johnson, "An Awesome Responsibility," 1990.

25. Gallup Poll on Nancy Reagan, *Gallup Poll Monthly,* Dec. 1981.

26. In general, the term *traditional* is not accurate in describing early first ladies given the fact that some early first ladies were quite progressive by any measure. And nearly all first ladies have been active, at least in a social capacity. However, many polls and studies of the first ladies use the term in contrast to "modern" or "active" first ladies. I try to avoid falling prey to this either/or dichotomy, but I did use the term *traditional* in my polls of presidential scholars and women in public life because I was trying to replicate the wording and focus of mass public opinion polling and because, though technically inaccurate, the description of certain first ladies as "traditional" is widely used and understood.

27. Gil Troy and other critics of active first ladies have maintained that the public rejects politically active first ladies and that such a partnership is flawed, dangerous, and ill conceived. See G. Troy, *Affairs of State,* 1997.

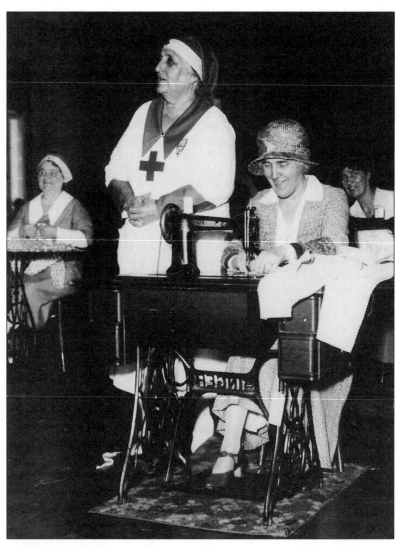

Many first ladies have championed important social issues. Here, Lou Hoover visits Red Cross workers (September 21, 1932) (collection of the Library of Congress).

7

Rating the Presidential Spouses

It is sad and telling that the press and public alike are unaware that Presidential wives since Abigail Adams have been wielding political influence.

—Edith Mayo, director,
Smithsonian Institution's first ladies exhibit

The formalization of a field of study of the presidential spouses would inform presidential scholarship. An inevitable area of research would be ranking or rating the first ladies. After all, several polls and scholars have attempted, with varying degrees of success, to rank the presidents.[1] These polls include the Schlesinger polls (1948 and 1962), the Maranell Accomplishment poll (1970), U.S. Historical Society poll (1977), the Chicago Tribune poll (1982), the Murray poll (1983), and the Sienna Research Institute poll (1994), to name a few. The presidential polls have identified the best and worst presidents or attempted a complete ranking of presidential performance. Most of the ratings are based on polls of presidential scholars and historians. Therefore, a poll of presidential scholars that assesses the first ladies, despite being more problematic, would serve a similar purpose. A ranking of presidential spouses would inform presidential scholarship, raising such research questions as whether or not the first lady rankings mirror or reflect the rankings of the presidents. It would also contribute to the new field of first lady scholarship by providing information on how recent spouses rate compared with early first ladies and how active and nontraditional spouses rate compared with inactive and traditional spouses.

171

Problems with Rating the First Ladies

The question of how one should go about ranking the first ladies is more problematic than the act of ranking the country's presidents. There are some shared concerns, including the problem of a small number of cases; after all, very few people have served as president or first lady. There is also high variation among those few cases. Such a study also lacks a single criterion by which to comprehensively assess or compare performance; there are also problems of comparability across the span of history.

The first ladies have been an especially varied lot, leading some to suggest that the only commonality shared by them is their marriage to someone who either would become the president or already was the president. (Edith Bolling, Julia Gardiner, and Frances Folsom all married sitting presidents: Woodrow Wilson, John Tyler, and Grover Cleveland, respectively.) But this statement is not entirely accurate; a closer inspection of the office will reveal some common approaches to and challenges of the position shared by many first ladies.[2]

Although most presidents married their wives (the future first ladies) prior to their White House years and had their wives serving with them in the White House, there are exceptions. For example, of the fifty-three women (as of 1999) who have served in a formal capacity as either first lady or hostess of the White House, only thirty-eight were actually married to the president. Several women, typically young daughters and nieces, served as "mistresses" or "proxy" first ladies, hostessing for ailing or deceased spouses (see Chapter 3). Thomas Jefferson and Andrew Johnson, for example, were assisted in social matters by their daughters, who filled in for, respectively, the deceased Mrs. Jefferson and the ill Mrs. Johnson. Likewise, a few sisters, cousins, and even two cabinet wives functioned as the surrogate hostess of the White House. Seven presidential spouses never served formally as first lady; five died prior to the presidential years (Martha Jefferson, Rachel Jackson, Hannah Van Buren, Ellen Arthur, and Alice Roosevelt) and two married the ex-presidents *after* their presidencies (Caroline Fillmore and Mary Lord Harrison). The problem thus arises as to who should be considered a first lady and thus eligible for the ranking. To that end, the ranking of presidential spouses does not consider spouses who either died prior to serving in the White House or married their spouses after his presidential term. Moreover, when a presidential spouse was alive during the White House years, only she was ranked, omitting those such as daughters and nieces who may have assisted in social hostessing. In the cases when a presidential spouse was not alive and a mistress served for a widowed president, such proxy or surrogate first ladies were deemed ineligible for ranking. This decision is premised on the unique relationship a spouse brings to the office. So little is known about surrogate first ladies that it would be highly difficult to assess their performance. Harriet Lane, James Buchanan's niece, who hosted for the bachelor president, is a unique case, and arguments exist for both including her and not including her. Unlike many surrogate hostesses, there is information available on Miss Lane, who hosted for Buchanan for years, both throughout his White House term and during his pre-presidential career. She is included in the ratings, but her status as a surrogate will be denoted.

The women of the White House also varied in age from new brides barely into their twenties to grandmothers who had been married to the president for decades (see Table 7.1). Some were well educated and others were not (see Box 7.1). They came from many regions of the nation (see Box 7.2) and from varied backgrounds, although interestingly, most presidential spouses brought considerably more wealth and social status into the marriage than did the presidents, leading some scholars to suggest that presidents tend to "marry up" or above themselves socially.[3] A look at the women who have served as first lady reveal a diverse group, with differences in life experiences, political ambition, and the nature of their marriage to the president. This diversity makes it difficult to study those who served as the president's spouse. Still, some similarities do emerge.

The presidential spouses are also more challenging to rank than the presidents because of the lack of knowledge and written documentation about them compared to that which exists for the presidents. There are also far fewer first lady scholars than presidential scholars; no formal field of study exists on the first lady; few systematic studies have been published on the first ladies; and scholarship on the first ladies is missing from textbooks, graduate training, and curricula in the fields of political science and history. Not surprisingly, then, many historians and political scientists lack significant knowledge by which to assess the first ladies. Additionally, and perhaps most problematically, there are no agreed-upon criteria by which to assess the first ladies. The Constitution is silent about her, there are no formal or legal precedents to which first ladies are to adhere, and her office is not official. The first lady is nonelected, nonappointed, and unpaid.

The presidential spouses cannot simply be rated by their hostessing talents or political activism because there is no single, primary role or responsibility for the first lady. It is thus difficult to assess the first lady or even the degree of influence she has held because societal norms deter presidential spouses from even giving the appearance of having influence or discussing her power openly.[4] Some first ladies may have been highly active, politically influential, and utilized nontraditional approaches while expanding the focus of the office, yet they may have been poor hostesses or their actions may have invited controversy that harmed the presidency. So, there is the problem as to whether such a spouse would be rated positively or negatively. A traditional wife who expressed no interest in politics or social

Table 7.1   First Ladies' Age Profile

First Lady	Age at Marriage	Spousal Age Difference	Age in White House	Age at Death	Years Surviving Spouse
Martha Washington	27 years, 199 days*	+ 246 days	57 years, 313 days	70 years, 355 days	+ 2 years, 159 days
Abigail Adams	19 years, 348 days	− 9 years, 12 days	52 years, 113 days	73 years, 351 days	− 7 years, 249 days
Martha Jefferson	23 years, 74 days*	− 5 years, 189 days	N/A	33 years, 322 days	− 43 years, 301 days
Dolley Madison	26 years, 118 days*	− 17 years, 65 days	40 years, 288 days	81 years, 53 days	+ 13 years, 14 days
Elizabeth Monroe	17 years, 231 days	− 10 years, 63 days	58 years, 247 days	62 years, 85 days	− 284 days
Louisa Adams	22 years, 164 days	− 7 years, 216 days	50 years, 20 days	77 years, 91 days	+ 4 years, 80 days
Rachel Jackson	24 years*	− 92 days	N/A	61 years, 190 days	− 16 years, 168 days
Hannah Van Buren	23 years, 350 days	− 93 days	N/A	35 years, 334 days	− 43 years, 169 days
Anna Harrison	20 years, 123 days	− 2 years, 166 days	65 years, 222 days	88 years, 215 days	+ 22 years, 327 days
Letitia Tyler	22 years, 137 days	− 228 days	50 years, 145 days	51 years, 302 days	− 19 years, 130 days
Julia Tyler	24 years, 53 days	− 30 years, 36 days	24 years, 53 days	69 years, 67 days	+ 27 years, 173 days
Sarah Polk	20 years, 119 days	− 7 years, 306 days	41 years, 181 days	87 years, 344 days	+ 42 years, 60 days
Margaret Taylor	21 years, 273 days	− 3 years, 301 days	60 years, 164 days	63 years, 331 days	+ 2 years, 40 days
Abigail Fillmore	27 years, 324 days	+ 1 year, 300 days	52 years, 111 days	55 years, 17 days	− 20 years, 343 days
Jane Pierce	28 years, 243 days	− 1year, 109 days	46 years, 357 days	57 years, 265 days	− 5 years, 310 days
Mary Lincoln	23 years, 326 days	− 9 years, 304 days	42 years, 81 days	63 years, 215 days	+ 17 years, 92 days
Eliza Johnson	16 years, 225 days	− 1 year, 279 days	54 years, 151 days	65 years, 103 days	+ 168 days
Julia Grant	22 years, 208 days	− 3 years, 274 days	43 years, 37 days	76 years, 322 days	+ 17 years, 144 days
Lucy Hayes	21 years, 124 days	− 8 years, 328 days	45 years, 188 days	57 years, 301 days	− 3 years, 206 days
Lucretia Garfield	26 years, 206 days	− 151 days	48 years, 320 days	85 years, 329 days	+ 36 years, 176 days
Ellen Arthur	22 years, 56 days	− 7 years, 329 days	N/A	42 years, 135 days	− 6 years, 310 days
Frances Cleveland	21 years, 316 days	− 27 years, 125 days	21 years, 226 days	83 years, 125 days	+ 39 years, 137 days

First Lady	Age at Marriage	Spousal Age Difference	Age in White House	Age at Death	Years Surviving Spouse
Caroline Harrison	21 years, 19 days	+ 323 days	56 years, 141 days	60 years, 24 days	– 8 years, 139 days
Ida McKinley	23 years, 231 days	– 4 years, 130 days	49 years, 269 days	59 years, 352 days	+ 5 years, 254 days
Edith Roosevelt	25 years, 118 days	– 2 years, 293 days	40 years, 39 days	87 years, 45 days +	29 years, 267 days
Helen Taft	25 years, 168 days	– 3 years, 109 days	48 years, 71 days	82 years, 140 days	+ 13 years, 75 days
Ellen Wilson	25 years, 40 days	– 3 years, 137 days	52 years, 293 days	54 years, 83 days	– 9 years, 181 days
Edith Wilson	43 years, 64 days*	– 15 years, 291 days	40 years, 140 days	89 years, 74 days	+ 37 years, 328 days
Florence Harding	30 years, 327 days*	+ 5 years, 79 days	60 years, 202 days	64 years, 98 days	+ 1 year, 111 days
Grace Coolidge	26 years, 274 days	– 6 years, 183 days	44 years, 212 days	78 years, 186 days	+ 24 years, 184 days
Lou Hoover	24 years, 318 days	+ 134 days	54 years, 340 days	69 years, 284 days	– 20 years, 289 days
Eleanor Roosevelt	20 years, 157 days	– 2 years, 254 days	48 years, 144 days	78 years, 27 days	+ 17 years, 209 days
Bess Truman	34 years, 135 days	– 281 days	60 years, 57 days	97 years, 247 days	+ 9 years, 296 days
Mamie Eisenhower	19 years, 229 days	– 6 years, 30 days	56 years, 68 days	82 years, 350 days	+ 10 years, 218 days
Jackie Kennedy	24 years, 46 days	– 12 years, 60 days	31 years, 176 days	64 years, 294 days	+ 30 years, 177 days
Lady Bird Johnson	21 years, 330 days	– 4 years, 107 days	50 years, 335 days	N/A	N/A
Pat Nixon	28 years, 97 days	+ 299 days	56 years, 310 days	81 years, 98 days	– 304 days
Betty Ford	30 years, 190 days*	– 4 years, 278 days	53 years, 123 days	N/A	N/A
Rosalynn Carter	18 years, 323 days	– 2 years, 321 days	49 years, 155 days	N/A	N/A
Nancy Reagan	30 years, 242 days	– 10 years, 120 days	59 years, 198 days	N/A	N/A
Barbara Bush	19 years, 213 days	– 361 days	64 years, 227 days	N/A	N/A
Hillary Clinton	27 years, 351 days	– 1 year, 68 days	45 years, 85 days	N/A	N/A

Note: Age in White House means age of the first lady on entering White House.
Spousal Age Difference: + indicates first lady is older than spouse; – indicates first lady is younger than spouse.
Years Surviving Spouse: + indicates first lady outlived spouse; – indicates she died prior to him.
Age at Marriage: * indicates second marriage for first lady.

Box 7.1   Education of First Ladies

First Ladies with a College Education

First Lady	School(s)
Lucy Hayes	Ohio Wesleyan University (graduated 1850)
Lucretia Garfield	Hiram College; Western Reserve Eclectic Institute; Geauga Seminary
Frances Cleveland	Wells College (graduated 1885)
Ellen Wilson	Rome Female College
Helen Taft	Miami University (Ohio)
Grace Coolidge	University of Vermont (graduated 1902)
Lou Hoover	San Jose Normal School; Stanford University (graduated 1898)
Jackie Kennedy	Vassar; Sorbonne; George Washington University (graduated 1951)
Lady Bird Johnson	University of Texas (graduated 1933)
Pat Nixon	University of Southern California (graduated 1937)
Betty Ford	Bennington College
Rosalynn Carter	Georgia Southwestern College
Nancy Reagan	Smith College (graduated 1943)
Barbara Bush	Smith College
Hillary Clinton	Wellesley College (graduated 1969); Yale Law School (graduated 1973)

First Ladies with a Formal or Finishing School Education

First Lady	School(s)
Anna Harrison	Clinton Academy; Mrs. Graham's Boarding School for Young Ladies
Julia Tyler	Chegary Institute
Sarah Polk	Moravian Female Academy; Abercrombie School; Daniel Elam School
Mary Lincoln	Mme. Mentelle's School
Julia Grant	St. Louis Boarding School
Caroline Harrison	Oxford Female Seminary
Ida McKinley	Brook Hall Seminary

Box 7.2   Birthplaces of the First Ladies

Birthplace (#)	First Ladies
New York (9)	Monroe, Van Buren,[a] J. Tyler, Fillmore, Cleveland, Eleanor Roosevelt, Kennedy, Reagan, Bush
Ohio (6)	Hayes, Garfield, C. Harrison, McKinley, Taft, Harding
Virginia (6)	Washington, Jefferson,[a] Jackson,[a] L. Tyler, Arthur,[a] Edith Wilson
Georgia (2)	Ellen Wilson, Carter
Illinois (2)	Ford, Clinton
Iowa (2)	Hoover, Eisenhower
Missouri (2)	Grant, Truman
Tennessee (2)	Polk, E. Johnson
Connecticut (1)	Edith Roosevelt
England (1)	L. Adams
Kentucky (1)	Lincoln
Maryland (1)	Taylor
Massachusetts (1)	A. Adams
Nevada (1)	Nixon
New Hampshire (1)	Pierce
New Jersey (1)	A. Harrison
North Carolina (1)	Madison
Pennsylvania (1)	Lane[b]
Texas (1)	C. Johnson
Vermont (1)	Coolidge

Notes: a. These women were wives of presidents but died prior to their husbands' presidencies.

b. Harriet Lane was not a first lady, but she served for her bachelor uncle, President James Buchanan.

---

causes may have achieved fame for her hostessing or even enhanced public opinion toward her spouse's presidency. A first lady may have been neither publicly popular nor active in the public dimensions of the office, yet it is possible that she was a great source of moral support for her husband in private. Her presence may have been a major factor in her husband's successes, even though this link may not have been readily apparent to the public.

Hence, in the absence of formal criteria by which to base the ranking or rating, the first ladies are assessed according to a general view of them by presidential scholars. This approach may not be perfect, but it may be less imperfect than other ranking schemes, and it is similar to how the presidents are often ranked.

Yet another challenge in rating presidential spouses is the changing nature of the office of the first lady and the evolving status of women in society. Clearly, the same standards cannot be used to judge a modern first lady, who is expected to champion social causes and serve in the highly public, mass media, televised age, and a nineteenth-century first lady. Women in an earlier day and age suffered from a restrictive environment and had fewer opportunities to be public figures. Women were not even legally permitted to vote until the passage of the Nineteenth Amendment in 1920. Whereas modern first ladies are encouraged to champion a social project that tends to garner a lot of media attention, early spouses were discouraged by both their husbands and society from speaking to reporters. Moreover, whereas early first ladies did not dare undertake such endeavors as campaigning, modern first ladies cannot contemplate withdrawing from campaigning and participation in social causes.

In addition to the problems of historical relevance, many variables influence the nature of the office, including each occupant's personality and disposition to public service, the events of the day and age, public views and expectations of women, the president's view of the first ladyship, and the nature of the presidential marriage and partnership. These variables point to the period of time that should be studied: the White House years, the first lady's entire life, or the time of her life in which she was affiliated with her husband? If the last time period is selected, should the first lady be assessed only during the years her partner spent in public service? Unfortunately, there does not seem to be an easy solution, and the researcher is left to offer—in the absence of any conclusive research—a ranking model that invites further research and corrective additions that may address these concerns.

One way to rate the first ladies is through their public popularity. It can be hypothesized that a first lady's popularity might carry over to the president's own popularity. Popular first ladies would thus be an asset to their husbands' presidencies. If this is the case, from the political perspective of the White House, spousal popularity may be the most viable way to rate first ladies. From this perspective, two dimensions of popularity would be assessed: the first ladies' public popularity and whether or not that popularity affects presidential approval ratings. Yet to limit an assessment of the office of the first lady to a single measure ignores the many duties and complexities associated with the office and the full range of ways in which

Table 7.2   Gallup's "Most Admired Women"

1948 Eleanor Roosevelt (1)		Betty Ford (4)
Bess Truman (5)	1969 Mamie Eisenhower (1)	Jackie Onassis (5)
1949 Eleanor Roosevelt (1)	Pat Nixon (3)	1984 Nancy Reagan (4)
1950 Eleanor Roosevelt (1)	Jackie Onassis (5)	Betty Ford (6)
1951 Eleanor Roosevelt (2)	1970 Mamie Eisenhower (1)	1985 Nancy Reagan (1)
1952 Eleanor Roosevelt (1)	Pat Nixon (2)	Betty Ford (7)
Mamie Eisenhower (3)	Jackie Onassis (5)	Jackie Onassis (9)
Bess Truman (10)	Lady Bird Johnson (6)	1986 Nancy Reagan (3)
1953 Eleanor Roosevelt (1)	1971 Pat Nixon (2)	Betty Ford (8)
Mamie Eisenhower (2)	Mamie Eisenhower (5)	Jackie Onassis (10)
Bess Truman (8)	Jackie Onassis (6)	1987 Nancy Reagan (1)
1954 Eleanor Roosevelt (1)	Lady Bird Johnson (7)	Betty Ford (7)
Mamie Eisenhower (2)	1972 Pat Nixon (1)	1988 Nancy Reagan (3)
1955 Eleanor Roosevelt (1)	Mamie Eisenhower (4)	Betty Ford (5)
Mamie Eisenhower (3)	Jackie Onassis (5)	Jackie Onassis (8)
1956 Eleanor Roosevelt (1)	1973 Pat Nixon (2)	Barbara Bush (10)
Mamie Eisenhower (3)	Mamie Eisenhower (6)	1989 Barbara Bush (3)
1957 Eleanor Roosevelt (1)	Lady Bird Johnson (7)	Nancy Reagan (4)
Mamie Eisenhower (6)	Jackie Onassis (8)	Betty Ford (7)
1958 Eleanor Roosevelt (1	1974 Betty Ford (2)	Jackie Onassis (10)
Mamie Eisenhower (4)	Pat Nixon (3)	1990 Barbara Bush (2)
1959 Eleanor Roosevelt (1)	Lady Bird Johnson (8)	Nancy Reagan (4)
Pat Nixon (7)	Jackie Onassis (9)	Jackie Onassis (9)
1960 Eleanor Roosevelt (1)	Mamie Eisenhower	Betty Ford (10)
Mamie Eisenhower (2)	(10)	1991 Barbara Bush (1)
Pat Nixon (6)	1977 Rosalynn Carter (1)	Nancy Reagan (4)
Jackie Kennedy (7)	Betty Ford (4)	Jackie Onassis (6)
1961 Eleanor Roosevelt (1)	Pat Nixon (6)	Betty Ford (10)
Jackie Kennedy (2)	Jackie Onassis (9)	1992 Barbara Bush (1)
Mamie Eisenhower (4)	1978 Betty Ford (1)	Hillary Clinton (4)
Pat Nixon (10)	Rosalynn Carter (2)	Jackie Onassis (8)
1962 Jackie Kennedy (1)	Pat Nixon (4)	1993 Hillary Clinton (1)
Mamie Eisenhower (4)	Jackie Onassis (6)	Barbara Bush (4)
Pat Nixon (10)	1979 Rosalynn Carter (1)	1994 Hillary Clinton (1)
1963 Jackie Kennedy (1)	Betty Ford (2)	Barbara Bush (4)
Lady Bird Johnson (2)	Pat Nixon (7)	1995 Hillary Clinton (2)
Mamie Eisenhower (5)	Jackie Onassis (10)	Barbara Bush (3)
1964 Jackie Kennedy (1)	1980 Rosalynn Carter (1)	Nancy Reagan (10)
Lady Bird Johnson (2)	Betty Ford (3)	1996 Hillary Clinton (2)
Mamie Eisenhower (7)	Nancy Reagan (8)	Barbara Bush (3)
1965 Jackie Kennedy (1)	Jackie Onassis (9)	Nancy Reagan (8)
Lady Bird Johnson (2)	1981 Nancy Reagan (1)	Rosalynn Carter (10)
Mamie Eisenhower (4)	Betty Ford (5)	1997 Hillary Clinton (1)
1966 Jackie Kennedy (1)	Jackie Onassis (6)	Barbara Bush (3)
Lady Bird Johnson (2)	Rosalynn Carter (7)	Nancy Reagan (10)
Mamie Eisenhower (7)	1982 Nancy Reagan (3)	1998 Hillary Clinton (1)
1968 Mamie Eisenhower (3)	Betty Ford (4)	Barbara Bush (5)
Lady Bird Johnson (4)	Rosalynn Carter (10)	
Jackie Onassis (5)	1983 Nancy Reagan (3)	

Note: Number in parentheses is the ranking. Poll not conducted in 1967.

the first lady contributes to the presidency and the president, and it fails to allow a better understanding of the nature of the first ladyship.

It is clear that first ladies are well represented in the annual Gallup poll of the U.S. public's most admired women (see Table 7.2). One or more first ladies are found in the top ten list in almost every year that the poll has been conducted; often a first lady ranked as the most admired woman. Many first ladies are found on the list in multiple years, often after they have completed their service in the White House. The Gallup polls make a strong argument for the popularity of first ladies and their preeminence as one of the nation's most admired women. The poll's results alone might be taken as evidence of the success of first ladies.

Rankings by Women in Public Life

Not only is the first lady admired by the U.S. public, but it appears that she is also highly admired by other well-known and powerful women in U.S. political life. The findings in my poll of women in public life[5] are revealed in Table 7.3, which lists those first ladies who were identified by at least 10 percent of the poll respondents as being among the first ladies they most admired. The results might be taken as an endorsement of the seven first ladies listed below.

Table 7.3   Most Admired First Ladies

First Lady	Percentage of Votes
Eleanor Roosevelt	50.0
Hillary Clinton	40.0
Jackie Kennedy	24.3
Rosalynn Carter	21.4
Barbara Bush	18.6
Betty Ford	12.9
Lady Bird Johnson	11.4

Source: R. P. Watson, Women in Public Life Poll, 1995–1996.
Note: Respondents could vote for more than one First Lady.

Rankings by Presidential Scholars

Several polls and studies have attempted to rank the presidents. These serve as models for conducting a poll of the presidential spouses. The major presidential polls rely on input from presidential scholars; the total number of respondents typically ranges from 49 to 93. The presidential scholars being surveyed are usually asked to rate the presidents according to broad standards. For example, the Schlesinger polls (1948 and 1962) used 55 and 75 scholars, respectively, and classified the presidents in five categories: "great," "near great," "average," "below average," and "failure."[6] The Maranell Accomplishment Poll assessed presidential prestige and accomplishment and ranked presidents from top to bottom based on the responses of 571 historians.[7] The U.S. Historical Society polled 93 historians in an effort to rank the ten greatest presidents.[8] The Chicago Tribune poll surveyed 49 top scholars in an attempt to rank the ten best and ten worst presidents.[9] And the Murray poll used 953 historians in ranking the presidents from top to bottom.[10]

Another approach to ranking the first ladies is to assess the first ladies on a variety of criteria. *Good Housekeeping* magazine did just that when it commissioned a poll of presidential scholars and asked them to rate twentieth-century first ladies on multiple functions and dimensions of the first ladyship.[11] This poll is useful because it is one of the very few attempts to assess first ladies and because the twelve criteria employed in the ratings offer a comprehensive assessment of the range of dimensions of the office. These criteria can be combined in such a way to pinpoint specific, important dimensions of the office, even though *Good Housekeeping* did not perform such an analysis. The twelve criteria can be identified along four basic dimensions of the office, each one with one or more variables or criteria for ranking. The first dimension, for example, pertains to performing the duties of the office and can be assessed by employing such criteria as the first lady's "duties as hostess" and her efforts as a "campaigner," a "leader in social causes," and in "improving the White House." The second dimension considers the first lady as a presidential partner and can be assessed by considering such criteria as her "influence on the president" and her "helpfulness to the president." The third dimension measures the first lady's personality and can be assessed with the criterion of her "charisma." The final dimension considers whether the first lady can be characterized as a traditionalist or activist, which can be assessed through such criteria as "the first lady as a feminist," "her inspiration to women," and "her interest in politics." These criteria or variables for assessing each of the four aspects of the first ladyship are not perfect. For example, it is possible that to traditional women, a traditionalist first lady might be an inspiration, whereas more progressive women would be less inclined to admire such a first lady. Likewise, the concept of the first lady as an "inspiration to women" may not be a perfect measure of the extent to which the first lady is nontraditionalist. But it is a reasonable tool for beginning to measure such aspects of the office. In the *Good Housekeeping* rating (see Table 7.4), each first lady is assessed on a 10-point scale, whereby a score of 10 is high and a score of 1 is low.

Table 7.4 The *Good Housekeeping* Rating

Rank	First Lady	Total Score	Host	Camp	Lead	Pol	Fem	Trad	W.H.	Infl	Help	Spoke	Char	Women
1.	Lady Bird Johnson	92	8	10	9	10	6	4	8	9	10	2	9	7
2.	Eleanor Roosevelt	89	8	10	10	10	10	0	0	5	8	10	10	8
3.	Rosalynn Carter	88	7	10	8	10	10	0	2	10	10	7	8	6
4.	Lou Hoover	83	10	3	9	8	8	2	8	5	10	5	7	8
5.	Jackie Kennedy	79	8	6	0	0	4	6	10	7	6	4	10	8
6.	Betty Ford	73	8	2	6	4	7	3	2	6	8	10	9	8
7.	Helen Taft	69	6	9	2	10	5	2	2	9	9	2	7	6
8.	Pat Nixon	63	10	8	0	0	0	9	10	4	8	0	6	8
9.	Bess Truman	60	2	7	0	10	0	10	4	7	10	0	6	4
9.	Florence Harding	60	6	5	0	10	0	8	6	8	10	2	5	0
11.	Edith Roosevelt	54	8	0	1	0	0	10	9	0	8	0	8	10
12.	Edith Wilson	53	1	8	0	8	6	0	0	10	8	0	6	6
13.	Grace Coolidge	52	10	0	0	0	0	10	7	0	6	2	9	8
13.	Mamie Eisenhower	52	10	8	0	0	0	10	3	0	8	0	8	5
15.	Ellen Wilson	48	4	3	10	4	0	7	5	0	7	0	6	2

Source: Good Housekeeping, July 1980, p. 120.

Key:
Host = Hostess
Camp = Campaigner
Lead = Leader in causes
Pol = Interest in politics

Fem = Feminist
Trad = Traditionalist
W.H. = Improving White House
Infl = Influence on president

Help = Helpfulness to president
Spoke = Outspokenness
Char = Charisma
Women = Inspiration to women

In this poll, Lady Bird Johnson was judged as—to borrow the terminology used in presidential ranking polls—the "greatest" first lady of 1900–1980, with Eleanor Roosevelt a close second and Rosalynn Carter a close third. Using the criteria relevant to the four measures discussed earlier, it is possible to break out those criteria so as to measure various types of first ladies by simply adding up the relevant scores. For instance, further rankings of specific responsibilities and functions of the first ladies can be derived from the *Good Housekeeping* poll by summing the scores of the variables relevant to each of these four dimensions and dividing by the total number of variables. This produces an average (mean) score for each of the first ladies.

Fitness for the Office

This first dimension measures the first lady's fitness to perform the roles and duties of the office based on four variables or criteria (hostess; campaigner; leader in causes; improving the White House). Again, Lady Bird Johnson leads the list. As is apparent from Table 7.5, roughly one-half of the first ladies scored above 5 and one-half scored below 5, a near even split in the fitness for the office by twentieth-century first ladies.

Table 7.5   Fitness for the Office

First Lady	Score
1. Lady Bird Johnson	8.75
2. Lou Hoover	7.50
3. Eleanor Roosevelt	7.00
4. Pat Nixon	7.00
5. Rosalynn Carter	6.75
6. Jackie Kennedy	6.00
7. Ellen Wilson	5.50
8. Mamie Eisenhower	5.25
9. Helen Taft	4.75
10. Betty Ford	4.50
11. Edith Roosevelt	4.50
12. Florence Harding	4.25
13. Grace Coolidge	4.25
14. Bess Truman	3.25
15. Edith Wilson	2.25

The First Lady as Presidential Partner

This dimension provides a measurement or possible determinant of the extent or existence of a presidential partnership based on two important variables or criteria: the first lady's influence on the president and her help-fulness to the president. Rosalynn Carter scored a perfect 10, and several first ladies were rated very highly (see Table 7.6), reinforcing the thesis that a partnership exists in the office. Five first ladies scored a 9 or higher out of a possible score of 10, and all but four were rated above 5.

Table 7.6   Presidential Partnership

First Lady	Score
1. Rosalynn Carter	10.0
2. Lady Bird Johnson	9.5
3. Edith Wilson	9.0
4. Helen Taft	9.0
5. Florence Harding	9.0
6. Bess Truman	8.5
7. Lou Hoover	7.5
8. Betty Ford	7.0
9. Eleanor Roosevelt	6.5
10. Jackie Kennedy	6.5
11. Pat Nixon	6.0
12. Edith Roosevelt	4.0
13. Mamie Eisenhower	4.0
14. Ellen Wilson	3.5
15. Grace Coolidge	3.0

This facet of the first ladyship brings to light the definition of what constitutes a presidential partner. Some first ladies, although quite capable, intelligent, and charismatic, were not true partners. A reason for this lack of a partnership is that their husbands often did not encourage or allow it to happen. Generally, these husbands were not known for their commitment to teamwork during their presidencies and did not allow or envision a partner-ship or helpmate role for their wives. The Coolidges provide a good exam-ple of this lack of partnership. Grace Coolidge was intelligent and popular (she received a score of 9 on the "charisma" scale; see Table 7.7), but her husband, Calvin, would not permit her to speak to reporters or in public, and he did not invite her opinion on political matters. In contrast, the Carters were full partners in all aspects of their lives, sharing in political decisionmaking and other business matters of the presidency.

Highly skilled hostesses might not necessarily be presidential partners. Mamie Eisenhower was a successful hostess and popular first lady but did not participate in the political side of her husband's presidency. She does not appear to have been interested in or inclined toward such activities, nor did Dwight Eisenhower encourage his wife's activism or interest in this area. First Lady Bess Truman was not especially active or charismatic and did not enjoy appearing in public. However, Bess was a full partner behind the scenes, where she helped Harry with every important decision he made in his career.

The First Lady's Personality

This dimension assesses the first lady's charisma using that particular variable in the rating. All fifteen first ladies were rated at least a 5 or higher; eight of them scored an 8 or higher (see Table 7.7). The twentieth-century first ladies were a charismatic group, something that cannot be said of many twentieth-century presidents, including Warren Harding, Calvin Coolidge, Woodrow Wilson, Herbert Hoover, Richard Nixon, Gerald Ford, Jimmy Carter, and George Bush.

Table 7.7   Personality and Charisma

	First Lady	Score
1.	Eleanor Roosevelt	10
	Jackie Kennedy	10
3.	Grace Coolidge	9
	Lady Bird Johnson	9
	Betty Ford	9
6.	Edith Roosevelt	8
	Mamie Eisenhower	8
	Rosalynn Carter	8
9.	Helen Taft	7
	Lou Hoover	7
11.	Ellen Wilson	6
	Edith Wilson	6
	Bess Truman	6
	Pat Nixon	6
15.	Florence Harding	5

Activist Rating

This measurement classifies the activist versus nonactivist first lady. First ladies are ranked from the perspective of the activist model of first ladies based on four variables or criteria (inspiration to women, role as feminist, interest in politics, and outspokenness). Again, it is not entirely accurate to dichotomize first ladies into such categories. Also, the activist approach is not necessarily new to the office; many early first ladies were active.

Seven of the fifteen first ladies were rated with scores of 5 or higher (see Table 7.8), suggesting that they could be classified as activist first ladies. Four first ladies in particular received high scores in this area: Eleanor Roosevelt, Rosalynn Carter, Betty Ford, and Lou Hoover.

Table 7.8   Activist First Ladies

First Lady	Score
1. Eleanor Roosevelt	9.5
2. Rosalynn Carter	8.25
3. Betty Ford	7.25
4. Lou Hoover	7.25
5. Lady Bird Johnson	6.25
6. Helen Taft	5.75
7. Edith Wilson	5.0
8. Jackie Kennedy	4.0
9. Bess Truman	3.5
10. Florence Harding	3.0
11. Edith Roosevelt	2.5
12. Grace Coolidge	2.5
13. Pat Nixon	2.0
14. Ellen Wilson	1.5
15. Mamie Eisenhower	1.25

The Siena Research Institute (SRI) conducted polls in 1982 and 1993 on the first ladies. The 1982 poll is believed to be the first poll ever to assess the first ladies.[12] Just as with presidential rankings, SRI polled scholars of the presidency to rank the first ladies. The poll provided respondents with a chronological list of the first ladies. Scholars were asked to assess each first lady on a five-point scale according to both an overall general impression of the first lady and specific criteria, including background, value to country, integrity, leadership, intelligence, being her own woman, accomplishments, courage, public image, and value to the president. The poll conducted in 1982 considered forty-two first ladies, including six surrogate first ladies who were nieces, sisters, or daughters of the president. Anna Harrison was included in the poll, despite the fact that her husband died after only a month in office. Based on feedback from its first poll, SRI decided not to include nonwives in its second poll.[13] The 1993 poll considered only established first ladies, defined as the president's wife.

The Watson ranking of presidential spouses is modeled on the presidential polls and loosely on the SRI first ladies poll because it employs a broad criterion for rating, ranks only spouses (and Harriet Lane), and is based on a poll of presidential scholars. This poll offers a ranking of the best and worst first ladies and a comprehensive ranking from top to bottom of all eligible first ladies. Two hundred presidential scholars (a list that includes political scientists and historians) were surveyed in 1996, eighty-seven of whom responded to the poll.[14]

Three presidential spouses died while serving in the White House: Letitia Tyler, Caroline Harrison, and Ellen Wilson. Three additional first ladies married their spouses while he was serving as president: Julia Tyler, Francis Cleveland, and Edith Wilson. Because all six of these individuals served as first lady, they were eligible for the rankings. The rankings do not include spouses who died prior to their husbands' presidencies (Martha Jefferson, Rachel Jackson, Hannah Van Buren, Ellen Arthur, and Alice Roosevelt). Anna Harrison and Lucretia Garfield were ranked, even though their spouses are sometimes not ranked in the presidential polls (both their husbands died shortly into their presidential terms). Those who married their husbands after his presidency were ineligible for ranking.

With consideration to the difficulty of rating presidential spouses, I used two separate assessment systems. The first lists the ten best and ten worst presidential spouses (one based on the first lady's average ranking scores by pollsters and scholars and the second based on the first lady's listing as successful or unsuccessful by the pollsters and scholars). The second assessment rates, from top to bottom, all the presidential spouses (based on each first lady's average score). All of these ratings are based on the rankings provided by the presidential scholars polled by the author.

Tables 7.9a and 7.9b list those first ladies the presidential scholars felt had been "especially successful." Tables 7.10a and 7.10b list those considered by the pollsters to be "unsuccessful" first ladies. The best and worst lists were calculated as follows: Tables 7.9a and 7.10a are based on the aggregate number of times a first lady was listed by the respondents as highly successful or unsuccessful. The first lady getting the most mentions in the poll is listed first, the first lady getting the second most mentions in the poll is listed second, and so forth. Tables 7.9b and 7.10b are based on the average (mean) score each first lady received (using a four-point scale).

In the Watson poll presidential scholars were asked to indicate their general impression or opinion of the first ladies. They were encouraged not to attempt to respond to a particular first lady with whom they were unfamiliar. Otherwise, this would have biased the poll. The rankings employ a four-point scale, ranging from "very favorable" to "very unfavorable." A score of 1 indicates very favorable and a score of 4 indicates very unfavorable. The SRI poll used a larger scale whereby scores closer to 100 indicated a better rating. Table 7.11 reveals the rankings by presidential scholars based on the overall arithmetic average (mean) score each first lady

Table 7.9a	**Top Ten (Most Successful) First Ladies**	**Table 7.9b**	**Top Ten First Ladies (average score)**

	Table 7.9a		Table 7.9b
1.	Eleanor Roosevelt	1.	Eleanor Roosevelt
2.	Barbara Pierce Bush	2.	Abigail Smith Adams
3.	Jacqueline Bouvier Kennedy	3.	Dolley Payne Madison
4.	Claudia "Lady Bird" Taylor Johnson	4.	Martha Dandridge Washington
5.	Rosalynn Smith Carter	5.	Elizabeth "Betty" Bloomer Ford
6.	Hillary Rodham Clinton	6.	Sarah Childress Polk
7.	Elizabeth "Betty" Bloomer Ford	7.	Julia Dent Grant
8.	Dolley Payne Madison		(tie with Harriet Lane)[a]
9.	Abigail Smith Adams	8.	Frances Folsom Cleveland
10.	Edith Bolling Galt Wilson	9.	Ellen Axson Wilson
		10.	Jacqueline Bouvier Kennedy

Source: Watson Presidential Scholar Poll, 1996–1997. Poll, 1996–1997.
Note: a. Harriet Lane was James Buchanan's niece.

Table 7.10a	**Bottom Ten (Least Successful) First Ladies**	**Table 7.10b**	**Bottom Ten First Ladies (average score)**

	Table 7.10a		Table 7.10b
1.	Mary Todd Lincoln	1.	Anna Tuthill Symmes Harrison
2.	Nancy Davis Reagan	2.	Mary Todd Lincoln
3.	Hillary Rodham Clinton	3.	Jane Means Appleton Pierce
4.	Edith Bolling Galt Wilson	4.	Florence Kling Harding
5.	Florence Kling Harding	5.	Helen Herron Taft
6.	Mamie Doud Eisenhower	6.	Nancy Davis Reagan
7.	Elizabeth "Betty" Bloomer Ford	7.	Mamie Doud Eisenhower
8.	Grace Goodhue Coolidge	8.	Ida Saxton McKinley
9.	Elizabeth "Bess" Wallace Truman	9.	Margaret Mackall Smith Taylor
10.	Rosalynn Smith Carter	10.	Letitia Christian Tyler

Source: Watson Presidential Scholar Poll, 1996–1997.

received. The Watson poll ranks on the basis of lowest to highest score, with the lower scores being the better scores. The SRI poll ranks in order of the highest to lowest score, the higher the score the better.

There is some consensus between the two polls on the best and worst first ladies. Not only did the Watson and SRI polls agree on these rankings, but the top and bottom scores were relatively far from their closest challengers. For example, at the bottom of the list Mary Lincoln appears to have little competition. The only cases marginally close to her in *both* polls were Jane Pierce, Nancy Reagan, and Florence Harding. Likewise, Eleanor

Table 7.11   Rankings of First Ladies

Watson Poll		SRI Poll	
First Lady	Score	First Lady	Score
1. Anna Eleanor Roosevelt	1.12	1. Eleanor Roosevelt	93.65
2. Abigail Smith Adams	1.34	2. Hillary Clinton	86.35
3. Dolley Payne Madison	1.40	3. Abigail Adams	83.63
4. Martha Dandridge Washington	1.52	4. Dolley Madison	77.42
5. Elizabeth "Betty" Bloomer Ford	1.52	5. Rosalynn Carter	77.38
6. Sarah Childress Polk	1.60	6. Lady Bird Johnson	77.28
7. Julia Dent Grant	1.67	7. Jackie Kennedy	74.67
8. Harriet Lane[a]	1.67	8. Barbara Bush	74.03
9. Francis Folsom Cleveland	1.75	9. Betty Ford	72.16
10. Ellen Axson Wilson	1.75	10. Edith Wilson	70.72
11. Jacqueline Bouvier Kennedy	1.88	11. Bess Truman	68.19
12. Lucretia Rudolph Garfield	2.00	12. Martha Washington	67.39
13. Abigail Powers Fillmore	2.00	13. Lou Hoover	63.90
14. Elizabeth McCardle Johnson	2.00	14. Edith Roosevelt	63.87
15. Edith Kermit Roosevelt	2.00	15. Lucy Hayes	62.82
16. Hillary Rodham Clinton	2.00	16. Louisa Adams	62.26
17. Claudia "Lady Bird" Taylor Johnson	2.01	17. Mamie Eisenhower	62.10
18. Elizabeth "Bess" Wallace Truman	2.03	18. Pat Nixon	61.78
19. Barbara Pierce Bush	2.06	19. Grace Coolidge	61.71
20. Rosalynn Smith Carter	2.08	20. Sarah Polk	61.30
21. Louisa Johnson Adams	2.20	21. Ellen Wilson	60.82
22. Lucy Webb Hayes	2.20	22. Frances Cleveland	60.35
23. Patricia Ryan Nixon	2.20	23. Elizabeth Monroe	60.13
24. Elizabeth Kortright Monroe	2.25	24. Eliza Johnson	59.98
25. Caroline Lavinia Scott Harrison	2.25	25. Helen Taft	59.94
26. Grace Goodhue Coolidge	2.27	26. Julia Grant	59.81
27. Lou Henry Hoover	2.43	27. Julia Tyler	59.36
28. Julia Gardiner Tyler	2.50	28. Lucretia Garfield	59.25
29. Edith Bolling Galt Wilson	2.50	29. Caroline Harrison	59.12
30. Letitia Christian Tyler	2.60	30. Letitia Tyler	58.62
31. Margaret Mackall Smith Taylor	2.66	31. Abigail Fillmore	58.62
32. Ida Saxton McKinley	2.80	32. Ida McKinley	58.53
33. Mamie Doud Eisenhower	2.82	33. Margaret Taylor	58.32
34. Nancy Davis Reagan	2.90	34. Jane Pierce	58.22
35. Helen Herron Taft	2.91	35. Florence Harding	55.15
36. Florence Kling Harding	3.06	36. Nancy Reagan	53.07
37. Jane Means Appleton Pierce	3.33	37. Mary Lincoln	52.62
38. Mary Todd Lincoln	3.45		
39. Anna Tuthill Symmes Harrison	3.60		

a. Harriet Lane was President Buchanan's niece.

Roosevelt was also rated far better than any other first lady, with only Abigail Adams and Dolley Madison even somewhat close in both polls.

These are both similarities and differences between the findings of these polls. When the first ladies are placed in three categories for comparison—(1) best/top; (2) average; and (3) worst/bottom (with the top and bottom twelve accounting for best and worst, respectively, and the rest of the first ladies considered average)—there are many similarities between the two polls. For instance, both polls ranked as the top first ladies Eleanor Roosevelt, Abigail Adams, Dolley Madison, Jackie Kennedy, Betty Ford, Hillary Clinton, and Martha Washington. Those ranked as average in both polls included Lucy Hayes, Louisa Adams, Pat Nixon, Bess Truman, Lou Hoover, Grace Coolidge, Edith Roosevelt, and Elizabeth Monroe. Both polls also included many of the same first ladies at the bottom: Mary Lincoln, Ida McKinley, Margaret Taylor, Jane Pierce, Florence Harding, and Nancy Reagan.

The notable differences between the two polls include Sarah Polk (6th in Watson, 20th in SRI); Julia Grant (7th in Watson, 26th in SRI); Frances Cleveland (9th in Watson, 22nd in SRI); Ellen Wilson (9th in Watson, 21st in SRI); Mamie Eisenhower (33rd in Watson, 17th in SRI); Edith Wilson (28th in Watson, 10th in SRI); and Rosalynn Carter (20th in Watson, 5th in SRI). The differences could point to a lack of knowledge of the first ladies by presidential scholars, something to which several scholars admitted when responding to the Watson poll. Yet there are enough similarities between the polls to validate their results and to provide a foundation for formalizing theory about the presidential spouses.

Building a Body of Theory: Hypotheses About the First Ladies

Using the Watson poll and SRI rankings, it is possible to test three hypotheses about the first ladies. Each hypothesis will advance theory that permits us a more systematic examination of the office. The following areas of research will be explored: (1) a comparison of the rankings of first ladies from different historical periods, in which I hypothesize that first ladies serving since 1933 and the early first ladies are ranked better than the first ladies serving in the period between the 1830s and 1932 (the top spots in the presidential polls are also filled largely by post-1933 presidents and early presidents such as Washington and Jefferson); (2) a comparison of the rankings of highly active, progressive first ladies with those of inactive, traditional first ladies, in which I hypothesize that traditional first ladies are ranked better than progressive first ladies (the latter group has been highly criticized and some presidential historians have maintained that an activist approach has been rejected by the public); and (3) a comparison between the rankings of presidential spouses and presidents, in which I hypothesize that the spousal rankings will approximate or mirror their respective husbands' ranking (a result that might indicate the existence of a partnership in the White House).

Modern Versus Early Spouses

For the purpose of analysis, it is helpful to categorize the presidential spouses historically into three groups: (1) early first ladies (1789–1833); (2) the middle years (1833–1933); and (3) modern spouses (1933–present). Such groupings will permit the testing of the first hypothesis. To measure the spousal and presidential rankings, both the Watson and SRI polls are used and the rankings of first ladies are categorized into three groups: (1) "best/top"; (2) average; and (3) "worst/bottom."

Among these categories, there appears to be both admiration for and animosity toward modern presidential spouses. The top ten first ladies from Table 7.9a, for example, are dominated by those spouses who have served since 1933. The list includes First Ladies Eleanor Roosevelt, Bush, Kennedy, Johnson, Carter, Clinton, and Ford, who were ranked one through seven, respectively. The top ten rankings in Table 7.9b also included Eleanor Roosevelt, Betty Ford, and Jackie Kennedy, but such early first ladies as Abigail Adams and Dolley Madison were also ranked highly. Interestingly, the bottom ten category (Table 7.10a) was also dominated by individuals from the post-1933 era: First Ladies Reagan, Clinton, Eisenhower, Ford, Truman, and Carter. The bottom ten rankings in Table 7.10b also included modern first ladies like Nancy Reagan and Mamie Eisenhower but was dominated by those in the "middle years," such as First Ladies Lincoln, Pierce, Harding, Taft, McKinley, and Taylor. Interestingly, First Ladies Hillary Clinton, Rosalynn Carter, and Betty Ford appeared in both the successful and unsuccessful lists, perhaps a sign of the controversial roles assumed by these presidential spouses and the widespread disagreement over the proper role for the first lady. However, such findings could simply reflect the poll respondents' increased familiarity with and focus on recent first ladies or their lack of knowledge of the first ladies.

The top-to-bottom ranking in Table 7.11 reveals mixed findings, with modern presidential spouses scoring throughout the rankings. It appears, however, that the top spots on the list are dominated by modern and early presidential spouses, whereas those of the middle years tended to be scored as either average or at the bottom of the list. This finding supports the hypothesis. However, recent first ladies like Nancy Reagan, Mamie Eisenhower, and Pat Nixon were ranked within the bottom 15 spots on the list.

The average (mean) group score for each of the three historical periods allows a comparison of the rankings by period. Table 7.12 shows the group averages for both the Watson and SRI polls. Early first ladies led the Watson poll with a high group average of 1.74, the modern first ladies came in second, and the middle group fared the worst, with an average score of 2.38. The SRI poll also rated the middle group lowest, with an average

Table 7.12   Average Scores of First Ladies by Period

Table 7.12   Average Scores of First Ladies by Period

	Watson Poll	SRI Poll
Early first ladies (1789–1833)	1.74	70.17
Middle years (1833–1933)	2.38	60.15
Modern spouses (1933–present)	2.06	72.79
Pre-twentieth century	2.17	61.99
Twentieth century	2.19	68.71

Note: Low rankings on the Watson poll indicate the best scores. High rankings on the SRI poll indicate the best scores.

score of 60.15, but the modern spouses had the highest group average and the early spouses came in second. It also benefits the analysis of historic periods to compare the ratings of twentieth-century first ladies with pre-twentieth-century first ladies. Whereas the Watson poll shows near even group averages between the twentieth- and pre-twentieth-century first ladies, the SRI poll reveals a higher rating for those serving in the twentieth century. Both polls support the hypothesis that early and recent first ladies are rated better than those serving in the interim period. It is possible to reject the null hypothesis that there is no relationship between the rating of first ladies and the period in time in which they served.

Active Versus Nonactive Spouses

It is difficult to assess activism and what constitutes a partnership approach to the first ladyship. For example, several spouses were quite active but through a traditional role of hostessing and serving as the president's confidante. The concept of activism is relative; the role of the presidential spouse has evolved as societal attitudes toward women have evolved. Because many presidential spouses can be classified as presidential partners, functioning as influential, activist first ladies, it might be more accurate to classify first ladies as either political or presidential partners or non-partners.[15] Some presidential spouses have wielded political influence both publicly and privately in their husbands' presidencies and political careers. Others were highly influential in social, public, and career matters without being overtly political. Thus those spouses functioning as presidential partners, as defined by influence, will be considered active or partner first ladies.

In determining what constitutes this category, one must consider the relativity of history and norms functioning to limit any political or public activism or influence by women in an earlier day and age. The list in Table 7.13 represents the author's rating of presidential spouses who are among the most influential, powerful, and active first ladies, both publicly and privately, and can be considered the best examples of a political or presidential partner first lady. Despite the difficulty of categorizing first ladies by activism in the office, a model for doing so is offered by O'Connor, Nye, and Van Assendelft, who consider such factors as the first ladies' role in writing speeches, traveling on behalf of the president, and acting as a policy advocate or adviser.[16] According to this study, participation in such activities constitutes political activism. This model was used in compiling the list in Table 7.13. In addition to the list of active/partner first ladies, Table 7.13 offers the first lady's average score on the 1–4 rating scale in the Watson poll as well as her rank in the Watson poll. This allows one to examine whether active/partner first ladies were popular or successful.

Table 7.13   The Most Active Spouses/Presidential Partners (rating score and rank)

Abigail Smith Adams (1.34, 2nd)	Anna Eleanor Roosevelt (1.12, 1st)
Dolley Payne Madison (1.40, 3rd)	Claudia "Lady Bird" Taylor Johnson (2.01, 17th)
Sarah Childress Polk (1.60, 6th)	
Helen Herron Taft (2.91, 35th)	Elizabeth "Betty" Bloomer Ford (1.52, 4th)
Ellen Axson Wilson (1.75, 9th)	
Edith Bolling Galt Wilson (2.50, 28th)	Rosalynn Smith Carter (2.08, 20th)
	Nancy Davis Reagan (2.90, 34th)
Florence Kling Harding (3.06, 36th)	Hillary Rodham Clinton (2.00, 12th)
Lou Henry Hoover (2.43, 27th)	

Note: First ladies are listed in chronological order. Score of 1 is the highest ranking.

With the exception of Martha Washington (tied for number four), the top six spots in the Watson ranking were all those who could be classified as activist/partners (Eleanor Roosevelt, Abigail Adams, Dolley Madison, Betty Ford, and Sarah Polk). However, three of the bottom six presidential spouses were also activist/partners (Florence Harding, Helen Taft, and Nancy Reagan). (The SRI poll findings are similar.) The average score for presidential spouses identified as activist/partners in the Watson poll is 2.04. Those not classified as such averaged 2.26 as a group. (The SRI poll again revealed similar findings.) (The activist/partner group averaged 70.9

a group, spouses functioning in an active capacity or as partners have tended to score better than inactive nonpartners or traditional spouses. There is also some evidence to suggest that activist/partner first ladies tend to rate very well or very poorly in the polls. These ratings signal that there may be some risks involved with such approaches to the office or that society and scholars are still uncertain about presidential spouses functioning in this capacity.

Yet these presidential partners on average are ranked quite positively (see Table 7.14), better than both the twentieth-century and pre-twentieth-century first lady group averages (see Table 7.12). This finding is interesting given the often brutal public, political, and media criticism that active or nontraditional first ladies have received.[17] Moreover, some recent scholarship has been highly critical of active first ladies and has suggested that the public has rejected the notion of presidential couples or partners.[18] Perhaps the public has rejected such first ladies, but those ranking the first ladies apparently have not. The findings in both polls fail to support the hypothesis that traditional or nonpartner first ladies would have the best ratings.

Table 7.14   Partners Versus Nonpartners (average scores)

	Watson Poll	SRI Poll
Partners	2.04	70.9
Nonpartners	2.26	61.8

Note: Low scores on the Watson poll indicate the best scores. High scores on the SRI poll indicate the best scores.

President Versus Spouse Rankings

The Murray study (1982) is among the most comprehensive of the presidential rankings. Professor Robert K. Murray, a professor of history at Pennsylvania State University, administered a seventeen-page, 155-question poll to 953 scholars. The Siena Research Institute presidential poll (1994) also provides one of the most comprehensive studies of presidential rankings.[19] Both polls provide a basis for comparing the rankings of presidents with the rankings of the presidential spouses. Table 7.15 lists the results of the presidential polls along with the corresponding rank of the president's spouse from the Watson and SRI polls.

The comparison reveals what may be a slight relationship between presidential and presidential spouse rankings. By placing the presidents and first ladies into three roughly numerically even categories—the best/top

Table 7.15   Rankings of Presidents and Presidential Spouses

Presidents	Presidential Spouses		Presidents	Presidential Spouses	
SRI Poll (1994)	Watson Poll (1997)	SRI Poll (1993)	Murray Poll (1982)	Watson Poll (1997)	SRI Poll (1993)
1. F. Roosevelt 1	1		1. Lincoln	38	37
2. Lincoln 38	37		2. F. Roosevelt	1	1
3. T. Roosevelt 12	14		3. Washington	4	12
4. Washington 4	12		4. Jefferson	N/A	N/A
5. Jefferson N/A	N/A		5. T. Roosevelt	12	14
6. Wilson 9, 28	21, 10		6. Wilson	9, 28	21, 10
7. Truman 18	11		7. Jackson	N/A	N/A
8. Eisenhower 33	17		8. Truman	18	11
9. Madison 3	4		9. J. Adams	2	3
10. Kennedy 11	7		10. L. Johnson	17	6
11. Jackson N/A	N/A		11. Eisenhower	33	17
12. J. Adams 2	3		12. Polk	6	20
13. L. Johnson 17	6		13. Kennedy	11	7
14. Polk 6	20		14. Madison	3	4
15. Monroe 24	23		15. Monroe	24	23
16. Clinton 12	2		16. J. Q. Adams	21	16
17. J. Q. Adams 21	16		17. Cleveland	9	22
18. McKinley 32	32		18. McKinley	32	32
19. Cleveland 9	22		19. Taft	33	25
20. Reagan 34	36		20. Van Buren	N/A	N/A
21. Taft 35	25		21. Hoover	27	13
22. Van Buren N/A	N/A		22. Hayes	21	15
23. Nixon 21	18		23. Arthur	N/A	N/A
24. Hayes 21	18		24. Ford	4	9
25. Carter 20	5		25. Carter	20	5
26. Garfield 12	N/A		26. B. Harrison	24	29
27. Arthur N/A	N/A		27. Taylor	39	33
28. W. H. Harrison 39	N/A		28. Tyler	30, 28	27, 31
29. Hoover 27	13		29. Fillmore	12	31
30. B. Harrison 24	29		30. Coolidge	26	19
31. Bush 19	8		31. Pierce	37	34
32. Ford 4	9		32. A. Johnson	12	24
33. Taylor 29	33		33. Buchanan	(7)	N/A
34. Tyler 30, 28	27, 30		34. Nixon	20	18
35. Fillmore 12	30		35. Grant	7	26
36. Coolidge 26	19		36. Harding	36	35
37. Pierce 37	34				
38. Grant 7	26				
39. Buchanan (7)	N/A				
40. A. Johnson 12	24				
41. Harding 36	35				

Sources: Watson Presidential Scholar Poll, 1996–1997; Siena Research Institute Poll, 1994.

Note: The Watson poll includes several ties. Harriet Lane was not ranked in the SRI poll but was listed in parentheses in the Watson poll. The Murray poll did not include presidents serving after 1981.

group, the average or middle group, and the worst/bottom group—it is possible to determine how many of the couples appear in the same category within their respective polls. This tests the hypothesis that presidential couples will be ranked similarly.

A comparison between the Watson poll of first ladies and the SRI presidential poll shows that nineteen of the presidential couples appeared in the same category in their respective polls and twenty did not. This represents a near even split between presidential couples who were similarly ranked and presidential couples who were not ranked similarly. However, four of the couples appearing in different categories were only one rank away from appearing in the same category, and one of the couples appearing in different categories was not a true presidential couple: President Buchanan and his niece Harriet Lane. Using the same categories (top, middle, and bottom), a comparison of the Watson first lady poll with the Murray presidential poll reveals that fifteen of the presidential couples appeared in the same categories and nineteen did not. Three couples that appeared in different categories were only one rank away from appearing in the same category. This near-even split is similar to that found between the Watson first ladies poll and the SRI presidential poll. A comparison of the SRI first lady poll and the Murray presidential poll found nineteen couples ranked in the same category and fourteen in different categories. Slightly more spouses were ranked similarly in this near even split, yet three spouses who were ranked in different categories were only one rank away from being in the same category. The final comparison, the SRI first lady poll and the SRI presidential poll, provided the strongest support for the hypothesis: twenty-three presidents and first ladies were ranked in the same categories and only thirteen appeared in different categories. See Table 7.16 for a summary of these comparisons.

In the polls, several of the presidential spouses were almost identically ranked. In the Watson first lady and Murray presidential polls, for example, the members of three presidential couples were ranked within only one to

Table 7.16   Comparing Presidents' and First Ladies' Rankings

Polls	Similar Rank	Different Rank
SRI PRES and Watson FL	19	20
Murray PRES and Watson FL	15	19
Murray PRES and SRI FL	19	14
SRI PRES and SRI FL	23	13

Note: PRES indicates presidential poll. FL indicates first lady poll. The different totals occur because each of the four polls contained a different number of first ladies and presidents under study.

three spots of each other at the top of the lists: Franklin and Eleanor Roosevelt (2nd, 1st); George and Martha Washington (3rd, 4th); and Woodrow Wilson and his first wife, Ellen (6th, 9th). John and Abigail Adams were only seven spots apart (9th and 2nd). Some husbands and wives ranked only a few positions apart from one another in the middle of the respective lists: John and Jackie Kennedy (13th, 11th); John Quincy and Louisa Adams (16th, 21st); Jimmy and Rosalynn Carter (25th, 20th); and Rutherford and Lucy Hayes (22nd, 21st). Other presidents and first ladies were similarly ranked but appeared near the bottom of the rankings: Benjamin and Caroline Harrison (26th, 24th); John Tyler and his first wife, Letitia (28th, 30th), and his second wife, Julia (28th); Calvin and Grace Coolidge (30th, 26th); Franklin and Jane Pierce (31st and 37th); and Warren and Florence Harding (36th, 36th). In contrast, the Lincolns were on opposite ends of their respective polls, Abe at the top (1st), Mary at the bottom (38th). Ulysses Grant was second from bottom (35th), whereas his wife, Julia, ranked seventh. And despite Woodrow Wilson's sixth-place ranking, his second wife Edith's ranking was twenty-eighth.

Further support for the hypothesis comes from calculating the average ranking scores of first ladies grouped according to their husbands' rank. For instance, the spouses of the top ten presidents had an average ranking themselves of 13.5 in the Watson first lady poll (SRI poll: 12.7 average ranking). Spouses of those presidents ranked in the middle group averaged 18.3 in rank in the Watson first lady poll (SRI poll: 16.9 ranking). The bottom ten presidents had spouses who averaged a ranking of 21.0 in the Watson poll (SRI poll: 27.8 ranking). Both first lady polls therefore offer similar averages for the ranking of first ladies when they are grouped according to their husbands' rankings.

Thus there may be some association between a president's success and his spouse's success, or perhaps vice versa. Both the Watson and SRI first lady polls reveal that almost one-half of the presidential couples were ranked similarly to their spouses. If the office is truly a partnership or copresidency, it would stand to reason that the president and the first lady ranked similarly in so many examples. This research question should be further examined.

Notes

1. A. B. Murphy, "Evaluating Presidents," 1985; J. P. Pfiffner, *The Modern Presidency,* 1993.

2. C. S. Anthony, *Saga,* 1990 and 1991; B. B. Caroli, *First Ladies,* 1987; E. Mayo, "The Influence," 1993.

3. P. F. Boller Jr., *Presidential Wives,* 1988.

4. K. O'Connor, B. Nye, and L. Van Assendelft, "Wives in the White House," 1997.

5. I conducted a poll of women in public life in 1995. Two hundred women were randomly selected and surveyed. The sample included women in senior positions in the Clinton administration, women serving in either the U.S. House or Senate, female federal judges, female governors and the wives of married, male governors, and women listed in the *Washingtonian* magazine's list of the most powerful political women in the District of Columbia. A variety of questions were included in the poll, including the respondents' views on several issues pertaining to the first ladies, and whom they considered successful and unsuccessful first ladies; the respondents were asked to rank all the first ladies.

6. A. Schlesinger Sr., "The U.S. Presidents," 1948; A. Schlesinger Sr., "Our Presidents," 1962.

7. G. Maranell and R. Dodder, "Political Orientation," 1970.

8. R. E. DiClerico, *The American President,* 1979.

9. *US News and World Report,* 1982.

10. R. K. Murray, "The Murray Poll," 1983.

11. The poll appeared in the July 1980 issue of the magazine (p. 120).

12. The Siena Research Institute is centered at Siena College in the state of New York. The institute has conducted both presidential and first lady polls.

13. SRI was kind enough to provide me with information on the poll, including a press release.

14. The questionnaire was mailed to a random list of current members of the American Political Science Association (APSA), the nation's leading academic organization in the field of political science. These members were either part of APSA's "presidency research" section or listed in APSA's directory as having the presidency as their area of specialization. The questionnaire offered respondents a list of first ladies and asked them to identify which first ladies they felt had been "especially successful" and those they believed were "unsuccessful." Using a four-point Likert scale ranging from "very favorable" to "very unfavorable," presidential scholars also indicated their general impressions or opinions of the first ladies. If the scholar was unfamiliar with a particular first lady, he or she had the option of not rating the person in question.

15. C. S. Anthony, "First Ladylike," 1993; C. S. Anthony, "The First Ladies," 1992; Anthony, 1991 and 1990; Caroli, 1987; B. H. Winfield, "Madame President," 1994.

16. O'Connor, Nye, and Van Assendelft, 1997.

17. J. S. Rosebush, *First Lady, Public Wife,* 1987; B. A. Weisberger, "Petticoat Government," 1993.

18. G. Troy, *Affairs of State,* 1997.

19. D. A. Lonnstrom and T. O. Kelly II, "Rating the Presidents," 1997.

8

The Future of the Office

> *The president's spouse has the potential to become an important component of the contemporary presidency.*
>
> —George C. Edwards and Stephen J. Wayne,
> *Presidential Leadership: Politics and Policymaking*

Barbara Bush's selection as the graduation speaker at Wellesley College brought a considerable amount of criticism from some of the graduating seniors at the prestigious women's college. Roughly 150 of the 600 members of the graduating class signed petitions protesting Mrs. Bush's selection on the grounds that she had never had a career of her own and had failed to distinguish herself in a capacity beyond being merely the wife of George Bush. The first lady went forward with her speech on June 1, 1990, and addressed these issues by sharing with the students the important lessons she had learned in life, emphasizing the value of being a wife and mother, and discussing her rich experiences as first lady. She closed her speech with what became a popular quote: "And who knows? Somewhere out in this audience may even be someone who will one day follow in my footsteps, and preside over the White House as the President's spouse. I wish him well!"[1]

What's in a Name?

Mrs. Bush's closing comment not only is entertaining but will likely prove true one day in the not too distant future. It is inevitable that the United States will one day elect a heterosexual, married woman as president, an event that will forever change the office of the first lady. There have been many instances in the country's history when an extraordinary event or the service of a particular presidential spouse occasioned a fundamental change in the office. The outbreak of the Civil War and the advent of televised coverage of politics, for example, influenced both the office of the president and the office of the first lady. The first ladyships of Dolley Madison and Eleanor Roosevelt also greatly shaped the evolution and nature of the office. The election of a married female to the presidency will mark another major change in the office. At that time, the nation will be forced to reconsider the duties, roles, and responsibilities of the first lady because the office has historically been defined in a feminine capacity. The only such precedent in the United States has been the election of a woman governor. In such cases, the governor's husband has not been expected to perform the types of duties expected of wives of male governors.[2] The prospect of a female president offers insights into the gendered component of the first ladyship, because many of the rules governing the office would change dramatically.

Former first lady Rosalynn Carter predicted that there will be a woman president and that this occurrence will force the nation to discuss her husband's role.[3] President Gerald Ford and other former residents of the White House echoed this prediction. It is likely that many of the first lady's primary duties, most notably that of serving as the nation's social hostess, would not be a central part of the duties of the first male occupant of the office. Relatedly, it is doubtful that society would pay attention to his wardrobe, changes in his hairstyle, or the advice he gives to the president. It is unclear what the male spouse of a female president would be required to do. Would he be expected to serve as social host for White House teas and receptions? To stand in reception lines greeting guests? To help plan the menu, entertainment, and seating arrangements for state dinners? The strict taboo against a first lady holding outside employment while in the White House would probably be abandoned for the "first gentleman." However, conflict of interest concerns would still prevail regarding the nature of any employment and income outside the White House. There are already signs that this taboo may be weakening. During the 1996 presidential campaign, Elizabeth Dole, the wife of Republican nominee Bob Dole, stated that she would consider retaining her position as head of the American Red Cross even if her husband were elected.

It appears inevitable that a man will one day occupy the office of presidential spouse. Of that occurrence Barbara Bush observed: "When a woman President is elected, her husband will be afforded the same luxury that former First Ladies were allowed—to define his own role." Mrs. Bush further noted: "When there is a male spouse serving in that occupancy, perhaps we can allow him to choose the title he prefers."[4]

Perhaps feminist author Germaine Greer best captures the nature of the issue in her criticism of the first ladyship: "No woman anywhere should be expected to relinquish her privacy and her own work, to diet and dress up and give interviews every day, simply because she has married a man who has a prospect of success in politics."[5] The same might be said of a male spouse of a female president.

The issue of a female president also raises the question of the appropriate title for her spouse. Clearly, the title *First Lady,* which hints at royalty and sexism and has itself been the topic of criticism, is not suitable. Abandoning the title would not be unprecedented. First ladies such as Jackie Kennedy and Rosalynn Carter requested to be addressed not as *First Lady,* but as "Mrs. Kennedy" and "Rosalynn," respectively. Moreover, the title was not used during the service of the first presidential spouses. Martha Washington was known as "Lady Washington" and subsequent spouses were referred to as "Presidentress" or simply "Mrs." When the president's spouse was either not living or incapable of fulfilling the social duties equated with the office, the proxy hostesses who served on her behalf were known as "Lady of the White House" or "Mistress of the White House." The title *First Lady* was thus not used in the original office and has changed over the history of the office (nor is it mandated by law or discussed in the Constitution). I have already suggested that the title *Presidential Spouse* be adopted for the future, but there are a variety of other possible titles, including *First Spouse* or, if a precise translation of the present title is considered, *First Man* or *First Gentleman.* Or the male spouse could simply be known as "Mr." Regardless of the title, it is safe to say that with the advent of the modern duties of the first lady, the political nature of the office, and the prospect of a man in the office, the end is near for a presidential spouse's service primarily as the nation's homemaker-in-chief.

Life After the White House

Yes, there is life after the White House. Many first ladies have lived long, productive lives after their service. In fact, a total of twenty-three of the first thirty-six first ladies outlived their husbands. Bess Truman lived until the age of ninety-seven, making her the longest-lived first lady. Bess also outlived her husband by many years. Some first ladies, such as Francis Cleveland and Jackie Kennedy, have even remarried and in so doing certainly moved beyond the White House phase of their lives. First Lady Sarah Polk never remarried, despite the fact that her husband died only three months after leaving the White House. In fact, Mrs. Polk wore black for the rest of her life, which was to last more than four decades after leaving the White House, and devoted herself to the memory of her husband, organizing his official papers, opening their home in Tennessee to political guests eager to share in his legacy, and turning the Polk home into a museum, even leaving the former president's study untouched and in the state that the president had last left it. She also continued her interest in politics. The former first lady met with leaders of both the North and the South prior to and during the Civil War but remained neutral on the subject. One of Sarah Polk's few interests outside of her husband's memory was a family-owned cotton plantation in Mississippi that she continued to manage from her home in Tennessee.

Several former first ladies returned as guests at the White House, the Capitol, and at the capital city's social events. Dolley Madison was warmly welcomed back to the Capitol and had a special seat of honor reserved for her in the congressional chamber. She remained a fixture in the nation's capital during the last years of her life. Four decades after her first lady-ship, Edith Wilson participated in President John F. Kennedy's 1961 inaugural. Frances Cleveland was also invited to political events in the capital city and continued her involvement in politics years after the death of her husband.

Frances Cleveland is unique among first ladies in that her first ladyship spanned two nonconsecutive presidential terms. After her husband's first term (1885–1889), the president was defeated in his bid for a second term by Benjamin Harrison. On leaving the White House, Frances told the White House staff to do its best to leave things pretty much as they were because she vowed that she and her husband would be back in another four years. Her vow proved prophetic: Grover Cleveland was elected to a second term four years later. Mrs. Cleveland remained active after this second term as first lady. She also served as a trustee of Wells College, her alma mater, for over fifty years and headed the school's endowment fund in 1922. Frances continued her political involvement by campaigning for Al Smith, the Democratic candidate for president in 1928, and her social activism by heading the Needlework Guild of America. Five years after her husband's death, in 1913, Frances remarried, this time to Thomas J. Preston Jr., a professor of archaeology.

Helen Taft is another first lady who continued her activism in politics after the White House. After Howard Taft's term as president, he began serving on the Supreme Court, the only president to do so, and Helen returned to monitoring political events in the capital and her old political projects, although she was slowed a bit due to poor health. Edith Roosevelt, wife of Teddy Roosevelt, opposed the presidential candidacy of her husband's distant cousin Franklin D. Roosevelt and campaigned against him by posing for photographs with his opponent and the opponent's wife. Lady Bird Johnson has enjoyed a productive retirement by becoming a member of the board of the National Geographic Society, campaigning for her son-in-law Charles Robb during his successful bids for governor and senator of Virginia, continuing her efforts toward conservation and beautification, and founding and heading the National Wildflower Research Center. For her long career in public service, Lady Bird Johnson was awarded the Congressional Gold Medal in 1988.

Eleanor Roosevelt remained perhaps the most politically active first lady after the White House. Indeed, many of her greatest accomplishments were achieved after her husband's death in 1945. She was appointed by President Harry Truman as part of the U.S. delegation to the UN, where she was instrumental in helping to draft the Universal Declaration of Human Rights. Eleanor was also active in Democratic Party politics and was a founder of the well-respected liberal organization Americans for Democratic Action.

Other former first ladies seem to have had enough of the limelight and political life. Jackie Kennedy avoided politics, Washington, D.C., and the paparazzi that denied her a private life. Her second marriage was to the Greek multimillionaire Aristotle Onassis, and during her marriage the former first lady split her time between New York City, Greece, and Paris. After Onassis's death, Jackie moved to New York City, became an editor for Viking Press, and later became an associate editor for Doubleday, one of the largest publishing houses in the country. In general, the former first lady took great efforts to avoid politics and recapture her private life: She did not participate in most of the commemorative anniversaries and ceremonies marking her husband's life and death; she declined interviews and wrote no memoirs. Jackie did, however, serve on the board of the American Ballet Theater and personally selected the famous architect I. M. Pei to design the John F. Kennedy Presidential Library.

First ladies have also accepted new challenges and overcome personal troubles. Lucretia Garfield recovered from her husband's assassination by throwing herself into new challenges and hobbies. After returning to her home in Ohio, the former first lady began writing poetry, continued to read prolifically, overcame her shyness by speaking to women's organizations, and translated the writings of the famous French author Victor Hugo. Pat Nixon survived a stroke in 1976, shortly after leaving the White House, and remained somewhat reclusive and private. Betty Ford overcame a personal addiction to drugs and alcohol in 1978, also shortly after leaving the White House, and went on to help establish the Betty Ford Center in Rancho Mirage, California, an organization dedicated to drug and alcohol rehabilitation. Mrs. Ford devoted herself to raising money and awareness for several worthy causes, including the fight against arthritis and cancer, medical conditions from which she personally suffered. Numerous first ladies traveled extensively after their White House years. Julia Grant and Mary Lincoln took trips to Europe; Helen Taft traveled within the hemisphere to Bermuda and Panama.

Several first ladies went on to write books and their memoirs, and recent first ladies become regulars on the college commencement speaker circuit. Eleanor Roosevelt wrote prolifically from the time she left the White House in 1945 to her death in 1962, publishing several books and magazine articles, and continuing the syndicated newspaper column she started as first lady. Betty Ford published two books, including her memoirs, *The Times of My Life;* Barbara Bush wrote her autobiography, *Barbara Bush: A Memoir;* and Edith Roosevelt penned two books: *Cleared for Strange Ports,* a travel book, and *American Backlogs,* a family history. Lady Bird Johnson published *A White House Diary* and coauthored the book *Wildflowers Across America.* Helen Taft wrote *Recollections of Full Years,* Edith Wilson wrote *My Memoir,* and Rosalynn Carter wrote her memoirs, *First Lady From Plains,* and with her husband coauthored a book on the merits of volunteerism and healthy, spiritual living. Mrs. Carter has also continued her efforts on behalf of mental health awareness and on behalf of the disadvantaged through her work for Habitat for Humanity. In 1988 Mrs. Carter organized a conference devoted to "Women and the Constitution" and several symposia on mental health. She was selected to serve on the boards of top corporations such as the Gannett Corporation, publisher of *USA Today.*

First ladies have demonstrated their commitment to public service, their leadership in the causes they advocated while serving as first lady, and their service to the nation by continuing their activism in their post–White House years. To be sure, many first ladies remained popular and visible figures throughout their lives, distinguishing themselves by a lifetime of public service.

The President's Spouse and Scholarship

The Future of Presidential Spouse Scholarship

The future of scholarship on the president's spouse looks promising. Academic and popular interest in the first ladies began to develop in the mid to late 1980s, in part because of the controversy surrounding Nancy Reagan. Other factors served to fuel scholarly interest in the first ladies around this time. Television specials about Nancy Reagan and the first ladies were produced, conferences were convened focusing on the first ladyship, and the increased availability of White House social files and the first ladies' personal papers in presidential libraries expanded interest in the office. By the late 1980s, groundbreaking books, such as Betty Boyd Caroli's *First Ladies* (1987) and Myra G. Gutin's *The President's Partner: The First Lady in the Twentieth Century* (1989), had been published and marked the beginning of serious scholarly study of the first lady. Other books, including James S. Rosebush's *First Lady, Public Wife: A Behind-*

the-Scenes History of the Evolving Role of First Ladies in American Political Life (1987) and Paul F. Boller Jr.'s *Presidential Wives: An Anecdotal History* (1988), contributed to this expanding literature base. By the close of the decade of the 1980s, a field of scholarship was beginning to take form.

During the 1990s, the field of study moved slightly closer to gaining acceptance and credibility in the academic community generally and, more specifically, among presidential historians and political scientists. Expanding on the works of Caroli and Gutin, Carl S. Anthony's two-volume *First Ladies: The Saga of the President's Wives and Their Power* (1990 and 1991) and Lewis L. Gould's *American First Ladies: Their Lives and Their Legacy* (1996) offered the field a comprehensive reference account of the first ladies. By the close of the decade, scholarly journals had begun to include articles on the first lady, and academic conferences addressed the subject through panels and papers devoted to the first lady. The state of the first ladyship at the turn of the century and the state of scholarship on the topic are the theme for an entire issue of *Social Science Journal*. Other important books have been written, including Margaret Truman's *First Ladies: An Intimate Group Portrait of White House Wives* (1996) and Gil Troy's *Affairs of State: The Rise and Rejection of the Presidential Couple Since World War II* (1997), both of which enjoyed wide readership among academic and commercial audiences.

Recent research has changed the way we think about the first lady. The office of the first lady is now a widely recognized institution in the White House and the U.S. political system. But the first lady remains the "unknown institution" in U.S. politics, not in terms of who she is—the first lady is popular and influential—but in terms of her office and the roles and responsibilities associated with it. This situation is rapidly changing; scholars have begun to examine such questions and pollsters and political reporters have made Hillary Clinton's activities and power a regular topic for the evening news and op-ed pages of the country's leading newspapers.

Recent scholarship has also revealed that many first ladies have had considerable influence on their husbands' careers and presidencies. It is no longer a bold statement to suggest that the office of the first lady has shaped the course of U.S. history. Likewise, a new view of the first lady as an activist political partner is beginning to emerge as we recognize the power that has been operating behind the throne of the U.S. presidency. Such awareness is certain to influence the way the public sees the president's spouse, the nature of future first ladyships, and, quite possibly, the role a spouse plays in determining the electorate's vote in future presidential elections. In the words of Bill and Hillary Clinton, voters may recognize that they are in fact getting "two for the price of one." This awareness will also influence the direction of presidential scholarship; the field will be forced to consider the first lady in studies of presidential character, decisionmaking, power, the history and development of the office, and the existence of a plural presidency.

As a subject worthy of scholarly consideration, the first lady is moving close to acceptance. However, the field still suffers from a lack of formalization. In particular it needs further development and testing of theories and models; a more systematic approach to the study of the first lady; a better understanding of the institution or office (its roles, political contributions, and the public expectations of the first lady); the incorporation of first lady studies into the mainstream field of presidential scholarship; and the incorporation of the subject into the academic curriculum, especially in political science and U.S. history.

In addition to these important considerations, future study of the first ladyship must consider the gendered component of the office and the prospects of a male "first spouse." Assumptions made about a female spouse's roles and responsibilities and those of a male spouse will provide insights on the nature of gender and politics and the status of women in U.S. society. Also, first lady scholarship should be inter- and cross-disciplinary, encompassing not only presidential scholarship and political science but history and women's studies as well.

Comparative studies of the international experiences of the spouses of political leaders would further contribute to our understanding of how different cultures treat powerful or public women. Comparative studies of the different historical experiences of first ladies would shed light onto the evolution of the status of women in different times and eras. A greater appreciation of the challenges faced by first ladies and their numerous contributions to their husbands' careers, the institution of the presidency, and the country would result from the formal, systematic study of the U.S. first ladies, and a more accurate assessment of the institution of the presidency and the history of women in the United States would emerge.

Scholarly study of the first ladies should find a receptive audience. The topic offers a fascinating way to study presidential politics, provides insights into presidential decisionmaking and character, and, more generally, examines the role and status of women in U.S. history. In response to the aforementioned issues surrounding first lady scholarship, I have attempted to offer various theoretical and conceptual models for studying the first lady. I have also made a call to advance the state of scholarship on the first lady in the twenty-first century.

The Classroom and Curriculum

Irrespective of the recent advent of a field of study of the first ladies, the fact remains that most popular textbooks on the presidency, U.S. politics,

U.S. history, and social studies rarely even mention the first lady. Likewise, the topic is omitted from the primary, secondary, and higher education curricula. It is time that teachers begin to incorporate the first lady into the classroom. More resources will be developed to assist teachers as the field matures as an academic discipline. Already, there are teacher-training conferences devoted to the subject, such as the summer program in American studies sponsored by the Louisiana State University at Shreveport,[6] and more programs like this need to be developed. The education journal *Social Studies* has also published an article for educators on the first ladies.[7] More educational journals must follow suit.

It appears that the first lady is not being discussed in the classrooms of primary, secondary, and higher education because most textbooks on history, civics, U.S. politics, and the presidency rarely mention her. Even a casual perusal of leading texts in these subject areas highlights the neglect. If the subject of the first lady is being taught, it appears that it is not given much time or attention, and the manner in which it is being discussed is suspect. To help address these questions and concerns, I conducted a poll in 1996 and 1997 wherein professors who taught courses on the presidency were surveyed about the extent to which the first lady appeared in their lectures.[8] This study sought to determine if the first lady was being included in the college curriculum. The first questions asked faculty who taught courses on the U.S. presidency and U.S. politics whether or not they devoted class time to the first ladies. The results are listed in Table 8.1.

Table 8.1   The First Lady in the College Classroom

	No	Yes	No Response
In U.S. presidency courses	26.4%	63.2%	10.4%
In U.S. politics courses	52.9%	27.6%	19.5%

Source: Watson Presidential Scholars Poll, 1996–1997.
Note: Scores rounded to nearest 0.1 percent.

Nearly two-thirds of the respondents indicated that they did incorporate the topic of the first lady into their U.S. presidency courses, whereas the first lady is discussed infrequently in courses on U.S. politics. As the data in Table 8.2 point out, however, the extent of class time devoted to the topic is nothing more than a casual mention. Of those checking the "other" category for the amount of class time spent on the topic, the responses ranged from discussing Eleanor Roosevelt during lectures on Franklin Roosevelt, to using Hillary Rodham Clinton as an example of how the

Table 8.2   Class Time Devoted to the First Lady

Course	Casual Mention	Part of Lecture	One Lecture	Two Lectures	Other
U.S. presidency	52.7%	25.5%	7.3%	3.6%	10.9%
U.S. politics	75.0%	20.8%	0%	0%	4.2%

Source: Watson Presidential Scholars Poll, 1996–1997.
Note: Scores rounded to nearest 0.1 percent.

office of the first lady has become politically active in the twentieth century, to an occasional reference to a president's wife throughout the academic term.

Another segment of the questionnaire addressed how much the presidential scholars knew about the first ladies. Even though it may bring into question the validity of my poll, it is important to note that in many instances respondents admitted to not knowing much about the presidential spouses. Several respondents left comments such as "I am unfamiliar with her"; "I don't know anything about the first ladies"; "I just don't know enough about [the first ladies] to discuss them in class or in a survey"; and "I have limited knowledge about the first ladies." Many respondents indicated that they knew almost nothing about the following presidential spouses: Martha Jefferson, Rachel Jackson, Hannah Van Buren, Anna Harrison, Letitia Tyler, Julia Tyler, Margaret Taylor, Abigail Fillmore, Jane Pierce, Harriet Lane (James Buchanan's niece), Lucretia Garfield, Ellen Arthur, Caroline Harrison, and Alice Roosevelt.

It is not surprising, then, that the first ladies are not being incorporated into the college political science or history classroom in significant ways. It is probable that the same can be said for the elementary- and secondary-level curricula. The first ladies are a topic, however, with which students are at least casually familiar. Most of them can recognize recent first ladies and they can observe the roles and influence of the first lady through the media. Evening news reports and newspaper articles now regularly devote attention to the first lady. Similarly, the new National First Ladies Library has a home page with pictures, biographical profiles, and other information readily accessible.[9] The White House also administers a home page filled with the first lady's speeches, pictures, activities, and, of course, biographical profile.[10] Many students learn U.S. history by studying the presidents and therefore are at least marginally familiar with the presidents and their accomplishments. The first ladyship is a dynamic, evolving, and highly political office that has emerged as an influential institution within and beyond the White House. Teachers can no longer afford to ignore the president's spouse.

The Future of the Office

Because the office has evolved with few guidelines to follow and many forces shaping it, it is hard to predict new developments. The fact that there are so few formal or legal parameters surrounding the first ladyship also makes it difficult to assess the future of the office. One step toward formalizing the duties of the office, if that is the direction the public desires, is to assign the first lady a salary. If the position eventually becomes a salaried office, then formal parameters, duties, and responsibilities for the job will ensue. This would obviously cause controversy. Former first lady Barbara Bush does not see the first ladyship as an office. She believes that its lack of formalization benefits first ladies, that the undefined role allows each first lady to define the office to suit her own vision.[11] Former first lady Rosalynn Carter echoes Mrs. Bush's sentiments: "I've always said I was glad I didn't have a salary. If you have a salary, then the position will become institutionalized and there will be duties that you have to perform. I was glad that I could do what I wanted to do."[12] With pay comes restrictions and unanswered questions about specific roles and responsibilities of the office. But an argument exists for paying the wife of the president. She has a large budget, staff, and offices and puts in more hours than many paid staffers. The demands of the office, intensity of public scrutiny, extensive travel and social obligations, and other factors make it one of the most demanding jobs in the world.

One force that will continue to shape the direction of the office is the evolving status of women in U.S. society. As the role of women continues to progress, the institution will respond to such changes, producing more political partners like Rosalynn Carter or Hillary Rodham Clinton. Perhaps the first lady will be permitted to have or retain her own career during her White House years and will not be fully responsible for the social affairs of the White House. Eleanor Roosevelt challenged our assumptions about women, the role of women in politics and society, and the nature of the presidential marriage. She helped her husband in many ways not thought possible before her tenure as first lady, and she accomplished all this under intense public scrutiny. Her actions produced changes in the nature of the office and the public's expectations of future first ladies. In fact, to a degree, all subsequent first ladies have served in the shadow of Eleanor.

The U.S. public has been exposed to a wide variety of approaches to the office and many different types of first ladies. Although the public is still uncertain about what it wants in a first lady, the public has seen many variations in the office and its occupant. Future first ladies now have a wider parameter for functioning because of such variations. The trailblazing by previous first ladies has made the job easier for future first ladies.

The first lady's staff and office seem to have become institutionalized within the White House to the point that there is little public or political opposition to the first lady having such staff and resources. It can be expected that the office will remain, with changes in composition reflecting changes in the particular approach of the sitting first lady. The existence of an organized, sizeable office will help future presidential spouses accomplish their agendas.

As various ethnic groups such as Hispanic Americans, African Americans, and Asian Americans make progress in U.S. society and the character of society becomes increasingly multicultural and integrated, it is probable that a non-Caucasian will soon serve as president or as the spouse of the president. This event might bring with it some changes to the office, but it is doubtful that those changes would be as substantive as would the changes brought on by a male presidential spouse. Thus the gender component of the office is more of a defining characteristic than the race component.

Certain aspects of the first ladyship appear to be unique to the United States. For instance, in the United States, no first lady has ever succeeded her husband after his death or political term (although such succession did happen historically in Congress; congressional wives have been selected to assume the duties of their deceased husbands for the remainder of their terms). Around the world, however, some wives and daughters of political leaders have assumed political office after the deaths of their husbands or fathers. The United States has not elected a a woman president, although several nations around the world have had female heads of state. In much of the world there is no institution similar to the U.S. first ladyship. Carla Voltolini, the wife of Italian president Sandro Pertini, retained her job as a psychologist during her husband's term in office, kept her maiden name, and did not even live in the Italian president's official residence. However, as U.S. influence grows around the world and U.S. culture remains the country's leading export, it is probable that characteristics of the U.S. first ladyship might begin appearing in other nations.

Although ill defined, the office of the first lady has at time held a great deal of power. First ladies have been public figures since Martha Washington and will continue to be well known. The first lady has emerged as a key player within the president's kitchen cabinet, or inner circle of powerful advisers. Presidential spouses can be expected to remain as powerful advisers as long as the particular presidential marriage is healthy.

Eleanor Roosevelt demonstrated the potential for the office and this potential remains.

Future first ladies can be expected to continue to advise presidents, make contributions to worthy social causes and U.S. politics, make a difference as campaigners, lead needed renovations and restorations of the White House, and continue to be among the most popular citizens of the republic. Future presidential spouses can be expected to assume official duties either as honorary chairs of committees or presidential projects or, with the weakening of the "Bobby Kennedy rule," may actually be appointed to office. There are precedents for such appointments. Bess Truman was paid to work as the head of her husband's Senate office, Lady Bird Johnson was not paid but still headed her husband's congressional office, Rosalynn Carter functioned as the honorary chair of her husband's task force on mental health reform, and Hillary Clinton ran her husband's health care task force. With first ladies fulfilling such important and visible policy roles, a provision may be created to allow the president's spouse to serve as head of a commission or task force.

Two key events that will surely shape the future of the office are the election of a married, heterosexual female to the presidency and the election of an unmarried president of either sex. It has been a long time since a widower or bachelor was elected to the White House. If this occurs again, it would provide a good test for the nature of the role of the president's spouse. It is possible that a surrogate host(ess) would be utilized for White House socials. Most likely, female family members would be called upon to assist with the social side of the presidency, and close family members of both sexes, such as children or parents, might assume some role in campaigning. However, it is unlikely that a full-time surrogate would be required. The White House staff of butlers, curators, chefs, and protocol officers are more than capable of fulfilling the social duties of the presidency. This raises an interesting point. When a first lady is present, she becomes the de facto head of White House social affairs and the White House staff, and is responsible for management of the executive building. Yet it is conceivable that if an unmarried president or a female president were elected, the social and hosting dimension of the presidency would instantly revert to the control of the professional staff that has been hired to manage such concerns. Although the first lady is a powerful, influential partner in the presidency and an outlet for extensive media coverage, an unmarried president can easily function without a first lady. The social affairs of the White House can proceed through the institutional mechanisms in place for such events. However, without a close political confidante, popular public figure, recognizable head of White House social affairs, and cocampaigner and spokesperson—that is, without a sitting first lady—the presidency may be worse off.

There is considerable speculation about when a woman will be elected president. Women have run for the presidency; however, their campaigns have been on a third-party platform and the bids have been largely symbolic. The first woman selected to the presidential ticket of a major political party was Geraldine Ferraro, Walter Mondale's running mate on the Democratic ticket in 1984, but the Mondale-Ferraro ticket was soundly defeated by the Reagan-Bush ticket. With a critical mass of women now serving or having served as governor, U.S. senator, or U.S. representative, there is a field of potential women presidential candidates who have the necessary political experiences and national exposure to make a serious run for the office. The question is whether or not the electorate is ready to vote for a woman. Most presidents have served in politics prior to their presidencies in such capacities as governor, senator, representative, diplomat, or secretary of state. Indeed, the U.S. public seems to require such political backgrounds in potential presidential candidates. Several of the early presidents—John Adams, Thomas Jefferson, James Madison, James Monroe, and John Quincy Adams—served as secretary of state or diplomat prior to becoming president. Such recent presidents as Ronald Reagan, Jimmy Carter, and Bill Clinton were governors before becoming president; George Bush and Richard Nixon served as vice president before their presidencies and both had also served in Congress. Lyndon Johnson and Gerald Ford were powerful members of Congress before being selected as vice president and then serving as president.

Historically, many great women governed. For instance, in ancient Egypt women of the courts and with aristocratic backgrounds were entitled to equal rights and status. From this society, many great queens emerged to rule Egypt: Hatshepsut, Nefertiti, Aahhotep, and, of course, Cleopatra. In England, Queen Elizabeth I's rule extended to many parts of the world, and Queen Liliu'okalani ruled the Kingdom of Hawaii before it was annexed by the United States. Internationally, there have been several women who have served as head of state. (Table 8.3 lists women who have served as heads of state.) The first woman elected as head of state was Sirimavo Bandaranaike, who became prime minister of Ceylon (now Sri Lanka) in 1960. By 1970 both India and Israel were governed by women. In 1988 Benazir Bhutto became prime minister of Pakistan, the first women to lead a Muslim nation. In 1997 five countries were being led by women. It is inevitable that the United States will one day be governed by a woman. Not only have women made progress in gaining prominent political offices in the United States, thus breaking down some of the cultural barriers precluding leadership by women, but first ladies have wielded great political power for much of the country's history. The precedent is not as distant as one might imagine.

Table 8.3   Female World Leaders

Name	Nation	Title	Years of Service
Sirimavo Bandaranaike	Ceylon	Prime minister	1960–1965; 1970–1977; 1994–
Indira Gandhi	India	Prime minister	1966–1977; 1980–1984
Golda Meir	Israel	Prime minister	1969–1974
Isabel Perón	Argentina	President	1974–1976
Elizabeth Domitien	Central African Republic	Prime minister	1975–1976
Maria de Lourdes Pintassilg	Portugal	Prime minister	1979
Lidia Gueiler	Bolivia	President	1979–1980
Margaret Thatcher	United Kingdom	Prime minister	1979–1990
Vigdis Finnbogadottir	Iceland	President	1980–
Mary Eugenia Charles	Dominica	Prime minister	1980–1995
Gro Brundtland	Norway	Prime minister	1981; 1986–1989; 1990–1996
Milka Planinc	Yugoslavia	President	1982–1986
Agatha Barbara	Malta	President	1982–1986
Maria Liberia-Peters	Netherlands Antilles	Prime minister	1984–1986; 1988–1994
Corazon Aquino	Philippines	President	1986–1992
Benazir Bhutto	Pakistan	Prime minister	1988–1990; 1993–1996
Ertha Pascal-Trouillot	Haiti	President	1990
Kazimiera Prunshiene	Lithuania	Prime minister	1990–1991
Violeta Chamorro	Nicaragua	President	1990–1996
Mary Robinson	Ireland	President	1990–
Edith Cresson	France	Prime minister	1991–1992
Khaleda Zia	Bangladesh	Prime minister	1991–1996
Hanna Suchocka	Poland	Prime minister	1992–1993
Kim Campbell	Canada	Prime minister	1993
Sylvie Kinigi	Bolivia	Prime minister	1993
Tansu Ciller	Turkey	Prime minister	1993–1996
Agathe Uwilingiyimana	Rwanda	Prime minister	1993–1994
Chandrika Kumaratunga	Sri Lanka	Prime minister and president	1994
Claudette Werleigh	Haiti	Prime minister	1995–1996
Hasina Wazed	Bangladesh	Prime minister	1996–
Ruth Perry	Liberia	President	1996–

Advice to First Ladies

Besides teachers, researchers, voters, and the U.S. public, another obvious group with a vested interest in learning about first ladies is first ladies themselves. In particular, prospective first ladies preparing to assume the office of the first lady would find it beneficial to learn as much as possible about previous first ladies, the challenges of the office, and public expectations of first ladies. Not surprisingly, journalists, scholars, and others who have studied the office have felt obliged to offer advice to prospective first ladies.

For instance, in an article appearing in *The New Yorker* titled "Free Advice," five historians were asked to offer advice to First Lady Hillary Clinton, who at the time was facing media criticism, public disapproval, and legal controversies.[13] In the article, author Ann Hollander suggested that the first lady did not have the confidence of Jackie Kennedy and that she was not free to be herself because her physical appearance was an issue with the press and the public. Author Simon Schama felt that the first lady was facing what other first ladies of the twentieth century had faced: the United States' obsession with the image of the president as a "traditional family man" and its expectation that the first lady be a "dutiful reflection of the husband's virtue." Teddy Roosevelt scholar Edmund Morris advised the first lady that the public wants a "human being" in the White House and that humor is an effective way of humanizing one's appearance. Morris felt that Mrs. Clinton's lack of a sense of humor was a problem. He cited former first lady Nancy Reagan, whom he called a "spoiled, rich apologist for the elite," as an example of a first lady who was somewhat successful in changing her image. She accomplished this with humor: Mrs. Reagan's strained relations with the media and her image as an aloof, queenlike first lady with excessively expensive tastes were dramatically improved during her appearance at the popular Gridiron Club Dinner in the capital city, where she made fun of herself by dressing as "Second-hand Rose" in a parody of her image. Author Robert Darnton advised the first lady that most people reduced political and policy issues to the personalities involved with the issues and therefore it is important to be well liked. The final historian offering advice in the article was Doris Kearns Goodwin, presidential scholar, historian, and author. Goodwin reminded readers and the first lady that Eleanor Roosevelt was an active, outspoken first lady who broke one precedent after another. She was the first presidential spouse to hold regular press conferences, testify before Congress, and write a daily newspaper column. Eleanor was criticized for these actions, but she was consistent and persistent in her approach. She dealt with the controversy by continuing to be a voice for the voiceless.

Other historians have offered general advice for incoming first ladies.

Historian Gil Troy has compiled a list of tips for first ladies.[14] From his study of presidential couples serving since Franklin and Eleanor Roosevelt, Troy concludes that the public has rejected the notion of a politically active first lady. He thus advises new first ladies (and first couples) to consider the following twelve concerns.

1. *Don't be yourselves, be who they want you to be.* First ladies must accept their role as a cultural and social leader and, as such, must project the symbol of traditional womanhood and marriage.
2. *Support each other, rely on each other, but don't forget who's boss.* First ladies and presidents must support each other and rely on each other, but they must not forget that the president is the leader who has been elected to public office. The president's spouse needs to create a safe haven for the president in the living quarters of the White House.
3. *Let the white glove pulpit resonate with the bully pulpit.* The first lady's speeches and public image should work as the president's chorus, echoing and supporting him.
4. *Treat the spouse's project as an integral part of the administration.* First ladies must be sure to select a project that is not controversial and relates to part of the presidency or the president's agenda.
5. *The less power you seem to want, the more you'll get and the more popular you shall be.*
6. *Never criticize the president, unless you both agree it's convenient.*
7. *Pioneers belong in the Wild West, and possibly in the West Wing, but certainly not the East Wing.* First ladies should play it safe and traditional.
8. *When in doubt, go retro.* Traditional roles and approaches to the first ladyship are best. The United States looks to such an image from the first lady and holds first couples to a higher standard than the rest of society. There is little room for error.
9. *Nothing is trivial and the personal is political, but don't take the political personally.* The first lady and presidential couple must define their personal boundaries while serving in such a public office.
10. *You get one mea culpa; use it well.*
11. *Take the long-term view of your marriage.*
12. *Keep up appearances—you set the standard now, and your marriage belongs to history.*

It is doubtful that the same advice would be given to a male spouse of a female president. Troy takes a very traditional view of the office and neglects the fact that several nontraditional or progressive first ladies have been very popular and enjoyed high public approval ratings. Notably absent in Troy's list is the role of partner played by presidential spouses. Troy feels that most scholars who have studied the first lady have spent too much time trying to justify her power and not enough time analyzing the nature of the marriage and what he sees as a rejection of the partnership approach.[15] But he is right to warn first ladies about the possibility of hostility arising from activism and the potential harm to the president's image of a controversial first lady. However, the role of partner is natural and healthy in many ways. The president is facing the most trying times and challenges of his life, the office is larger than any one person, and many issues are so sensitive that they cannot be confided in with anyone but a spouse, on immediate family member, or a lifelong friend. Presidents benefit from having a trusted confidante, a loyal supporter, a business helpmate, and a political ally. Future spouses should be encouraged to share in their spouse's work, decisions, and challenges. Troy is also right in suggesting that they should remember that there are distinct roles that are to be fulfilled in the public sphere and distinct roles that are best delegated to the private sphere. An absent or unhelpful first lady is more of a liability to a president than a capable, ready, and willing partner. The first lady and president need to assess the state of their marriage and consider their own talents and limitations in designing a role for the spouse.

Not all the advice offered to first ladies has been serious and somber. Some advice has been lighthearted and humorous but still helpful. Journalists have also written on the matter. In an article appearing in the magazine *Ladies' Home Journal*, writer Diana McLellan gives just such advice.[16]

1. *As the nation's top hostess, don't be stingy.* Entertain in a manner that will make America proud.
2. *Do let White House guests dance and enjoy themselves at social functions and be sure to dance yourself.* Presidents Ronald Reagan, Lyndon Johnson, and Gerald Ford all danced at White House events and were applauded for it. In fact, these presidents often initiated such fun activities and appeared to genuinely enjoy themselves at White House socials. Consequently, guests also enjoyed themselves. Rosalynn Carter and Barbara Bush, however, were often stiff and unsocial, did not dance, and did not appear to enjoy themselves.
3. *Do include your family in White House celebrations.*
4. *Don't do anything official on Saturdays and remember to have a social and private life.*
5. *Do fulfill the role of wife by supporting and protecting the president.*

6. *As first lady, don't forget the women of Washington, D.C.* Be sure to have social functions for women.

7. *Do expect criticism and get a really good press secretary.*

The first ladyship presents a wide array of challenges for the occupant of the office, some political and some personal. The prospect of assuming the office would be bewildering for even the most prepared presidential spouses. Thus I must jump on the bandwagon of my colleagues and offer my advice to future first ladies.

1. *Expect criticism.* The first lady should not expect to please all of the people all of the time. After all, the office is filled with paradoxes. First ladies have been criticized for being simultaneously too extravagant and too informal, too young and too old, and the list goes on. The first lady should not criticize public figures or the press because the public does not take kindly to such actions by the first lady unless they are directly in defense of her husband.

2. *All things in moderation.* Considering the first point, the first lady would be wise to seek moderation when determining her role, which activities to undertake, and how to balance her time between the various political and social requirements of the office. The first lady should play it safe by not taking on too much of any one approach or activity.

3. *Promote yourself and your accomplishments.* The first lady should hire good public relations people and promote her causes, travels, and appearances. Again, it is wise to practice moderation and humility in these endeavors. However, the country wants to get to know its first lady, and the appearance of an active, dedicated, hardworking spouse will be a success for the first lady and for the president. It will also prevent the media or the first lady's critics from defining her because she will already have established a rapport with and base of support in the public.

4. *Balance the social and political.* The public permits and now expects first ladies to be involved in political activities such as campaigning and advising presidents. However, if the public perceives a first lady solely by these activities, this perception could create problems. If a first lady pays as much attention to the social roles of the office, it reduces her vulnerability to criticism of her power or political activism. Both roles are important and first ladies should attempt to achieve a balance in their prioritization of these two broad areas of service.

5. *Select a project. Promote it and enjoy it.* Recent first ladies have been identified with a pet project. These projects improve the first lady's image and allow her to make many meaningful contributions to a worthy social cause. First ladies should select a project that supports their husbands' platforms (it would be a lose-lose situation should a first lady select

a project at odds with the president's or party's agenda) and something about which both the president and the first lady feel strongly. Promote the project and enjoy it. In the harsh world of presidential politics, a meaningful project can be a relief from the grind of politics and can be personally rewarding. Such projects are unique because they bypass the usual bureaucracy of government and the first lady does not have to obtain the support of Congress to pursue them. Yet because they have the benefit of credibility owing to their affiliation with the first lady, these projects can significantly help the particular issue at hand.

6. *Practice making speeches.* A first lady will be required to make many speeches. As with the president and the bully pulpit, the white glove pulpit is often a source of great power. Learn how to master the media, your visual image, and public opinion.

7. *Travel with and campaign for the president.* The public has grown to expect first ladies to support the president. The first lady can be a major benefit to the president, his popularity, and his agenda (and her own agenda) on the campaign trail.

8. *It is okay to be politically active, as long as you are frank about it.* The public is not afraid of a politically active first lady per se, but it is concerned about unchecked power and influence that occurs beyond the purview of public introspection. Oftentimes the media and the public assume the worst. Perception is reality in politics and even suspicion fuels criticism. A first lady can thus be active in political and policy affairs, but she should be forthcoming about her interest and activism. Such participation in political matters can occur under the guise of loyal support of her husband. Relatedly, the political activism should not be directed toward an issue that is highly controversial.

9. *Be yourself.* The first lady should approach the office in a way in which she is comfortable. She should not try to be Eleanor Roosevelt if she is not Eleanor Roosevelt. If a first lady explains her approach to the people, they will understand.

10. *Respect and give credit to the public.* Too many political figures err by not giving the public credit. The public will understand, forgive, and support a public figure as long as it perceives that that person is being forthright, honest, and open. The public is capable of understanding issues better than is often believed. The people deserve to know what is going on and want to get to know their leaders personally. If the first lady obliges this interest, she will earn their trust and support.

11. *White House social affairs are important.* The nation loves a great hostess. Social hosting is a win-win situation: It is rarely controversial, and it generally receives positive media coverage. The first couple has an obligation to continue the tradition of hosting social affairs. Only in times of war and economic crisis have these affairs been minimized. Such events

can often fulfill a viable political role, improving political relations with guests, foreign nations, and the public.

12. *Keep the White House as the people's house.* The first lady should try not to limit the public's access to this national monument and living museum. It is incumbent upon the first couple to tend to necessary White House renovations and restorations. Many first couples have reaped considerable political mileage by showcasing a restored White House. All guests and visitors to the White House remember the experience.

13. *Create a private life for you and your family.* The demands of the White House are considerable for not only the president but the president's family. To be most effective, the president needs to have a private life and a relaxing environment to give him respite from the challenges of governing the nation. This is also true for the first lady and the entire first family. The living quarters of the White House should be a place where the first family can escape the pressures of the White House. The first lady can help by ensuring that the first family has some personal space free from distractions and time away from politics. The first family should try to retain hobbies, take vacations together, and eat meals together. Many presidents and first ladies have suffered from poor health directly related to the demands and stress associated with the job.

14. *Assist the president with cabinet selections and staffing.* Presidents often form committees to assist them with staffing concerns, especially prior to taking office. Successful staffing is a key to a successful administration. In politics, however, everyone has a political agenda, and there are consequences and reasons behind every staffing decision and piece of advice offered to the president by aides. There is also the concern of selecting a staff that works well together. The first lady is one of the few confidantes of the president who can say no to him and offer advice with no political strings attached. As such, her advice in politically sensitive staffing decisions is invaluable.

15. *Be the president's confidante.* Many aides find it difficult to disagree with the president, to be completely frank with him, or to offer advice irrespective of the political consequences. The president must worry about the loyalty of aides, his advisers' ulterior political objectives, and the possibility that an aide will leak a story or write a tell-all book after leaving office. In the first lady the president finds his most loyal, trusted confidante, someone with whom he can discuss sensitive matters openly, someone who will say no to him, and someone who will keep the conversation confidential. The first lady can help the president by being his top political confidante and sounding board.

16. *Beware of the president's enemies.* First ladies must be aware that some presidential aides (and enemies and the press) will use the first lady to get to the president. Advisers recognize that the first lady influences the

president and therefore may try to influence the first lady in hopes of ultimately influencing the president. Likewise, the president has many political enemies and the media is always looking for an interesting story. First ladies should be careful of the proverbial wolf in sheep's clothing.

17. *Be a spokesperson for women.* Women are beginning to turn out to vote in greater numbers than men. A first lady can bring women into the president's political party and to the president by being the voice of women. She can accomplish this through her political activities, her social causes, and social hostessing. The first lady should not neglect women. She should appear at women's events and organizations. Given the comparative lack of women in positions of power, the first lady is in a unique position to make a difference on important issues of interest to women.

18. *Know the institution of the first ladyship.* The first lady should study the history of the first ladyship. She can learn from the experiences, stories, and successes of previous first ladies. The institution has a proud heritage and it is an honor to follow in the steps of such legends as Martha Washington, Abigail Adams, and Eleanor Roosevelt.

19. *Surround yourself with a good staff.* This advice is true of anyone in a position of leadership, power, or public trust: Find energetic, competent, politically astute, and loyal staffers. The first lady should attempt to hire a staff that shares her vision for the office. Included within the staff should be someone who knows the first lady well and aides responsible for a wide variety of matters, including public relations, policy matters and the first lady's project, speechwriters, scheduling and advance aides, and individuals with a talent for organization.

20. *Have fun.* If a first lady is enjoying her service, this will become apparent to her staffers, the press, and the public and it will work to her benefit. The first lady has the unparalleled opportunity of living in a national museum, to witness firsthand history in the making and the affairs of a nation, to meet some of the most powerful and interesting people of the world, to travel around the country and the world, and to experience the luxury of state dinners and the world's best chefs and entertainers. Perhaps most important, she has an opportunity to make a difference.

Notes

1. B. Bush, *Barbara Bush,* 1994, p. 540.

2. L. L. Gould, *Governors' Wives,* 1968.

3. I interviewed Rosalynn Carter in 1998. She and her aide were kind enough to furnish me with responses to my questions.

4. I interviewed Barbara Bush in 1998. She and her aide Quincy Hicks were kind enough to furnish me with responses to my questions.

5. G. Greer, "Abolish her," 1995, p. 27.

6. The Louisiana State University campus in Shreveport runs an American studies summer program for teachers featuring courses on the presidents and the first ladies.

7. R. P. Watson, "Incorporating the First Ladies," 1998.

8. I conducted a poll of presidential scholars in 1996. Two hundred scholars who taught courses on the presidency were surveyed and 87 responded. The questionnaire asked respondents about the extent to which they included the topic of the first ladies in their course lectures.

9. Opened in June 1998, the National First Ladies Library is located at the former home of First Lady Ida McKinley (The Saxton McKinley House) in Canton, Ohio.

10. The Web site may be accessed at *www.Whitehouse.gov.*

11. My interview with Barbara Bush and Quincy Hicks, 1998.

12. My interview with Rosalynn Carter and her aide, 1998.

13. J. Kornbluth, "Free Advice," 1995, p. 34.

14. G. Troy, *Affairs of State,* 1997.

15. Troy, 1997.

16. D. McLellan, "What Every New First Lady Should Know," 1993, p. 182.

First Lady Frances Cleveland (front row, center) poses with the wives of her husband's cabinet members (1897). First ladies such as Mrs. Cleveland have often been the driving force behind getting women appointed to administrative positions (collection of the Library of Congress).

Appendix:
Profiles of the First Ladies

Martha Dandridge Custis Washington

Presidential Years: 1789–1797
Born: June 2, 1731; Williamsburg, Virginia
Died: May 22, 1802; Mount Vernon Plantation, Virginia
Buried: Mount Vernon, Virginia
Parents: Frances Jones and Colonel John Dandridge (plantation owner)
Marriage: 1st marriage: June 1749 to Colonel Daniel Parke Custis in New Kent County, Virginia (widowed 1757)
2nd marriage: January 6, 1759, to George Washington in New Kent County, Virginia
Children: 1st marriage: Daniel, 1751–1754; Frances, 1753–1757; John ("Jacky"), 1754 or 1755–1781; Martha ("Patsy"), 1756 or 1757–1773
Education: No formal education

Abigail Smith Adams

Presidential Years: 1797–1801
Born: November 11, 1744; Weymouth, Massachusetts
Died: October 28, 1818; Quincy, Massachusetts
Buried: Quincy, Massachusetts
Parents: Elizabeth Quincy and the Reverend William Smith (Congregational minister)

Marriage:	October 25, 1764, to John Adams in Weymouth, Massachusetts
Children:	Abigail Amelia, 1765–1813; John Quincy, 1767–1848; Susanna, 1768–1770; Charles, 1770–1800; Thomas Boylston, 1772–1832
Education:	No formal education

Martha Wayles Skelton Jefferson

Martha died nineteen years prior to Jefferson's presidency

Born:	October 19, 1748; Charles City County, Virginia
Died:	September 6, 1782; Monticello Plantation, near Charlottesville, Virginia
Buried:	Monticello, Virginia
Parents:	Martha Eppes and John Wayles (plantation owner)
Marriage:	1st marriage: November 20, 1766, to Bathurst Skelton (died 1770)
	2nd marriage: January 1, 1772, to Thomas Jefferson in Williamsburg, Virginia
Children:	1st marriage: infant son, 1767–1771
	2nd marriage: Martha ("Patsy") Washington, 1772–1836; Jane Randolph, 1774–1775; infant son, 1777; Mary ("Maria," "Polly"), 1778–1804; Lucy Elizabeth, 1780–1781; Lucy Elizabeth, 1782–1785
Education:	No formal education

Dorothea "Dolley" Payne Todd Madison

Presidential Years:	1809–1817
Born:	May 20, 1768; New Garden, North Carolina
Died:	July 12, 1849; Washington, D.C.
Buried:	Montpelier Plantation, Virginia
Parents:	Mary Coles and John Payne (plantation owner)
Marriage:	1st marriage: January 7, 1790, to John Todd in Philadelphia, Pennsylvania (died 1793)
	2nd marriage: September 15, 1794, to James Madison in Harewood, Virginia
Children:	1st marriage: John Payne, 1792–1852; William Temple, 1793
Education:	No formal education

Elizabeth Kortright Monroe

Presidential Years:	1817–1825
Born:	July 30, 1768; New York, New York
Died:	September 23, 1830; Oak Hill, Virginia
Buried:	Richmond, Virginia
Parents:	Hannah Aspinwall and Captain Lawrence Kortright (British army officer)
Marriage:	February 16, 1786, to James Monroe in New York, New York
Children:	Eliza Kortright, 1786–1835; James Spence, 1799–1800; Maria Hester, 1803–1850
Education:	No formal education

Louisa Catherine Johnson Adams

Presidential Years:	1825–1829
Born:	February 12, 1775; London, England
Died:	May 15, 1852; Washington, D.C.
Buried:	Quincy, Massachusetts
Parents:	Catherine Nuth and Joshua Johnson (U.S. consul)
Marriage:	July 26, 1797, to John Quincy Adams in London, England
Children:	George Washington, 1801–1829; John, 1803–1834; Charles Francis, 1807–1886
Education:	No formal education

Rachel Donelson Jackson

Rachel died in the interim between Jackson's election and his inauguration

Born:	June 15, 1767; Halifax County, Virginia
Died:	December 22, 1828; Nashville, Tennessee
Buried:	Nashville, Tennessee
Parents:	Rachel Stockley and Colonel John Donelson (surveyor, land owner)
Marriage:	1st marriage: March 1, 1784 or 1785, to Lewis Robards (separated 1790)
	2nd marriage: August 1791, remarried January 17, 1794, to Andrew Jackson
Children:	2nd marriage: adopted nephew Andrew Jr.
Education:	No formal education

Hannah Hoes Van Buren

Hannah died 18 years prior to Van Buren's presidency

Born:	March 8, 1783; Kinderhook, New York
Died:	February 5, 1819; Albany, New York
Buried:	Kinderhook, New York
Parents:	Maria Quakenboss and John Hoes
Marriage:	February 21, 1807, to Martin Van Buren
Children:	Abraham, 1807–1873; John, 1810–1866; Martin, 1812–1855; infant son; Smith Thompson, 1817–1876
Education:	No formal education

Anna Tuthill Symmes Harrison

Presidential Years:	1841 (Anne never lived in the White House)
Born:	July 25, 1775; Walpack Township, New Jersey
Died:	February 25, 1864; North Bend, Ohio
Buried:	North Bend, Ohio
Parents:	Anna Tuthill and John Cleves (judge)
Marriage:	November 25, 1795, to William Henry Harrison in North Bend, Ohio
Children:	Elizabeth Bassett, 1796–1846; John Cleves Symmes, 1798–1830; Lucy Singleton, 1800–1826; William Henry, 1802–1838; John Scott, 1806–1840; Mary Symmes, 1809–1842; Carter Bassett, 1811–1839; Anna Tuthill, 1813–1865; James Findlay, 1814–1817
Education:	Clinton Academy in Long Island, New York Mrs. Graham's Boarding School for Young Ladies, in New York, New York

Letitia Christian Tyler

Presidential Years:	1841–1842
Born:	November 12, 1790; New Kent County, Virginia
Died:	September 10, 1842; Washington, D.C.
Buried:	Cedar Grove, Virginia
Parents:	Mary Brown and Colonel Robert Christian (plantation owner)
Marriage:	March 29, 1813, to John Tyler in New Kent County, Virginia
Children:	Mary, 1815–1848; Robert, 1816–1877; John, 1819–

1896; Letitia, 1821–1907; Elizabeth, 1823–1850; Anne
Contesse, 1825; Alice, 1827–1854; Taxwell, 1830–1874
Education: No formal education

Julia Gardiner Tyler

Presidential Years: 1844–1845
Born: May 4, 1820; Gardiners Island, New York
Died: July 10, 1889; Richmond, Virginia
Buried: Richmond, Virginia
Parents: Julia McLachlan and David Gardiner (senator)
Marriage: June 26, 1844, to John Tyler in New York, New York
Children: David Gardiner, 1846–1927; John Alexander, 1848–
                     1883; Julia Gardiner, 1853–1935; Robert Fitzwalter,
                     1856–1927; Pearl Taylor, 1860–1947
Education: Chegary Institute (finishing school) in New York, New
                     York

Sarah Childress Polk

Presidential Years: 1845–1849
Born: September 4, 1803; Murfreesboro, Tennessee
Died: August 14, 1891; Nashville, Tennessee
Buried: Nashville, Tennessee
Parents: Elizabeth and Captain Joel Childress (plantation
                     owner)
Marriage: January 1, 1824, to James K. Polk in Murfreesboro,
                     Tennessee
Children: None
Education: Boarding school in Nashville, Tennessee; Moravian
                     Female Academy in Salem, North Carolina

Margaret "Peggy" Mackall Smith Taylor

Presidential Years: 1849–1850
Born: September 21, 1788; Calvert County, Maryland
Died: August 18, 1852; Pascagoula, Mississippi
Buried: Louisville, Kentucky
Parents: Ann Mackall and Major Walter Smith (plantation
                     owner)

Marriage:	June 21, 1810, to Zachary Taylor in Jefferson County, Kentucky
Children:	Ann Mackall, 1811–1875; Sarah Knox, 1814–1835; Octavia Pannel, 1816–1820; Margaret Smith, 1819–1820; Mary Elizabeth ("Betty"), 1824–1909; Richard, 1826–1879
Education:	No formal education

Abigail Powers Fillmore

Presidential Years:	1850–1853
Born:	May 13, 1798; Stillwater, New York
Died:	March 30, 1853; Washington, D.C.
Buried:	Buffalo, New York
Parents:	Abigail Newland and Lemuel Powers (Baptist preacher)
Marriage:	February 5, 1826, to Millard B. Fillmore in Moravia, New York
Children:	Millard Powers, 1828–1889; Mary Abigail, 1832–1854
Education:	Some schooling in New Hope, New York

Jane Means Appleton Pierce

Presidential Years:	1853–1857
Born:	March 12, 1806; Hampton, New Hampshire
Died:	December 2, 1863; Andover, New Hampshire
Buried:	Concord, New Hampshire
Parents:	Elizabeth Means and the Reverend Jesse Appleton (Congregational minister and university president)
Marriage:	November 19, 1834, to Franklin Pierce in Amherst, Massachusetts
Children:	Franklin, 1836; Frank Robert, 1839–1843; Benjamin, 1841–1853
Education:	No formal education

Mary Todd Lincoln

Presidential Years:	1861–1865
Born:	December 13, 1818; Lexington, Kentucky

Died:	July 16, 1882; Springfield, Illinois
Buried:	Springfield, Illinois
Parents:	Eliza Parker and Robert Todd Smith (merchant, plantation owner)
Marriage:	November 4, 1842, to Abraham Lincoln in Springfield, Illinois
Children:	Robert Todd, 1843–1926; Edward Baker, 1846–1850; William Wallace, 1850–1862; Thomas ("Tad"), 1853–1871
Education:	Mme. Mentelle's School in Lexington, Kentucky

Eliza McCardle Johnson

Presidential Years:	1865–1869
Born:	October 4, 1810; Leesburg, Tennessee
Died:	January 15, 1876; Greeneville, Tennessee
Buried:	Greeneville, Tennessee
Parents:	Sarah Phillips and John McCardle (shoemaker)
Marriage:	May 17, 1827, to Andrew Johnson in Greeneville, Tennessee
Children:	Martha, 1828–1901; Charles, 1830–1863; Mary, 1832–1883; Robert, 1834–1869; Andrew, 1852–1879
Education:	No information available

Julia Dent Grant

Presidential Years:	1869–1877
Born:	January 26, 1826; St. Louis, Missouri
Died:	December 14, 1902; Washington, D.C.
Buried:	New York, New York
Parents:	Ellen Wrenshaw and Colonel Frederick Dent (judge, plantation owner)
Marriage:	August 22, 1848, to Ulysses S. Grant in St. Louis, Missouri
Children:	Frederick Dent, 1850–1912; Ulysses Simpson, 1852–1929; Ellen Wrenshaw, 1855–1922; Jesse Root, 1858–1934
Education:	Misses Mauro's Boarding School in St. Louis, Missouri

Lucy Ware Webb Hayes

Presidential Years:	1877–1881
Born:	August 28, 1831; Chillicothe, Ohio
Died:	June 25, 1889; Fremont, Ohio
Buried:	Fremont, Ohio
Parents:	Maria Cook and Dr. James Webb (physician)
Marriage:	December 30, 1852, to Rutherford Hayes in Cincinnati, Ohio
Children:	Birchard Austin, 1853–1926; James Webb Cook, 1856–1934; Rutherford Platt, 1858–1927; Joseph Thompson, 1861–1863; George Crook, 1864–1866; Fanny, 1867–1950; Scott Russell, 1871–1923; Manning Force, 1873–1874
Education:	Wesleyan Female College; Ohio Wesleyan University (Delaware, Ohio), graduated 1850

Lucretia Rudolph Garfield

Presidential Years:	1881
Born:	April 19, 1832; Hiram, Ohio
Died:	March 14, 1918; South Pasadena, California
Buried:	Cleveland, Ohio
Parents:	Arabella Mason and Zeb Rudolph (farmer, community leader)
Marriage:	November 11, 1858, to James A. Garfield in Hiram, Ohio
Children:	Eliza Arabella, 1860–1863; Harry Augustus, 1863–1942; James Rudolph, 1865–1950; Mary ("Molly"), 1867–1947; Irvin McDowell, 1870–1951; Abram, 1872–1958; Edward, 1874–1876
Education:	Geauga Seminary (Ohio); Western Reserve Eclectic Institute (now Hiram College) in Hiram, Ohio

Ellen Lewis Herndon Arthur

Died just prior to Arthur's vice presidency

Born:	1837; Culpepper County, Virginia
Died:	January 12, 1880; Albany, New York
Buried:	Albany, New York
Parents:	Elizabeth Hansbrough and William Lewis Herndon (naval officer)

Marriage:	October 25, 1859, to Chester A. Arthur in New York, New York
Children:	William Lewis, 1860–1863; Chester Alan, 1864–1937; Ellen Herndon, 1871–1915
Education:	No formal education

Frances Folsom Cleveland

Presidential Years:	1886–1889; 1893–1897
Born:	July 21, 1864; Buffalo, New York
Died:	October 29, 1947; Princeton, New Jersey
Buried:	Princeton, New Jersey
Parents:	Emma C. Harmon and Oscar Folsom (lawyer)
Marriage:	1st marriage: June 2, 1886, to Grover Cleveland in Washington, D.C.
	2nd marriage: February 10, 1913, to Professor Thomas J. Preston Jr. in Princeton, New Jersey
Children:	1st marriage: Ruth, 1891–1904; Esther, 1893–1980; Marion, 1895–1977; Richard Folsom, 1897–1974; Francis Grover, 1903
Education:	Wells College in Aurora, New York, graduated 1885

Caroline Lavinia Scott Harrison

Presidential Years:	1889–1893
Born:	October 1, 1832; Oxford, Ohio
Died:	October 25, 1892; Washington, D.C.
Buried:	Indianapolis, Indiana
Parents:	Mary Potts Neal and the Reverend Dr. John W. Scott (Presbyterian minister, founder of Oxford Female Institute
Marriage:	October 20, 1853, to Benjamin Harrison
Children:	Russell Benjamin, 1854–1936; Mary Scott, 1858–1930
Education:	Oxford Female Institute in Oxford, Ohio

Ida Saxton McKinley

Presidential Years:	1897–1901
Born:	June 8, 1847; Canton, Ohio
Died:	May 26, 1907; Canton, Ohio
Buried:	Canton, Ohio

Parents:	Catherine Dewalt and James A. Saxton (banker)
Marriage:	January 25, 1871, to William McKinley in Canton, Ohio
Children:	Katherine, 1871–1875; Ida, 1873
Education:	Finishing school; studied in Europe; Brook Hall Seminary in Media, Pennsylvania

Edith Kermit Carow Roosevelt

Presidential Years:	1901–1909
Born:	August 6, 1861; Norwich, Connecticut
Died:	September 30, 1948; Oyster Bay, New York
Buried:	Oyster Bay, New York
Parents:	Gertrude Tyler and Charles Carow (financier, investor)
Marriage:	December 2, 1886, to Theodore Roosevelt in London, England
Children:	Theodore, 1887–1944; Kermit, 1889–1943; Ethel Carow, 1891–1977; Archibald Bulloch, 1894–1979; Quentin, 1897–1918
Education:	Miss Comstock's Finishing School in New York, New York

Helen Herron Taft

Presidential Years:	1909–1913
Born:	June 2, 1861; Cincinnati, Ohio
Died:	May 22, 1943; Washington, D.C.
Buried:	Arlington National Cemetery; Arlington, Virginia
Parents:	Harriet Collins and John W. Herron (judge)
Marriage:	June 19, 1886, to Howard Taft in Cincinnati, Ohio
Children:	Robert Alfonso, 1889–1953; Helen Herron, 1891–1987; Charles Phelps, 1897–1983
Education:	Miss Nourse's School in Cincinnati, Ohio; University of Cincinnati

Ellen Louise Axson Wilson

Presidential Years:	1913–1914
Born:	May 15, 1860; Savannah, Georgia

Died:	August 6, 1914; Washington, D.C.
Buried:	Rome, Georgia
Parents:	Margaret Hoyt and the Reverend Samuel Axson (Presbyterian minister)
Marriage:	June 24, 1885, to Woodrow Wilson in Savannah, Georgia
Children:	Margaret Woodrow, 1886–1944; Jessie Woodrow, 1887–1933; Eleanor Randolph, 1889–1967
Education:	Rome Female College in Rome, Georgia; Art Student's League in New York, New York

Edith Bolling Galt Wilson

Presidential Years:	1915–1921
Born:	October 15, 1872; Wytheville, Virginia
Died:	December 28, 1961; Washington, D.C.
Buried:	Washington, D.C.
Parents:	Sallie White and William Bolling (judge)
Marriage:	1st marriage: April 30, 1896, to Norman Galt in Wytheville, Virginia (died January 28, 1908) 2nd marriage: December 18, 1915, to Woodrow Wilson in Washington, D.C.
Children:	None
Education:	Martha Washington College in Abington, Virginia; Powell's School in Richmond, Virginia

Florence Kling Harding

Presidential Years:	1921–1923
Born:	August 15, 1868; Marion, Ohio
Died:	November 21, 1924; Marion, Ohio
Buried:	Marion, Ohio
Parents:	Louisa Bouton and Amos Kling (banker)
Marriage:	1st marriage: 1880 to Henry DeWolfe in Marion, Ohio (divorced in 1885) 2nd marriage: July 8, 1891, to Warren Harding in Marion, Ohio
Children:	1st marriage: Eugene Marshall, 1880–1915
Education:	Cincinnati Conservatory of Music

Grace Anna Goodhue Coolidge

Presidential Years: 1923–1929
Born: January 3, 1879; Burlington, Vermont
Died: July 8, 1957; Northampton, Vermont
Buried: Plymouth, Vermont
Parents: Lemira Barrett and Andrew Goodhue (mechanical engineer)
Marriage: October 4, 1905, to Calvin Coolidge in Burlington, Vermont
Children: John 1906–; Calvin Jr., 1908–1924
Education: University of Vermont, graduated 1902

Lou Henry Hoover

Presidential Years: 1929–1933
Born: March 29, 1874; Waterloo, Iowa
Died: January 7, 1944; New York, New York
Buried: West Branch, Iowa
Parents: Florence Weed and Charles Henry (banker)
Marriage: February 10, 1899, to Herbert Hoover in Monterey, California
Children: Herbert Clark, 1903–1969; Allan Henry, 1907–1993
Education: Leland Stanford College (now Stanford University), graduated 1898

Anna Eleanor Roosevelt Roosevelt

Presidential Years: 1933–1945
Born: October 11, 1884; New York, New York
Died: November 7, 1962; New York, New York
Buried: Hyde Park, New York
Parents: Anna Hall and Elliott Roosevelt (investor)
Marriage: March 17, 1905, to Franklin D. Roosevelt in New York, New York
Children: Anna Eleanor, 1906–1975; James, 1907–1991; Franklin, 1909; Elliot, 1910–1990; Franklin Jr., 1914–1988; John Aspinwall, 1916–1981
Education: Private tutors; Allenwood School in London, England

Elizabeth "Bess" Virginia Wallace Truman

Presidential Years: 1945–1953
Born: February 13, 1885; Independence, Missouri
Died: October 18, 1982; Independence, Missouri
Buried: Independence, Missouri
Parents: Madge Gates and David Wallace (farmer, businessman)
Marriage: June 28, 1919, to Harry S Truman in Independence, Missouri
Children: Mary Margaret, 1924–
Education: Barstow School for Girls in Kansas City, Missouri

Mamie Geneva Doud Eisenhower

Presidential Years: 1953–1961
Born: November 14, 1896; Boone, Iowa
Died: November 1, 1979; Washington, D.C.
Buried: Abilene, Kansas
Parents: Elivera Carlson and John Doud (business owner, meat-packer)
Marriage: July 1, 1916, to Dwight D. Eisenhower in Denver, Colorado
Children: Doud Dwight, 1917–1921; John Sheldon Doud, 1922–
Education: Miss Walcott's Fashionable School in Colorado

Jacqueline Lee Bouvier Kennedy Onassis

Presidential Years: 1961–1963
Born: July 28, 1929; South Hampton, New York
Died: May 19, 1994; New York, New York
Parents: Janet Lee and John Bouvier III (lawyer, stockbroker)
Marriage: 1st marriage: September 12, 1953, to John F. Kennedy in Newport, Rhode Island (died November 22, 1963)
                 2nd marriage: October 20, 1968, to Aristotle Onassis in Skorpios, Greece
Children: 1st marriage: Caroline Bouvier, 1957–; John Fitzgerald Jr. 1960–; Patrick Bouvier, 1963
Education: Holton-Arms School in Washington, D.C.; Miss Porter's School in Farmington, Connecticut; Vassar

College, 1947–1948; The Sorbonne in Paris, 1948–1949; George Washington University, graduated 1951

Claudia "Lady Bird" Taylor Johnson

Presidential Years:	1963–1969
Born:	December 22, 1912; Karnack, Texas
Died:	N/A
Buried:	N/A
Parents:	Minnie Pattillo and Thomas Taylor (planter, merchant)
Marriage:	November 17, 1934, to Lyndon B. Johnson in San Antonio, Texas
Children:	Lynda Bird, 1944–; Lucy ("Luci") Baines, 1947–
Education:	St. Mary's School for Girls in San Antonio, Texas; University of Texas, graduated 1933

Patricia Ryan Nixon

Presidential Years:	1969–1974
Born:	March 16, 1912; Ely, Nevada
Died:	June 22, 1993; San Clemente, California
Buried:	California
Parents:	Katharine Bender and William Ryan (miner)
Marriage:	June 21, 1940, to Richard M. Nixon in Riverside, California
Children:	Patricia, 1946–; Julie, 1948–
Education:	University of Southern California, graduated cum laude 1937

Elizabeth "Betty" Bloomer Ford

Presidential Years:	1974–1977
Born:	April 8, 1918; Chicago, Illinois
Died:	N/A
Buried:	N/A
Parents:	Hortense Neahr and William Bloomer (salesman)
Marriage:	1st marriage: 1942 to William C. Warren in Grand Rapids, Michigan (divorced 1947)

<table>
<tr><td></td><td>2nd marriage: October 15, 1948, to Gerald R. Ford in Grand Rapids, Michigan</td></tr>
<tr><td>*Children:*</td><td>2nd marriage: Michael Gerald, 1950–; John Gardner, 1952– ; Steven Meigs, 1956–; Susan Elizabeth, 1957–</td></tr>
<tr><td>*Education:*</td><td>Calla Travis Dance Studio; Bennington School of Dance in Vermont, 1936–1937</td></tr>
</table>

Rosalynn Smith Carter

Presidential Years:	1977–1981
Born:	August 18, 1927; Plains, Georgia
Died:	N/A
Buried:	N/A
Parents:	Frances "Allie" Murray and Wilburn Smith (mechanic)
Marriage:	July 7, 1946, to Jimmy Carter in Plains, Georgia
Children:	John William, 1947–; James "Chip" Earl III, 1950–; Donnel Jaffery, 1952–; Amy Lynn, 1967–
Education:	Georgia Southwestern College in Americus

(Anne Francis) Nancy (Robbins) Davis Reagan

Presidential Years:	1981–1989
Born:	July 6, 1921 or 1923; New York, New York
Died:	N/A
Buried:	N/A
Parents:	Edith "Dee" Luckett and Kenneth Robbins (car salesman); mother divorced Robbins and married Dr. Loyal Davis, who adopted Nancy
Marriage:	March 4, 1952, to Ronald Reagan in Riverside, California
Children:	Patricia Ann, 1952–; Ronald Prescott, 1958–
Education:	Girls Latin School in Chicago, Illinois; Smith College, in Northampton, Massachusetts, graduated 1943

Barbara Pierce Bush

Presidential Years:	1989–1993
Born:	June 8, 1925; Rye, New York
Died:	N/A

Buried:	N/A
Parents:	Pauline Robinson and Marvin Pierce (publisher)
Marriage:	January 6, 1945, to George Bush in Rye, New York
Children:	George Walker, 1946–; Pauline "Robin" Robinson, 1949–1953; John Ellis, 1953–; Neil Mellon, 1954–; Marvin Pierce, 1956–; Dorothy Walker, 1959–
Education:	Ashley Hall Finishing School in Charleston, South Carolina; Smith College in Northampton, Massachusetts

Hillary Rodham Clinton

Presidential Years:	1993–2001
Born:	October 26, 1947; Chicago, Illinois
Died:	N/A
Buried:	N/A
Parents:	Dorothy and Hugh Rodham (fabric store owner)
Marriage:	October 11, 1975, to Bill Clinton in Fayetteville, Arkansas
Children:	Chelsea Victoria, 1980–
Education:	Wellesley College, graduated 1969; Yale Law School, graduated 1973

Bibliography

Adams, Charles Francis, ed. *Memoirs of John Quincy Adams,* Vols. I–IV. (Philadelphia: J. B. Lippincott, 1874–1877).

Adams, Louisa. *Record of a Life,* or *My Story.* (1825).

———. *Adventures of a Nobody.* (1840).

Aikman, Lonnelle. *The Living White House.* (Washington, DC: White House Historical Association, 1991).

Akers, Charles W. *Abigail Adams: An American Woman.* (Boston: Little, Brown, 1980).

Ames, Mary Clemmer. "A Woman's Letter from Washington." *The Independent* (March 5, 1877): 2.

Ammons, Harry. *James Monroe: The Quest for National Identity.* (Charlottesville, VA: University of Virginia Press, 1990).

Anderson, Alice E., and Hadley V. Baxendale. *Behind Every Successful President: The Hidden Power and Influence of America's First Ladies.* (New York: Shapolsky Publishers, 1992).

Anderson, Judith Icke. *William Howard Taft: An Intimate History.* (New York: Norton, 1981).

Anthony, Carl Sferrazza. "First Ladies, Third Degree: Hillary Clinton's Predecessors in the Hot Seat." *Washington Post* (March 24, 1994): C1, C8.

———. "First Ladylike, After All: Hillary's Merely the Latest in a Long Line of Partners Who Pitch In." *Washington Post* (January 31, 1993): F1.

———. "Office Politics and the First Ladies: Wanting Her Own Space Is Nothing New." *Washington Post* (1993): B1–3.

———. "The First Ladies: They've Come a Long Way, Martha." *Smithsonian* 23 (1992): 135–158.

———. "Skirting the Issue: First Ladies and African Americans." *American Visions* 7 (1992): 28–32.

———. *First Ladies: The Saga of the President's Wives and Their Power,* Vols. 1–2. (New York: William Morrow, 1990–1991).

Arnett, Ethel Stephens. *Mrs. James Madison: The Incomparable Dolley.* (Greenville, NC: Piedmont Press, 1972).

Avery, Patricia A. "Life After the White House: How First Families Adjust." *U.S. News and World Report* (June 25, 1984): 39–41.

Ayers, B. Drummond, Jr. "The Importance of Being Rosalynn." *New York Times* (June 31, 1979): 39.

Baker, Jean H. *Mary Lincoln: A Biography.* (New York: Norton, 1987).

Baker, Ray Stannard. *Woodrow Wilson: Life and Letters,* Vols. 1–4. (New York: C. Scribner's Sons, 1927–1939).

Barber, James David. *The Presidential Character: Predicting Performance in the White House.* (Englewood Cliffs, NJ: Prentice-Hall, 1985).

Barnes, Fred. "Nancy's Total Makeover." *New Republic* (September 16, 1985): 19.

Barzman, Sol. *The First Ladies.* (New York: Harper, 1970).

Bauer, K. Jack. *Zachary Taylor: Soldier, Planter, Statesman of the Old Southwest.* (Baton Rouge: Louisiana State University Press, 1985).

Beasely, Maurine. *The White House Press Conferences of Eleanor Roosevelt.* (New York: Garland Press, 1983).

Benze, James G., Jr. "Nancy Reagan: China Doll or Dragon Lady?" *Presidential Studies Quarterly* 20 (Fall 1990): 777–790.

Betts, Edwin Morris, and James Adam Bear, eds. *The Family Letters of Thomas Jefferson.* (Columbia: University of Missouri Press, 1966).

Black, Allida M. *Casting Her Own Shadow: Eleanor Roosevelt and the Shaping of Postwar Liberalism.* (New York: Columbia University Press, 1996).

———. "Championing and Champion: Eleanor Roosevelt and the Marian Anderson 'Freedom Concert.' *Presidential Studies Quarterly* 20 (Fall 1990): 719–736.

———, ed. *What I Want to Leave Behind: The Essential Essays of Eleanor Roosevelt.* (New York: Columbia University Press, 1995).

Boller, Paul F., Jr. *Presidential Wives: An Anecdotal History.* (New York: Oxford, 1988).

Bond, Beverley W., ed. *The Intimate Letters of John Cleves Symmes and His Family, Including Those of His Daughter Mrs. William Henry Harrison, Wife of the Ninth President of the United States.* (Cincinnati: Historical and Philosophical Society of Ohio, 1956).

Boner, Floelle Youngblood. "Six Widows of Presidents." *National Republic* (October 1933): 5–6, 24.

Borrelli, Anne, and Janet M. Martin. *The Other Elites.* (Boulder, CO: Lynne Rienner, 1997).

Brady, Patricia. "Martha Washington," in Lewis L. Gould, ed., *American First Ladies.* (New York: Garland, 1996), pp. 2–16.

Brandon, Dorothy. *Mamie Doud Eisenhower: A Portrait of a First Lady.* (New York: Scribner's, 1954).

Brendon, Piers. *Ike: His Life and Times.* (New York: Harper, 1986).

Briggs, Emily. *The Olivia Letters.* (New York: 1906).

Brogan, Hugh, and Charles Mosley. *American Presidential Families.* (New York: Maximilian, 1993).

Brown, Harry J., and Frederick D. Williams, eds. *The Diary of James A. Garfield,* Vols. 1–4. (East Lansing: University of Michigan Press, 1967–1981).

Brown, Stuart Gerry, ed. *The Autobiography of James Monroe.* (Syracuse, NY: Syracuse University Press, 1959).

Burns, Paul A. "Profiles: the First Lady." *New Yorker* (May 15, 1926): 17–18.

Burrell, Barbara. *Public Opinion, the First Ladyship, and Hillary Clinton.* (New York: Garland, 1997).

Bush, Barbara. *Barbara Bush: A Memoir.* (New York: Scribner's Sons, 1994).

Butterfield, L. H., Marc Friedlaender, and Mary-Jo Kline, eds. *The Book of Abigail and John: Selected Letters of the Adams Family, 1762–1784.* (Cambridge: Harvard University Press, 1975).

Carlson, Margaret. "Hillary." *Vanity Fair* (June 1993): 111–116, 166–170.

———. "The Center of Power: The First Lady Wants More Than Clout." *Time* (May 10, 1993): 29–33.

———. "The Silver Fox." *Time* (January 23, 1989).

Caroli, Betty Boyd. *First Ladies.* (New York: Oxford University Press, 1987).

Carpenter, Liz. *Ruffles and Flourishes.* (College Station: Texas A&M Press, 1992).

Carter, Jimmy. *Keeping Faith: The Memoirs of Jimmy Carter.* (New York: Random House, 1982).

Carter, Jimmy, and Rosalynn Carter. *Everything to Gain.* (New York: Random House, 1987).

Carter, Rosalynn. *First Lady from Plains.* (Boston: Houghton-Mifflin, 1984).

Cleaves, Freeman., ed. *Old Tippecanoe: William Henry Harrison and His Time.* (Norman: University of Oklahoma Press, 1969).

Clinton, Hillary Rodham. *It Takes a Village.* (New York: Simon & Schuster, 1996).

"Comparison of Mrs. McKinley and Mrs. Bryan." *Harper's Bazaar* (August 11, 1900): 954–956.

Conant, Jennet, and Eleanor Clift. "First Ladies in Waiting: What's a Woman's Place?" *Newsweek* (August 17, 1987): 20–21.

Coolidge, Grace. "The Real Calvin Coolidge." *Good Housekeeping* (June 1935): 41–42, 198–210.

———. "When I Became the First Lady." *American Magazine* (September 1929). *(*Also appears in *Good Housekeeping,* April–June, 1935.)

Corbitt, Katherine. "Louisa Catherine Adams: The Anguished 'Adventures of a Nobody,'" in Mary Kelley, ed., *Women's Being, Women's Place: Female Identity and Vocation in American History.* (Boston: Houghton Mifflin, 1979), pp. 67–84.

Corcoran, Katherine. "Pilloried Clinton." *Washington Journalism Review* (January–February 1993): 27–29.

Corwin, Edward S. *The President: Office and Powers* (New York: New York University Press, 1984).

Cronin, Thomas E., and Michael A. Genovese. *The Paradoxes of the American Presidency.* (New York: Oxford University Press, 1997).

Crook, W. H. *Memories of the White House: The Home Life of Our Presidents from Lincoln to Roosevelt.* (Boston: 1911).

Curran, Robert. *The Kennedy Women.* (New York: Lancer, 1964).

Custis, George W. P. *Recollections and Private Memoirs of Washington.* (Washington, DC: W. H. Moore, 1859).

Cutts, Lucia B. *Memoirs and Letters of Dolly Madison.* (Boston: Houghton Mifflin, 1886).

Daggett, Mabel Porter. "Woodrow Wilson's Wife." *Good Housekeeping* (March 1913): 316–323.

———. "The Woman in the Background." *The Delineator* (March 1909): 393–396.

David, Lester. *The Lonely Lady of San Clemente: The Story of Pat Nixon.* (New York: World Publishing, 1978).

David, Lester, and Irene David. *Ike and Mamie: The Story of the General and His Lady.* (New York: World Publishing, 1981).

Deaver, Michael. *Behind the Scenes.* (New York: Morrow, 1987).

DePauw, Linda Grant, and Conover Hunt. *Remember the Ladies: Women in America.* (New York: Viking Press, 1976).

DiClerico, Robert E. *The American President.* (Englewood Cliffs, NJ: Prentice-Hall, 1979).

Diller, Daniel C., and Stephen L. Robertson. *The Presidents, First Ladies, and Vice Presidents: White House Biographies, 1789–1997.* (Washington, DC: Congressional Quarterly Press, 1997).

Dobbin, Muriel. "Reflections on Life in a Fishbowl." *U.S. News and World Report* (September 28, 1987): 37–38.

Durest-Lahti, Georgia, and Rita Mae Kelly. *Gender Power, Leadership, and Governance.* (Ann Arbor: University of Michigan Press, 1995).

Edwards, George C., III, and Stephen J. Wayne. *Presidential Leadership: Politics and Policy Making.* (New York: St. Martin's Press, 1994).

Edwards, George C., III, John H. Kessel, and Bert A. Rockman, eds. *Researching the Presidency: Vital Questions, New Approaches.* (Pittsburgh: University of Pittsburgh Press, 1993).

Eisenhower, Dwight. *At Ease: Stories I Tell to Friends.* (Garden City, NY: Doubleday, 1967).

Eisenhower, Julie Nixon. *Pat Nixon: The Untold Story.* (New York: Simon & Schuster, 1986).

———. *Special People.* (New York: Simon, 1977).

Enders, Jackie. "Who Needs First Ladies?" *Washington Post* (May 31, 1990).

Ferrell, Robert H., ed. *Dear Bess: The Letters from Harry to Bess Truman.* (New York: Norton, 1983).

Feuss, Claude M. *Calvin Coolidge: The Man from Vermont.* (Hamden, CT: Archon, 1965).

Fields, Joseph E., ed. *"Worthy Partner": The Papers of Martha Washington.* (Westport, CT: Greenwood, 1994).

"First Ladies, First Impressions." *Vogue* (October 1988): 219.

"First Ladies: The Veterans of America's Second Toughest Job." *Life* (July 1986): 107–114.

"A First Lady of Priorities and Proprieties." *Time* (January 5, 1981): 25.

"For Mrs. Reagan, Gifts Mean High Fashion at No Cost." *New York Times* (January 16, 1982): 15.

Ford, Betty. *Betty: A Glad Awakening.* (Garden City, NY: Doubleday, 1987).

———. *The Times of My Life.* (New York: Harper, 1978).

Ford, Gerald R. *A Time to Heal: The Autobiography of Gerald R. Ford.* (New York: Harper, 1979).

Fuller, Helen. "The Powerful Persuaders: Lady Bird's Trip Through the South." *New Republic* (October 24, 1964): 11.

Furman, Bess. *White House Profile.* (Indianapolis: Bubbs Merrill, 1951, 1957).

———. "Independent Lady from Independence." *New York Times* (June 9, 1946): 17.

Gates, Henry L. "Hating Hillary: Hillary Clinton Has Been Trashed Right and Left—But What's Really Fueling the Furies?" *The New Yorker* (February 26, 1996): 116–132.

Geer, Emily Apt. *First Lady: The Life of Lucy Webb Hayes.* (Kent, OH: Kent State University Press, 1984).

George, Alexander L., and Juliette L. George. *Presidential Personality and Performance* (Boulder, CO: Westview, 1998).

Gerson, Noel B. *The Velvet Glove: A Life of Dolley Madison.* (Nashville, TN: T. Nelson, 1975).

Ginsberg, Benjamin. *The Captive Public.* (New York: Basic Books, 1986).

Goodwin, Doris Kearns. *No Ordinary Time: Franklin and Eleanor Roosevelt, The Home Front in World War II.* (New York: Simon & Schuster, 1994).

———. "Hillary and Eleanor." *Mother Jones* (January–February 1993).

Gordon, Frances McGregor. "The Tact of Mrs. Woodrow Wilson." *Collier's* (March 8, 1913): 13.

Gould, Lewis L. "Modern First Ladies and the Presidency." *Presidential Studies Quarterly* 20 (1990): 677–683.

———. "First Ladies." *The American Scholar* 55 (1986): 528–535.

———. *Governors' Wives: Women of Influence.* (Madison, WI: LaFollette Institute of Public Affairs, 1968).

———, ed. *American First Ladies: Their Lives and Their Legacy.* (New York: Oxford University Press, 1996).

Graf, LeRoy P., and Ralph W. Haskins, eds., *The Papers of Andrew Johnson,* Vols. 1–2. (Knoxville: University of Tennessee Press, 1967–1983).

Grayson, Benson Lee. *The Unknown President: The Administration of President Millard Fillmore.* (Washington, DC: University Press of America, 1981).

Greer, Germaine. "Abolish Her: The Feminist Case Against First Ladies." *The New Republic* (June 26, 1995): 21–27.

Gutin, Myra G. *The President's Partner: The First Lady in the Twentieth Century.* (New York: Greenwood Press, 1989).

Hagedorn, Herman. *The Roosevelt Family of Sagamore Hill.* (New York: Macmillan, 1954).

Hartzell, Josiah. *Sketch of the Life of Mrs. William McKinley.* (Washington, DC: 1896). (Campaign literature.)

Hatch, Alden. *First Lady Extraordinary.* (New York: Dodd, Mead, 1961). (Written with the help of Edith Wilson.)

Hay, Peter. *All the President's Ladies: Anecdotes of the Women Behind the Men in the White House.* (New York: Viking, 1988).

Healy, Donna Dixon. *America's First Ladies: Private Lives of the Presidential Wives.* (New York: Atheneum, 1988).

Hecht, Marie. *John Quincy Adams: A Personal History of an Independent Man.* (New York: Macmillan, 1972).

Henney, Elizabeth. "Presenting: Mrs. Eisenhower." *Washington Post* (August 2, 1942).

Hershey, Leonore. "Pat Nixon." *Ladies' Home Journal* (February 1972): 89–95.

Heymann, C. David. *A Woman Named Jackie.* (New York: Signet Books, 1990).

Hickok, Lorena. *Eleanor Roosevelt: Reluctant First Lady.* (New York: Free Press, 1962).

Hill, George Griswald. "The Wife of the New President." *Ladies' Home Journal* (March 1909): 7.

"Hillary Clinton, Trail-blazer." *The Economist* (December 5, 1992): 30.

Hoff-Wilson, Joan. *Herbert Hoover: Forgotten Progressive.* (Boston: Little, Brown, 1975).

Holloway, Laura C. *Ladies of the White House.* (New York: U.S. Publishing Co., 1870).

Holman, Hamilton. *Zachary Taylor: Soldier of the Republic.* (Hamden, CT: Anchor Books, 1966).

Hoogenboom, Ari. *Rutherford B. Hayes: Warrior and President.* (Lawrence: University Press of Kansas, 1995).

"Hoover's Silent Partner." *Literary Digest* 105 (September 8, 1917): 50–52.

Hoover, Herbert. *The Memoirs of Herbert Hoover,* Vols. 1–3. (New York: Macmillan, 1951–1952).

Hoxie, R. Gordon. "About This Issue." *Presidential Studies Quarterly* 20 (1990): 672–675.

Hunter, Marjorie. "Mrs. Carter Supports Health Aid in Senate Debut." *New York Times* (February 8, 1979): B9.

"In Defense of First Ladies." *The New Republic* (July 31, 1995): 4.

Jackson, Donald, and Dorothy Twohig, eds. *The Diaries of George Washington,* Vols. 1–6. (Charlottesville: University of Virginia, 1976–1979).

Johnson, Claudia A. "Lady Bird." *A White House Diary.* (New York: Holt, 1970).

Johnson, Claudia A. "Lady Bird," with Carlton B. Lees. *Wildflowers Across America.* (New York: Abbeville Press, 1988).

Johnson, Faye Lind. "An Awesome Responsibility: Rosalynn Carter as First Lady." *Presidential Studies Quarterly* 20 (Fall 1990): 769–776.

Keckley, Elizabeth. *Behind the Scenes: Thirty Years a Slave and Four Years in the White House.* (New York: G. W. Carleton, 1868).

Kelley, Kitty. "How Barbara Bush Zapped My Books: Was There Political Pressure at the Smithsonian First Ladies Show?" *Washington Post* (October 2, 1994): C5.

Kennedy, Rose Fitzgerald. *Times to Remember.* (Garden City, NY: Doubleday, 1974).

Kilian, Pamela. *Barbara Bush: A Biography.* (Thorndike, ME: Thorndike, 1992).

King, Norman. *Hillary: Her True Story.* (New York: Birch Lane Press, 1993).

Klapthor, Margaret Brown. *The First Ladies.* (Washington, DC: White House Historical Association, 1994).

Koenig, Louis W. *The Chief Executive* (New York: Harcourt Brace Jovanovich, 1975).

Kornbluth, Jesse. "Free Advice: Five Historians Comment on Hillary Clinton." *The New Yorker* (January 30, 1995): 34.

Lash, Joseph P. *Eleanor and Franklin: The Story of Their Relationship, Based on Eleanor Roosevelt's Private Papers.* (New York: Norton, 1971).

"The Last Word on First Ladies." *U.S. News and World Report* (March 30, 1992).

Leech, Margaret. *In the Days of McKinley.* (New York: Harper, 1959).

Leighton, Frances Spatz. *The Search for the Real Nancy Reagan.* (New York: Macmillan, 1987).

"Letters of Mrs. James K. Polk to Her Husband." *Tennessee Historical Quarterly* (June 1952).

Leven, Phyllis Lee. *Abigail Adams: A Biography.* (New York: St. Martin's Press, 1987).

Link, Arthur S., et al., eds. *The Papers of Woodrow Wilson* (69 volumes). (Princeton, NJ: Princeton University Press, 1966–1994).

Lonnstrom, Douglas A., and Thomas O. Kelly II. "Rating the Presidents: A Tracking Study." *Presidential Studies Quarterly* 27 (Summer 1997): 591–598.

Mann, Judy. "A Lesson for First Ladies." *Washington Post* (March 14, 1992): B8.

———. "First Ladies for Our Times." *Washington Post* (December 11, 1992): E3.

Maranell, Gary, and Richard Dodder. "Political Orientation and Evaluation of Presidential Prestige." *Social Science Quarterly* 51 (September 1970): 418.

Mayer, Dale C. "An Uncommon Woman: The Quiet Leadership Style of Lou Henry Hoover." *Presidential Studies Quarterly* 20 (Fall 1990): 685–698.

———. *Lou Henry Hoover: Essays on a Busy Life.* (Worland, WY: High Plains Publishing, 1994).

Mayo, Edith. "The Influence and Power of First Ladies." *Chronicle of Higher Education* (September 15, 1993): A52.

McAdoo, Eleanor Wilson, ed. *The Priceless Gift: The Love Letters of Woodrow Wilson and Ellen Axson Wilson.* (Westport, CT: Greenwood, 1975).

McAneny, Leslie. "'First Lady' Contest: No News Is Good News for Elizabeth Dole." *The Gallup Poll Monthly* (April 1996): 16–17.

———. "President Clinton, Mother Teresa Are 1995's 'Most Admired.'" *The Gallup Poll Monthly* (December 1995): 34–35.

McLellan, Diana. "What Every New First Lady Should Know." *Ladies Home Journal* (January 1, 1993): 182.

Means, Marianne. *The Women in the White House.* (New York: Random House, 1963).

Middleton, Harry. *Lady Bird Johnson: A Life Well Lived.* (Austin: University of Texas Press, 1992).

Mitchell, Stewart, ed. *New Letters of Abigail Adams, 1788–1801.* (Boston: Little, Brown, 1947).

Montgomery, Ruth. *Mrs. LBJ.* (New York: Holt, 1964).

Moore, Charles. *The Family Life of George Washington.* (Boston: Houghton Mifflin, 1926).

Moore, David W. "Public Uncertain over First Lady's Role." *Gallup Poll Monthly* (March 1994): 11–13.

Morris, Sylvia Jukes. *Edith Kermit Roosevelt.* (New York: Random House, 1980).

Moughan, Anthony, and Barry C. Burden. "The Candidates' Wives," in Herbert Weisberg, ed., *Democracy's Feast.* (Chatham, NJ: Chatham House Publishers, 1995).

"Mrs. Ford Scored on Equality Plan." *New York Times* (February 21, 1975): 32.

"Mrs. Ford to Continue Equal Rights Lobbying." *New York Times* (February 15, 1975): 31.

"Mrs. Hoover Calls for Relief Workers." *New York Times* (November 28, 1932): 3.

"Mrs. Hoover's International Housekeeping." *Literary Digest* 99 (November 24, 1928): 39–46.

"Mrs. McKinley–Mrs. Bryan: A Comparison." *Harper's Bazaar* (July 7, 1990): 954–956.

"Mrs. Taft's Plans for the White House." *Ladies' Home Journal* (March 1909): 6, 72.

Mundy, Alicia. "The Two Mrs. Clintons." *Media Week* 6 (May 20, 1996): 28–31.

Murphy, Arthur B. "Evaluating Presidents of the United States," in *The American Presidency,* David C. Kozak and Kenneth N. Ciboski, eds. (New York: Nelson-Hall, 1985), pp. 437–448.

Murray, Robert K. "The Murray Poll." *Journal of American History* (December 1983).

———. *Warren G. Harding and His Administration.* (Minneapolis: University of Minnesota Press, 1969).

Nagel, Paul C. *The Adams Women: Abigail and Louisa Adams, Their Sisters and Daughters.* (New York: Oxford University Press, 1987).

Neal, Steve. *The Eisenhowers: Reluctant Dynasty.* (Garden City, NY: Doubleday, 1978).

Nelson, Anson, and Fanny Nelson. *Memorials of Sarah Childress Polk.* (New York: 1892).

Nelson, Michael. *The Presidency: A History of the Office of the President of the United States from 1789 to the Present.* (New York: Smithmark Publishers, 1996).

———. *The Presidency, A to Z: A Ready Reference Encyclopedia.* (Washington, DC: Congressional Quarterly Press, 1996).

Nevins, Allan, ed. *Letters of Grover Cleveland.* (Boston: Houghton Mifflin, 1933–1934).

———. *Grover Cleveland: A Study in Courage.* (New York: Dodd, Mead & Co., 1932).

———. *The Diary of John Quincy Adams 1794–1845: American Political, Social, and Intellectual Life from Washington to Polk.* (New York: Longmans, Green & Co., 1928).

"New First Ladies." *Christian Science Monitor* (December 8, 1992): 19.

"New Mistress of the White House." *Current Opinion* 54 (March 1913): 195–196.

Nichols, Roy F. *Franklin Pierce: Young Hickory of the Granite Hills.* (Philadelphia: University of Pennsylvania Press, 1958).

Nixon, Richard. *The Memoirs of Richard Nixon.* (New York: Warner, 1978).

Nordham, George W. *George Washington's Women: Mary, Martha, Sally and 146 Others.* (Philadelphia: Dorrance, 1977).

O'Connor, Karen, Bernadette Nye, and Laura Van Assendelft. "Wives in the White House: The Political Influence of First Ladies." *Presidential Studies Quarterly* 26 (1997): 835–853.

O'Hagan, Ann. "Women of the Hour No. 3: Mrs. Roosevelt." *Harper's Bazaar* (May 1905): 412–416.

Parks, Lillian Rogers. *My Thirty Years Backstairs at the White House.* (New York: Fleet, 1961).

The Personal Memoirs of Julia Dent Grant. (New York: Putnam, 1975).

Pessen, Edward. *The Log Cabin Myth: The Social Backgrounds of the Presidents.* (New Haven, CT: Yale University Press, 1984).

Pfiffner, James P. *The Modern Presidency.* (New York: St. Martin's, 1993).

Pillsbury, Stanley R. "The First Lady of the Land," in *Dictionary of American History.* (New York: Scribner, 1976), p. 26.

Pollit, Katha. "The Male Media's Hillary Problem." *The Nation* (May 17, 1993): 657–660.

"The President's Partner." *Newsweek* (November 5, 1979).

Prindiville, Kathleen. *First Ladies.* (New York: Macmillan, 1964).

Pryor, Helen. *Lou Hoover: Gallant First Lady.* (New York: Dodd, Mead, 1969).

"Public Portraits." *Public Opinion* (March–April 1989): 37–39.

Quaife, Milo Milton, ed. *The Diary of James K. Polk During His Presidency, 1845 to 1849,* Vols. 1–4. (Chicago: A. C. McClurg & Co., 1910).

Radcliff, Donnie. *Hillary Rodham Clinton: A First Lady for Our Time.* (New York: Warner Books, 1993).

———. "First Ladies, Second to None." *Washington Post* (December 8, 1992): D1.

———. *Simply Barbara Bush: A Portrait of America's Candid First Lady.* (New York: Warner Books, 1989).

Reagan, Nancy. *My Turn: The Memoirs of Nancy Reagan.* (New York: Random House, 1989).

Reagan, Nancy, with Bill Libby. *Nancy.* (London: Robertson, 1981).

Reagan, Ronald. *An American Life: Memoirs of Ronald Reagan.* (New York: Pocket Books, 1990).

Regan, Donald T. *For the Record: From Wall Street to Washington.* (San Diego: Harcourt Brace Jovanovich, 1988).

Richards, Laura E. *Abigail Adams and Her Times.* (New York: D. Appleton & Co., 1928).

Riis, Jacob. "Mrs. Roosevelt and Her Children." *Ladies' Home Journal* (August 1902): 5–6.

Robbins, Jhan. *Bess and Harry: An American Love Story.* (New York: Putnam, 1980).

Roberts, Roxanne, and Donnie Radcliff. "And First Ladies All in a Row . . . National Garden Fundraiser Honors White House Spouses." *Washington Post* (May 12, 1994): C1.

Robertson, Nan. "First Lady Is Torched in South." *New York Times* (October 7, 1964): 33.

———. "First Lady Booed in South Carolina." *New York Times* (October 8, 1964): 32.

Robertson, Stephen L. "The First Ladies," in Michael Nelson, ed., *The Presidency: A History of the Office of the President of the U.S. from 1789 to the President.* (New York: Smithmark Publishers, 1996), pp. 188–199.

Roosevelt, Edith. *Cleared for Strange Ports.* (New York: C. Scribner's Sons, 1927).

———. *American Backlogs.* (New York: C. Scribner's Sons, 1928).

Roosevelt, Eleanor. *The Autobiography of Eleanor Roosevelt.* (New York: Harper, 1961).

———. *This I Remember.* (New York: Harper, 1949).

———. *This Is My Story.* (New York: Harper, 1937).

Rose, Richard. "Evaluating Presidents," in George C. Edwards II, John H. Kessel, and Bert A. Rockman, eds., *Researching the Presidency: Vital Questions, New Approaches.* (Pittsburgh: University of Pittsburgh Press, 1993), pp. 453–484.

Rosebush, James S. *First Lady, Public Wife: A Behind-the-Scenes History of the Evolving Role of First Ladies in American Political Life.* (New York: Madison Books, 1987).

Rosenthal, A. M. "The First Ladyship." *The New York Times* (March 11, 1994): B8.

Ross, Ishbel. *An American Family: The Tafts—1678–1964.* (Westport, CT: Greenwood, 1977).

———. *Grace Coolidge and Her Era: The Story of a President's Wife.* (New York: Dodd, Mead, 1962).

———. *The General's Wife: The Life of Mrs. Ulysses S. Grant.* (New York: Dodd, Mead, 1959).

Rozell, Mark. In James P. Pfiffner and R. H. Davidson, eds., *Understanding the Presidency.* (New York: Longman, 1997).

Russell, Francis. *The Shadow of Blooming Grove: Warren G. Harding in His Times.* (New York: McGraw-Hill, 1968).

Ryan, Mary C., and Nancy Kegan Smith. *Modern First Ladies: Their Documentary Legacy.* (Washington, DC: National Archives Records Administration, 1989).

Sakol, Jeannie. "All the President's Wives." *New Woman* (January 1, 1989): 72–75.

Saunders, Frances Wright. *First Lady Between Two Worlds: Ellen Axson Wilson.* (Chapel Hill: University of North Carolina Press, 1985).

Schachtman, Tom. *Edith and Woodrow: A Presidential Romance.* (New York: G. P. Putnam's Sons, 1981).

Schlesinger, Arthur, Jr. *A Thousand Days: John F. Kennedy in the White House.* (Boston: Houghton Mifflin, 1965).

Schlesinger, Arthur, Sr. "The U.S. Presidents." *Life* (1948).

———. "Our Presidents: A Rating by 75 Scholars." *New York Times Magazine* (July 29, 1962).

Seager, Robert, II. *And Tyler Too: A Biography of John and Julia Gardiner Tyler.* (New York: McGraw-Hill, 1963).

Seale, William. *The President's House: A History,* Vols. 1–2. (Washington, DC: White House Historical Assoc., 1986).

Selden, Charles A. "Six White House Wives and Widows." *Ladies' Home Journal* (June 1927): 18–19, 109–110, 112–113, 115.

Sellars, Charles G. *James K. Polk: Constitutionalist, 1843–1846.* (Princeton, NJ: Princeton University Press, 1966).

———. *James K. Polk: Jacksonian 1795–1843.* (Princeton, NJ: Princeton University Press, 1957).

Seltzer, Richard A. *Mistakes that Social Scientists Make.* (New York: St. Martin's, 1996).

Severence, Frank H., ed. *Millard Fillmore Papers,* Vol. 1. (Buffalo: Buffalo Historical Society, 1907).

Shepherd, Jack. *Cannibals of the Heart: A Personal Biography of Louisa Catherine and John Quincy Adams.* (Boston: Little Brown, 1980).

Sidey, Hugh. "Second Most Powerful Person," *Time* (May 7, 1979): 22.

Sievers, Harry J. *Benjamin Harrison,* Vols. 1–3. (Dobbs Ferry, NY: Oceana Publications, 1969).

Simon, John Y., ed. *The Papers of Ulysses S. Grant,* Vols. 1–20. (Carbondale, IL: Southern Illinois University Press, 1967).

Smith, K. B. "The First Lady Represents America." (1997).

Smith, Marie D. *The President's Lady: An Intimate Portrait of Mrs. Lyndon B. Johnson.* (New York: Random House, 1964).

Smith, Richard Norton. *An Uncommon Man: The Triumph of Herbert Hoover.* (New York: Simon & Schuster, 1984).

Smithsonian Institution, First Ladies Exhibit at the Museum of American History, Washington, DC.

Taft, Mrs. William Howard (Helen Herron Taft). *Recollections of Full Years.* (New York: Dobb, Mead & Co., 1914).

Tarpley, Webster Griffin, and Anton Chaitkin. *George Bush: The Unauthorized Biography.* (Washington, DC: Executive Intelligence Review, 1992).

Taylor, Lloyd C., Jr. "A Wife for Mr. Pierce." *New England Quarterly* 28 (September 1955): 339–348.

"The 10 Best and 10 Worst Presidents." *U.S. News and World Report* (January 25, 1982): 29.

Thayer, Mary Van Renssalaer. *Jacqueline Kennedy: The White House Years.* (Boston: Little Brown, 1967).

Thomas, Norman C., Joseph A. Pika, and Richard A. Watson. *The Politics of the Presidency.* (Washington, DC: Congressional Quarterly Press, 1993).

Tobin, Leesa E. "Betty Ford as First Lady: A Woman for Women." *Presidential Studies Quarterly* 20 (Fall 1990): 761–768.

"Traveling with Pat Nixon." *U.S. News and World Report* (June 30, 1969): 9.

Troy, Gil. *Affairs of State: The Rise and Rejection of the Presidential Couple Since World War II.* (New York: The Free Press, 1997).

Truman, Harry. *Memoirs,* Vols. 1–2. (Garden City, NY: Doubleday, 1955).

Truman, Margaret. *First Ladies: An Intimate Group Portrait of White House Wives.* (New York: Random House, 1996).

———. "When Your Husband Is the President." *Parade Magazine* (October 8, 1995): 4–6.

———. *Bess W. Truman.* (New York: MacMillan, 1968; New York: Pocket Books, 1974).

Turim, Gayle. "First Ladies Restored to Prominence." *Americana* (April 1992): 54–57.

Turner, Justin G., and Linda Levitt Turner. *Mary Lincoln—Her Life and Letters.* (New York: Knopf, 1972).

Tyler, Julia Gardiner. "To the Duchess of Sutherland and the Ladies of England." *Southern Literary Messenger* (February 19, 1853): 120–126.

———. "Reminiscences." *Richmond Dispatch* (July 21, 1889).

Van der Heuvel, Gerry. *Crowns of Thorns and Glory: Mary Todd Lincoln and Varina Howell Davis: The Two First Ladies of the Civil War.* (New York: E. P. Dutton, 1988).

Wallace, Sarah Agnes. "Letters of Mrs. James K. Polk to Her Husband." *Tennessee Historical Quarterly* (June 1952): 180–288.

Warner, Judith. *Hillary Clinton: The Inside Story.* (New York: Signet Books, 1993).

Watson, Robert P. "Ranking the Presidential Spouses." *Social Science Journal* 36 (January 1999): 117–136.

———. "Incorporating the First Ladies into the Classroom." *Social Studies* 89 (July–August 1998): 165–170.

———. "The First Lady Reconsidered: Presidential Partner and Political Institution." *Presidential Studies Quarterly* 27 (Fall 1997): 805–818.

Weaver, Judith L. "Edith Bolling Wilson as First Lady: A Study in the Power of Personality, 1919–1920." *Presidential Studies Quarterly* 15 (Winter 1985): 33–50.

Weidenfeld, Sheila Rabb. *First Lady's Lady: With the Fords at the White House.* (New York: Putnam, 1979).

Weisberger, Bernard A. "Petticoat Government: First Ladies Have Been Under Fire Ever Since Albert Gallatin Called Abigail Adams 'Mrs. President.'" *American Heritage* 44 (1993): 18–20.

West, J. B. *Upstairs at the White House.* (New York: Warner Books, 1974).

"What Ex-First Ladies Are Doing Now." *U.S. News and World Report* (November 1, 1982): 8.

Whitney, Janet. *Abigail Adams.* (Boston: Little, Brown, 1947).

Whitton, Mary Ormsbee. *First First Ladies, 1789–1865.* (New York: Hastings House, 1948).

"Who Best as First Lady?" *The Gallup Poll Monthly* (August 1996): 24.

"Who Runs America?" *U.S. News and World Report* (April 14, 1980): 39.

Wicker, Tom. "Speaking for Carter." *New York Times* (July 24, 1979): A15.

Wikander, Lawrence E., and Robert H. Ferrell, eds. *Grace Coolidge: An Autobiography.* (Worland, WY: High Plains Publishing, 1992).

Williams, T. Harry., ed. *Hayes: The Diary of a President, 1876–1881.* (New York: D. McKay, 1964).

Wills, Gary. *Reagan's America: Innocents at Home.* (New York: Doubleday, 1987).

Wilson, Edith Bolling. *My Memoir.* (New York: Bobbs-Merrill, 1939).

Wilson, Joan Hoff, and Marjorie Lightman. *Without Precedent: The Life and Career of Eleanor Roosevelt.* (Indianapolis: Indiana University Press, 1984).

Winfield, Betty Houchin. "Madame President: Understanding a New Kind of First Lady." *Media Studies Journal* 8 (1994): 59–71.

———. "The Legacy of Eleanor Roosevelt." *Presidential Studies Quarterly* 20 (Fall 1990): 699–708.

Withey, Lynne. *Dearest Friend: A Life of Abigail Adams.* (New York: Free Press, 1981).

"The Women We Admire." *Public Opinion* (March–April 1989): 40.

Woodward, Bob. *The Agenda: Inside the Clinton White House.* (New York: Simon & Schuster, 1994).

Wooten, James T. "Mrs. Carter Sees Role Widening." *New York Times* (March 15, 1977).

Index

About the Book

Although unpaid, unelected, and unappointed, first ladies have been functioning as powers behind the throne of the U.S. presidency since the nation was founded. This groundbreaking study shows clearly that the first lady is an influential force in presidential politics and a subject worthy of serious scholarly attention.

Watson traces the first lady's role, from the time it was ignored by the framers of the Constitution through its development into today's powerful political institution, complete with office, staff, and budgetary resources rivaling those of key presidential advisers. He also examines the paradoxes surrounding activism in the office. His intriguing study reveals a fascinating history and reassesses the significance of the presidential spouse.

Robert Watson is associate professor of political science at the University of Hawaii–Hilo.